THE
RED
RIPPER

THE
RED
RIPPER

Peter Conradi

A DELL BOOK

To Roberta

Published by
Dell Publishing
a division of
Bantam Doubleday Dell Publishing Group, Inc.
666 Fifth Avenue
New York, New York 10103

ISBN: 0-440-21603-6

Printed in the United States of America

Acknowledgments

Sometimes the very fact of being a foreigner can make it much more difficult to work as a journalist in Russia; sometimes it can open all sorts of doors. It was the latter which turned out to be the case during research for this book.

Police and investigators from the Public Prosecutor's Office impressed me time and time again with their willingness to talk openly of their roles in the affair. Chikatilo's former colleagues and neighbors surprised me with the warmth of their welcome when I turned up out of the blue at their homes after a long trek across the Russian countryside.

I should like to thank Amurkhan Yandiyev, Andrei Tkachenko, Vladimir Kazakov, Yevgeny Bakin, Mikhail Fetisov, Viktor Burakov, Aleksandr Bukhanovsky, as well as countless other people in Rostov and Moscow. A special mention is due also to Peter Sobiecki and to Lyudmila Vinnikova for their unswerving dedication—and to my agent, Andrew Nurnberg, for the lunch in a Moscow hotel which started off the whole project.

Above all, I should like to thank my wife, Roberta, not just for her valuable literary criticism, but also for her enduring support and patience which, as always, helped me through the most difficult moments.

The hands of the bus station clock showed eight P.M. through the cracked glass, but it was still warm outside, a typical summer evening, on September 13, 1984, in the south of Russia. He looked around for a second: Grim-faced workers hurried home after their shifts, young couples lingered for a few moments, tramps settled down with their bottles of vodka for the evening. He had been on duty all day, and his eyes were beginning to blur.

It was the way the man moved that first caught his eye. Inspector Aleksandr Zanasovski of the Rostov-on-Don police had been shadowing him for several hours now as he weaved his way through the crowd. Furtive yet nervous, the inspector watched like a hunter stalking his prey.

He had seen the man for the first time two weeks earlier in the railroad station on the other side of the main square. A tall, powerful man wearing thick glasses and a neat suit, he was in his late forties or early fifties perhaps, and carried a bulky briefcase in his hand.

He had been trying to pick up women there as well—and with persistence. Zanasovski had never seen anything like it before. In the hour he spent watching him, the man must have spoken to a dozen or more; a few words here or a smile and he was off to the next one, almost as soon as he had started. Then, after an hour, he had gone outside and started to do the same at the bus stop. It was then that Zanasovski had challenged him and asked him to come to the small one-man police post inside the bus station for a routine document check. He could still remember the name: "Chikatilo, Andrei Romanovich." A strange kind of name, Ukrainian, perhaps. It certainly wasn't an Ivanov or a Yakovlyev. According to his passport, he was married with two kids and was head of the supply department in one of the city's main factories. He was also a graduate of the philological faculty of the city's university. Zanasovski had no cause to detain him. But that did not stop him from asking the man what he had been up to.

"I was waiting to go home and was bored," the man had replied. "I wanted to talk to someone. And anyway, I like young people. I used to be a teacher. I'm interested in them: where they live, what they do, what their hobbies are."

One of the girls he had been trying to talk to confirmed the story. "He asked me things like where I studied and where I was going," she said.

And now two weeks later, here was this man again, and he was behaving in exactly the same way.

In ordinary times, Zanasovski would probably have thought nothing more about it: a middle-aged married man out to cheat a little on his wife. But the summer of 1984 did not count as ordinary times in Rostov. Somewhere out there was a serial killer. The city was full of rumors and fear. The pressure was on to find him before he struck again.

The more Zanasovski watched this man, the more suspicious his behavior seemed. "This time we're not going to let him go," he breathed to his young colleague who was standing watch with him.

It had been more than two years now since they had found the first body. The girl, named Lyuba Biryuk, had been thirteen years old, a nice kid from a nice family. She was the niece of an officer from the local Criminal Investigation Department. It made it almost like losing a member of the family. Her remains had been found on a wooded path beside the road in Donskoi, a little village about twenty miles north of Rostov.

A murder was nothing out of the ordinary. The Rostov region had always had one of the highest crime rates in the country. It was a matter of simple geography: Rostov was a kind of frontier town, it attracted all sorts, good and bad. An average of at least three hundred people were killed every year in the area. That meant almost one murder a day. But Biryuk's killing was different. She was a child. And there were the injuries themselves—more than thirty deep stab wounds, as well as horrible blows around the eyes. The policeman who was called to the scene had never seen anything like it.

Since then, the murders had continued but the police seemed no closer to catching the culprit. The theories were many, but the evidence was scarce. It had taken them two weeks to find Biryuk's body. By then the trail was already cold. A body decomposes quickly under a southern sun, which can easily send the temperature up to 95 degrees or more. The police found other bodies that had lain there for months and were already little more than skeletons. No one had noticed when the others were missing; no one had even bothered to report their absence to the police.

Many of them were down-and-outs or drunks or prostitutes or kids who had run away from home. Even working out who they were was a nightmare. Some had to be sent to a special institute in Moscow where experts tried to remodel the faces.

There had been only one real sighting of the killer. In March that year, another child, Dima Ptashnikov had been murdered just outside the nearby town of Shakhti, and a woman claimed to have seen the boy going off with a strange man. But if anything, it only added to the confusion. The police had already put a couple of suspects behind bars for early murders. Two young men from a local hostel for the mentally retarded had been arrested and confessed. So what to make of this latest killing? Was it part of the series, and if so what about the men they had already jailed? Whichever way you looked at it, the whole thing was a disaster. Worst of all, the bosses in Moscow were beginning to take notice of it.

It wasn't meant to be like this in the Soviet Union. Crime was supposed to be going down. Or rather, that was the official line. But it was difficult to believe when you were out on the beat, particularly in Rostov. If you asked any ordinary policemen, they would say just the opposite. People seemed more dishonest—and more violent. Even so, serial killings were something else. They were something that happened in America, like unemployment, homelessness and corruption; the kind of things that they showed you on the television news or you read about in the international pages or *Pravda*. They were not the kind of crimes you would find in Rostov. But now, a serial killer was precisely what they seemed to have on their hands, and Zanasovski felt he might just be the man to catch him. But the sun was already going down. It was going to be a long night. He could feel it.

After talking with a couple of women in the bus station, the man walked outside and boarded one of the city's rickety red-and-white trolleybuses going toward the airport. Zanasovski motioned to his young partner, and they jumped on. The vehicle was full but not packed and there was room to move between the passengers swinging on the frayed ceiling straps. The man wasn't wasting a moment. As Zanasovski watched in fascination from the other side of the bus, the man was moving around, trying to catch the eye of the female passengers.

Two stops later, the man got off, crossed the road and got on another bus going back toward the city. So did the two policemen. Then he got off that bus as well and boarded another. And so it went. All the time he was trying to speak to women, but not in an aggressive way. You couldn't really say that he was harassing them. He was smiling, a pleasant middle-aged man in a thick suit and tie despite the summer heat.

"More and more I knew that this was the man," Zanasovski said later. He had already had that feeling two weeks before when he had first questioned him. Now it was even stronger. But still, it was too early to pounce. He had to stay with him for just a few more hours. Zanasovski hovered in the shadows, using all the skills he had acquired in two years of catching pickpockets.

The man got off the bus at Voroshilovsky Street and walked along Bolshaya Sadovaya Street, the city's main thoroughfare. He headed toward the Central Restaurant, a strange neo-Stalinist columned affair occupying the ground floor of the Central Hotel. Inside, the usual live band was pumping out the Beatles. Couples gyrated on the dance floor, their tables piled high with the customary cold starters and the obligatory bottles of vodka and sweet champagne. The man didn't go inside; he wasn't interested in eating or drinking, let alone dancing.

There were some women outside around the doorway—the usual type you could find hanging around there every night: slightly overweight, peroxide blond hair and already drunk by eight o'clock. The man approached them once, then backed away and tried again. Zanasovski could see that there was something holding him back, probably the men who were standing there as well.

The man was behaving very cautiously. He didn't seem to want any trouble or to be noticed. It wasn't his style. He gave up and walked toward a nearby cafe. It was a depressing place, full of drunks as well. Not the kind of place you could imagine for a normal middle-aged man on an evening out. The man was inside for only a few minutes before coming out and setting off again.

By now it was ten P.M. and the man headed for Rostov's Gorky Park, a green area that bears little relation to its much larger and grander namesake in Moscow. Just a stretch of grass and a few monuments of the usual Communist heroes. On sunny summer days, it can be a pleasant place to sit and watch the world go by. By night it is transformed into one of the city's worst crime spots. The main pathways are just about safe, especially at a closing time of the local movie theater when a stream of people walk through on their way home. But you have to be mad to stray onto one of the side paths.

The man sat for more than an hour on a bench watching women walk past—if watching was the right word for it. This was not a man idly admiring pretty girls. He looked ill at ease and agitated, his head turning back and forth as if he were trying to figure his chances. For all Zanasovski's skill in keeping out of sight, perhaps the man realized that he was being watched. Maybe the whole thing was just a show, a game to string Zanasovski along.

Then the man was on the move again. This time back toward the main station square, first to the small suburban train terminus and then into the larger mainline station next door.

The dirt and the smell mugged Zanasovski's senses as he followed the man into the hall. If Rostov marks the point where Europe meets Asia, then the dividing line runs through the station itself: the gateway to the Caucasus, they call it. All the trains traveling north to the great plains of Russia have to pass by it, as do those heading south toward Turkey. Every few minutes another one pulls in. Although it was late, there were still people everywhere: men in checked shirts and tight suits, sitting snoring on the benches; swarthy Caucasian women in head scarves trying to keep one eye on their children and the other on their bundles. And then the vagrants, the down-and-outs and the cheap prostitutes who would go with anyone in return for a bite to eat or a couple of sips of vodka.

The man went upstairs and sat down next to a girl on a bench and began to talk. They sat there for about an hour before she stood up abruptly and walked away. Zanasovski slipped off after her. What had the man wanted? he asked. Nothing much, she replied, and went off. Meanwhile, the man had moved on, wandering over to the bench opposite and sitting down next to another girl. She must have said something sharply to him, because he stood up immediately and left.

It was already past three A.M. and Zanasovski was exhausted. But the man showed no sign of tiring at all. He looked as if he were driven by some great energy as he paced the building, searching. It was getting more difficult for him to find people to talk to, now. Most of them were already asleep, so he moved yet again, this time to the bus station.

The man had not committed any crime, but it was clear to Zanasovski that he was searching for women. The hunt had already lasted for more than seven hours, and he hadn't found anyone. But with the patience and determination of a hunter, he had not given up.

At last his persistence seemed to be rewarded. A girl in a brown track suit, maybe just eighteen or nineteen, came in, sat down on a bench and then laid her head down. She looked young enough to be the man's daughter, but it didn't deter him. He went over and sat down on the bench next to where her head lay. The two policemen then sat down a couple of benches away and pretended to go to sleep. This oddest of odd couples started to talk. The girl was lying down. The man was sitting up straight, and as he talked, he was keeping an eye on what was happening in the hall around him. They must have stayed like that for twenty minutes or more. Through his half-closed eyelids, Zanasovski could see the man's gestures; he was obviously flirting with the girl and paying her compliments.

She stood up, said something to him and laid back down again. He took off his jacket, covered her head and his lap with it, and edged closer to her. Her face was hidden but the man's was not. It was clear from his expression what was happening under the jacket.

Just after five A.M. the girl stood up and walked out. The man followed. She went to the ladies' toilet, he to the men's. The two detectives lurked outside for about ten minutes. Then, the man emerged, hurrying toward the exit which led back to the main railway station. He went to the nearby tram stop and took the number five. It was the first tram of the day and there were only a few people aboard, bleary-eyed workers headed for the early shift. The man got off at the central market. Still, he seemed to be searching.

Zanasovski had seen enough. The man's behavior was more than just suspicious. As for what had happened with the girl on the bench in the bus station, that was easily grounds enough for pulling him in and charging him.

He walked up behind the man and put his hand on his shoulder. As the man turned, his whole face broke out into sweat. Although Zanasovski was wearing different clothes, the man seemed immediately to recognize him as the policeman who had checked his papers two weeks before.

"I have arrested plenty of people in my time, but never seen anything like this," the detective said later. He showed the shaken man his police identification card, and then led him to the small police post in the market.

By this time, the man's shock had turned to anger. He protested as they walked together through the crowds of market traders beginning to set up their stalls in the watery, early morning sunshine. Why had he been arrested? What were the grounds? What did they want with him? But after all that he had seen, Zanasovski was firm enough in his convictions simply to ignore him. When they arrived at the post, Zanasovski told the duty officer to fill out the warrant giving him authority to carry out a search.

The man's jacket contained some personal documents, papers connected with a business trip he had just completed for his factory, and some receipts. So far, nothing. Then they made him open his briefcase. Zanasovski could scarcely believe his eyes. Inside was a kitchen knife with a plastic handle and an eight-inch blade, some lengths of rope, and a jar of vaseline. When he looked at the tip of the knife, he noticed that the end of it was bent as if it had been used for hacking through something hard—like bone, perhaps.

Zanasovski felt vindicated. First the strange behavior, then the contents of the suitcase; it all fit into place. Plus there was the fact that the man was registered as living in the town of Shakhti, the scene of several of the murders. Zanasovski could barely contain the excitement in his voice when he called the duty officer at his home station in the Pervomaisky district of the city.

"I think I have found the man we are looking for," he said. A few minutes later a squad car arrived and took Zanasovski and the man back to the station. It was already seven A.M. and Zanasovski had been on duty all night. They told him to go home and get some rest.

After more than thirty murders of unparalleled cruelty, one of the world's deadliest and yet most unlikely of serial killers had finally been arrested. It had taken more than six years to track him down as he crisscrossed the south of Russia leaving a trail of death behind him. Now, on September 14, 1984, it appeared that it was all over. Andrei Chikatilo, a soft-spoken grandfather of forty-eight years and a former literature teacher, was under lock and key. And that, it seemed, was that.

2

The village of Yablochnoye is a settlement like any of the tens of thousands of others scattered across the vast territory of the former Soviet Union: little more than a collection of wooden houses set around a communal well in the middle of rolling fields. The region of the Ukraine in which it lies was always a rich one. Ever since the tsars added the territory to their empire at the end of the seventeenth century, it had been their breadbasket: its black, fertile earth and temperate climate were the dream of any farmer. Come harvesttime, wagonload after wagonload of corn would head northward to feed Moscow, St. Petersburg, and the other great cities of central Russia. The peasant farmers of Yablochnoye, which means literally "apple," sent their fair share of grain, too, along with fruit from their orchards.

But by the middle of the 1930s, this natural bounty had long since been replaced by misery. The countryside was in chaos, the granaries empty, and the pigs and cattle slaughtered. Everywhere there were soldiers and hated agents of the secret police, the NKVD. Worse than anything, there was famine, terrible famine the likes of which the people had never seen. And into this misery, in the year of 1936, was born a baby boy: Andrei Romanovich Chikatilo.

The reason for the suffering was simple: Josef Stalin, and his headlong drive to bring Communism to the countryside. The two revolutions of 1917 had swept away the tsar and brought to power Lenin and his revolutionary cohorts. But these had been essentially urban revolutions which had left untouched vast areas of the old Russian empire. Even the ensuing years of civil war among Bolsheviks and their opponents did little to change this. Different factions came and went, but for much of the 1920s, village life away from the capital continued much as it always had done. For most rural dwellers, the Bolsheviks' bold promise of electrification remained little more than a dream; many probably did not realize that Nicholas II and the royal family had been driven from the throne and murdered. By the end of the 1920s, all this was to change.

The impulse came partly from the worsening situation in the cities, which were brimming with the urban proletariat in whose proud name the revolution had been made. Several years of private enterprise under Lenin's so-called New Economic Policy had done much to repair the damage caused by the upheavals of the civil war, but it wasn't enough. Although the harvests were good, the so-called middle peasants and their richer cousins, the kulaks, were handing over far less grain to the state than was needed. It was clear that the fledgling Soviet Union was heading toward a serious grain crisis.

Stalin, who was by now maneuvering himself into a position of absolute control, was angry. It was not just the lack of food that annoyed him, but also the attitude of the country dwellers. For a man who was used to seeing everything in black and white, the peasants, and the kulaks in particular, were a symbol of everything that he hated: rich, traditionalist and, worst of all, independent. They were continuing to live out their lives oblivious of the changes going on around them.

The first blow came on December 27, 1929, just a week after the Soviet Union had celebrated Stalin's fiftieth birthday with the pomp that was to become typical of the personality cult built around him. In a speech to a conference of Marxist students, the Soviet leader launched a second revolution that was to be every bit as dramatic as that of twelve years before. "Either we go backward to capitalism or forward to socialism," he declared. And this, he told his audience, would mean collectivization: sweeping away the mass of individual peasant holdings that had existed for centuries and grouping their owners into collective or state farms. For Stalin, the process would accomplish two goals: First, the amount of food requisitioned from the countryside could be sharply increased; second, it would provide a pretext for the upheaval of the countryside. Asked about the suffering involved, the dictator replied with a characteristically blunt Russian proverb: "When the head is cut off, why cry over a few hairs?"

Inevitably, the hardest hit were the kulaks themselves. Stalin had vowed to "liquidate them as a class." In reality, they were wiped out as individuals. And the assault was not just against the rich. Possession of just one cow or horse was often enough to turn a lowly peasant into a so-called class enemy. Hundreds of thousands of them, together with their children and elderly relatives were shipped in unheated railway cars across the vast plains of the Ukraine and Russia toward remote parts of the Urals, Siberia, and Kazakhstan. Many of them died en route; many more when they arrived at their final destinations, which were often uninhabitable locations in the forests, mountains, and steppes. But others stayed behind and fought. Resistance was particularly strong in the Ukraine and in the North Caucasus; so strong, in fact, that the only way for Stalin to subdue them was to send in regular units of the Red Army, backed by air power.

The results were disastrous. Even those peasants who did not fight followed a policy of passive resistance, killing their cows, pigs, and sheep as a sign of protest at the regime. As many as 150 million head of cattle were destroyed in the period from 1929 to 1934, dealing a massive blow to the country's food supplies. Although Stalin tried in 1930 to ease the pace of collectivization a little, it was already too late. In 1921–22, the country had already been devastated by a "natural" famine. The man-made one of 1932 was far worse. And ironically, it was the south of Russia and the Ukraine, once the country's most prosperous areas, which were hit the hardest.

But Stalin did not want to be bothered with details. His government did little or nothing to stop the hunger. Instead, the government contributed directly to its spread, using it as a weapon in the civil war against the peasantry. In 1932, R. Terekhov, one of the leaders of the Ukrainian Communist Party, complained at a party meeting of the terrible situation that was developing in the villages of his republic. An angry Stalin retorted by accusing him of "telling fables" and suggesting he give up his party job in favor of one as a writer of fiction.

In a perverse way, the dictator succeeded. The structure of traditional rural society was destroyed; the sturdy independent peasants of old were replaced with a new species, the collective-farm worker: lazy, disinterested, and increasingly divorced from the soil, but at the same time dependent on the new regime and its local representatives. And Terekhov's report was anything but a fable: as the famine reached its peak, millions of people died, many of them literally in the fields or on the village streets, casualties of Stalin's war against his own people. In their desperation, many of them were also driven over the line which separates men from beasts. Stories of cannibalism abounded.

No family was immune to the horrors, whether natural or man-made. That went even for those like Chikatilo's family. His father, Roman, was no kulak. He was a simple landless peasant, but with a quick mind and a ready kind of wit. He adapted to the new situation and found work on a collective farm as a laborer. Once their second child, Tatyana, was born, his wife also went back into the fields. The family was not enjoying what anyone outside the Soviet Union would describe as a normal life; but then they weren't starving either. And in the context of the horrors of the 1930s that, in itself, was something.

As the decade progressed, things became a little better. Year by year, the harvests began to improve and production crept upward again. Living standards, though, were still well below those the peasants had enjoyed in what were then being described by officials as the bad old days of the tsars. But even this slight improvement could not last. Hitler's army was moving east, bringing in its wake blood and destruction. In 1939, in an attempt to buy himself time, Stalin made a pact with Hitler: the two dictators divided up the unfortunate countries squeezed between them. But Hitler had no intention of keeping his promise; two years later, in the early morning hours of June 22, 1941, his tanks smashed into the Soviet Union, ending the short-lived alliance between the twin evils of Fascism and Communism. Like millions of other men of his generation, Roman Chikatilo was called up by the Red Army and sent off to the front.

In looking back at those first years of Andrei Chikatilo's youth, psychiatrists have searched for any single incident or event which could have been responsible for the horrific course that his life was to take. Collectivization and then war were not peculiar to him; they were suffered by all his generation. His relationship with his mother, a deeply religious woman, also appears to have been normal—at least as far as it is possible to tell all these years later. Until Roman Chikatilo was sent off to fight, the same held true of Andrei's relationship with his father. There was one incident, however, which stuck in Chikatilo's mind, and which he recalled to a psychiatrist named Aleksandr Bukhanovsky, who was to work with him after his arrest more than fifty years later.

In 1934, some two year before Chikatilo's birth, his cousin disappeared from the village, apparently kidnapped. But there was no ransom demand. Such was the level of hunger that the rumors went around that the boy had been killed and eaten. The family came to believe it. At least, that was what Chikatilo's mother told her own five-year-old son a few years later. Why she chose to tell such a horrible tale to her child is not clear. Maybe it was simply in order to keep him from straying too far from the family home. But whatever the reason, it made a deep impression, both horrifying and yet also fascinating him. Was this the beginning of an obsession with death and with cannibalism which was to grow in the inner reaches of Chikatilo's consciousness for the rest of his life? Bukhanovsky believes it may have been the starting point. "What Chikatilo lived through in his childhood was dreadful," he said. "When he started telling me about his life, it was already the story of his illness."

Such a piece of news was bound to have an impact on any child, however normal he was. And Chikatilo was not completely normal. Even though nothing was detected at the time, those who examined him decades later found traces of some lesions on his brain. Alone, they would have meant nothing. But combined with other experiences which he was to have in the years that followed, they may have been enough to lay the basis for the horrors he was to perpetrate.

In fact, from the moment that Chikatilo began primary school, there were already the first signs of the psychological hang-ups and complexes which were later to gather force. Children who sat in class with him in the little building in the nearby town of Suny remember a shy, introverted and, above all, secretive little boy who never quite fit in with the others. From the very first day, he had problems making friends. As far as fellow pupils were concerned, he always seemed to be dreaming. Chikatilo, in return, found them unfriendly and thought they were picking on him. Most of all though, he was worried that they would find out about his secrets: like the fact that, until the age of twelve, he was still wetting his bed at nights and, worst of all, his chronic shortsightedness.

The shortsightedness became an obsession. He hadn't really been aware of it while he was still at home, but once he went to school he realized that he could barely read the blackboard. Still, he could not bring himself to tell his teachers. As far as he was concerned, it was his fault and so he just sat and suffered in silence, always afraid that he was going to be caught. Nor did he tell his family, for fear of being mocked as an *ochkarik*—or "four eyes"—by the other children. And even if he had, where would his mother have found glasses in rural Ukraine in the middle of the Second World War? Amazingly, he was not to get his first pair until he was thirty. "At school I was an object of ridicule and could not defend myself," he wrote later. "If I didn't have a pen or ink, I used to sit and cry."

But there was worse to come. For children of his generation, the war was no faraway, abstract thing. It was being fought out virtually around them. With much of Ukraine occupied by the Nazis, there was shooting and killing everywhere. Chikatilo himself remembered years afterwards seeing corpses, blood, even parts of human bodies. He also remembered the revulsion that he felt. But to a little boy growing up, war had another, more attractive side, too: the heroism. The heroism of the young Soviet partisans who drove the Nazi divisions from their hideouts in the woods—actions which the children themselves mimicked in their play. The atrocities that the partisans committed were often every bit as horrible as those perpetrated by the occupiers. But right was on their side, and eventually the Germans were driven away.

The stories of these partisans were dutifully recorded by the patriotic journalists and novelists of the day, and as Chikatilo got older he began to lap them up. He devoured any accounts that he could get his hands on. By far his favorite, though, was a celebrated book called *Molodaya Gvardiya*—literally the Young Guard—a Stalin prize-winner published immediately after the war, which was required reading for all. Its bloody tale of a group of young Communist partisans who eventually gave their lives in the struggle against the Nazis fired his imagination. In his daydreams, he began to imagine himself in the heroic role of one of the partisans roaming the woods. When his commander gave the order, he would catch a lone German scout, tie him against a tree and then beat him ruthlessly until he gave up his secrets.

Postwar reality turned out differently, and not just because of the famine which again swept the Ukraine in 1946–47, causing almost as much misery as that of the early 1930s. There was also the problem of his father. Far from being a hero who had fought selflessly for his country to the death, Roman Chikatilo had been captured by the Nazis almost immediately after the war began and had been sent to a concentration camp. He was liberated after 1945 by American G.I.s, and came home with his own share of war stories, which he told with a kind of bloodthirsty gusto. But it wasn't enough. In the eyes of his small son, it was as if his father had brought shame on the family.

In a bizarre way, the state, too, seemed to agree. In the last dark days before Stalin's death in 1953, any contact with the outside world, even as prisoner of war, made a person suspect. Had his father been killed, Chikatilo would have been the son of a hero. As it was he was the son of a virtual "enemy of the people." Unlike many others, Roman managed to avoid imprisonment for his "crime." As a laborer in an obscure village, he was far from the center of attention of the hated agents of the NKVD, who were preparing the last purge of those Stalin considered his enemies. But his position in the village became a sensitive one, providing another reason for the growing Andrei to avoid his classmates and for them to avoid him. It could not have come at a more difficult time.

The onset of puberty was to add another layer to Chikatilo's complexes. From mocking him purely because of his shortsightedness, his classmates began to find other reasons; one claimed that Chikatilo's breasts were too big and started calling him *baba*—a derogatory Russian word for woman, a cry soon taken up by the others. Standing next to him at the urinal, another boy had the impression that his foreskin was an odd shape. This, too, was soon broadcast to the rest of the school. Most other boys would have laughed it all off. But not Chikatilo.

Chikatilo was not ugly. Instead, he was growing up into a tall, well-built adolescent. His nickname eventually became "Andrei Sila"—Andrew the Strong. When it came to playground fights or other shows of strength, he was easily the toughest. As he became older, he could proudly claim to be the strongest in the whole school. By the simple action of grabbing a seat in the front row of the classroom, he was also coming to terms with his myopia. Teachers recall him as having been good in class and a keen and intelligent reader of Chekhov, Dostoyevski, and the other Russian writers. Fellow students marveled at his incredible memory. He could remember events and even long strings of meaningless numbers.

Equally important, Chikatilo was also showing signs of becoming the kind of model citizen with which Stalin hoped to fill his brave, new Communist world. He swallowed all the propaganda which was pumped into the students with an appetite which staggered even his teachers. When they told the children of the imminence of the victory of the world revolution, he believed it with all his heart, moving quickly to read Marx, Engels, and Lenin. He even memorized the name of the leaders of each country's Communist Party, however insignificant, and insisted on writing them in whenever he had to draw maps during geography classes.

This ideological fervor began to bring rewards: When he reached the age of sixteen, Chikatilo became editor of the school's "wall newspaper"—the equivalent of a school magazine—and a member of the school committee. He was also given the important post of agitator for political information, who was responsible for explaining and interpreting the news in the Communist-dominated press for his fellow students. When Stalin died in 1953, it was Chikatilo's job to read them out the long, flowery official tributes published in *Pravda*.

Yet all this was little more than an attempt by Chikatilo to prove himself and to overcome a chronic inferiority complex which was to be reinforced by his first halting contacts with girls. He was literally ter-

rified of them. By the age of fifteen and sixteen, when
other boys were settling into their first tentative relationships, the timid Chikatilo would blush even if he
had to sit down next to a female in class. He preferred
to get up and find another place instead. The ease
with which the others used to put their arms around
the girls made him jealous, but at the same time also
revolted him. He found their overfamiliarity shameful.

He was losing himself more and more in the fantasy
world of books. And within this world he found a kind
of romantic love, divorced from the sordid reality of
postwar rural Soviet life. It was a first sign of retreat
from reality, harmless to start with, but potentially
dangerous. As his frustration with women continued,
the retreat into his fantasies was to increase dramatically.

Not that he did not try to see what he was missing.
In the spring of 1954, a few months before he turned
eighteen, Chikatilo was at home alone when the doorbell rang. It was Tanya Bala, a friend of his younger
sister. She made no attempt to leave when he told her
that Tatyana was not there. She was just thirteen
years old, but seemed much older. To his eyes, she
already looked like a woman as she stood there with
her short skirt and a few inches of thigh visible above
her stocking tops. She looked at him provocatively,
and he could not resist. He became aroused and threw
himself on her. Neither took off their clothes, let alone
tried to have intercourse. Instead, they just lay for a
few minutes on the floor pressed closely together.
Afterward, he felt ashamed. Rather than relish his
first sexual experience, he felt revolted by it. He vowed
to remain "pure" until he married, dedicating himself
in the meantime to the pursuit of knowledge.

As Chikatilo grew, so did the chip on his shoulder.
An intelligent teenager, he dreamed of studying law
at the prestigious Moscow State University. He could

have made it; his decision to devote himself to his studies seemed to be paying off. His school reports were full of fours and fives—the highest grades possible—while the extensive extracurricular activities in school and in the Komsomol, the Communist Youth League, distinguished him from the other boys. For all its faults, Soviet society was still one of enormous opportunity in which even a poor country boy could still make it to a university.

Before then he had seen Moscow only in pictures. When he went there for his exams, the real thing made a dramatic impression on him—even though his parents had so little money that he had to sleep at the railway station. In between the various university entrance exams, he wandered through the wide streets dreaming of his future as a student and gazing in awe at the huge new Gothic-style buildings which seemed to be springing up everywhere. Maybe success would have finally helped him to shake off the feelings of rejection and worthlessness. But he had no chance to find out. Soon after he had returned home to his village, he was told that he hadn't been accepted by the university.

Chikatilo was shattered. He was convinced that he had been rejected only because of his father's war record. It was obvious to him that there could be no place at the university for the son of a virtual "enemy of the people," and he began to hate his father because of it. The truth was different. The law faculty, which at that time was being attended by another young man from the south called Mikhail Gorbachev, was one of the most popular and difficult to enter in the country. Competition for places was fierce, and others had simply done better on the entrance exam. The uncomfortable nights spent sleeping on the hard benches at the railway station had clearly taken their toll.

After this came one of the unusual swings that

would characterize Chikatilo for much of the rest of his life. Rather than trying for a lesser university, he settled for a lower-level technical education. The teenager who had dreamed of a glittering career as a lawyer instead signed up at the local technical college for a course in communications engineering. During that time, he also had his first real love affair, and again it was with a friend of his sister.

Tatyana Narizhnad took a liking to the young Chikatilo, and a romance flowered. She was seventeen, he was nineteen, and both were eager to experiment with sex. They tried twice, but their attempts ended in failure. Somehow, Chikatilo was holding back. Although he was attracted to her, he became chronically embarrassed whenever they were alone. They did not try again. The whole thing lasted something under two months, and then they went their separate ways. He graduated a few months later and was sent by the Young Communist League for his first work experience as a so-called young specialist to the grim industrial city of Nizhni-Tagil, about 800 miles due east of Moscow.

For a boy from the south it was a dark experience. The first winter, with temperatures plunging well below freezing, took him by surprise. Without proper clothing, he often came close to frostbite. But the initial impression he made on his workmates and bosses was a good one. They all remembered him as a keen, determined young man out to do well for himself.

At the same time, he was also trying to come to terms with his sexual drive. Putting his adolescent pledge of celibacy behind him, he tried several times to have sex with local girls in Nizhni-Tagil but things always went wrong: he would never get an erection at the right moment. The attitude of the girls didn't help. Often, they mocked him as he struggled with his own inadequacy, making things worse. He became paranoid that they would tell everyone else that he was impotent. The whole thing began to obsess him, and he became convinced there was something physically wrong with him, that he was not like the other boys. The cheerfulness that his workmates had first noticed in him began to fade. It was replaced by ever-deeper bouts of depression, during which he sometimes contemplated suicide. The only way out seemed to lie through work: in a sign of his almost obsessive quest for self-improvement, he began studying in the evening in a correspondence course offered by the Moscow Electrotechnical Institute.

It wasn't all gloom. In 1957, Moscow hosted a huge international youth festival and Chikatilo managed to persuade his bosses to allow him to go. It was a typical display of Communist pomp. The country's new leader Nikita Khrushchev was determined to improve the image of the country. For the young people who took part, particularly those from the provinces, it was an amazing experience, not least because of all the foreigners who poured into the city. Chikatilo later remembered those days as some of the happiest of his life—even though his poverty again meant that he had to sleep on a bench at the railway station. But he didn't care. He even made friends with an Austrian boy the same age he was, and they later became pen pals. When he went back to Nizhni-Tagil and told his friends, he reveled in their jealousy. But that was it. Later that year, Chikatilo was called up for military service and drafted into a communications unit, where he could make use of his training.

The three years he spent in the army were hard, although in a way not very different from his days in Nizhni-Tagil. Relations with his fellow recruits were not good. Although they all lived together day and night, he stayed aloof from the others and found it difficult to make friends. Part of it was because he always had the impression that people were making fun of him behind his back. Nor had things gotten any better with girls. There had been plenty of them around and it was easy to meet them whenever he went out with the other soldiers. But he didn't feel any more of a man in his uniform than he had felt before. When the end of the evening came and they started to pair off into couples, Chikatilo began to panic. He was convinced that he could not perform sexually, and the more he believed it, the more it became true. In the end, he began to skip the outings, preferring to stay in the barracks listening to the radio or reading his beloved political literature. Rumors of his impotence began to get around. To his horror, some of the soldiers began to claim that he was gay.

There was an incident at that time that left a deep impression on him. While he was sitting cuddling a girl during a date, she suddenly made clear that she had had enough and tried to push his arms away. But for a moment, he wouldn't let her go. He enjoyed the feeling of tension as she pushed against him and tried in vain to unlock his muscular arms. After just a few seconds, he gave up and released her; but in the middle of the struggle he could feel himself ejaculating in his trousers. It was only a single insignificant incident, but it was enough. The first dangerous link in his subconscious between sexual enjoyment and physical violence had been made in his mind.

3

The country into which Chikatilo emerged at the beginning of the 1960s was changing rapidly. Stalin was long since dead and the so-called thaw initiated by his successor, Nikita Khrushchev, was in full swing. In the legendary "secret speech" to a closed session of the Twentieth Party Congress in February 1956, the new leader had spoken of the abuses of power and the crimes of a man he had once served so loyally, and denounced the cult of personality which had been built up around Stalin. Released gradually to the Soviet Union and then to the rest of the world, the speech was like a bombshell. Khrushchev had no intention of abandoning the Communist system, let alone the absolute power that he enjoyed within it. He was determined, however, to put an end to the unbridled terror which had characterized the Stalin years, and he began to rehabiliate many of its victims.

The Russians had things of which to be proud, too. On April 18 of that year, Yury Gagarin blasted off on the first manned space flight, becoming a hero at home and creating fears in the United States that Americans had critically underestimated the strength of their cold war enemy. Living standards, too, were rising, although they were still way below those of the rest of Europe. While Khrushchev's boast to overtake and "bury" the West remained nothing more than empty rhetoric, at least the famines of the 1930s were a thing of the past.

Upon leaving the army, Chikatilo returned to his family in Yablochnoye. But there was little for him to do there. He was now twenty-four, could boast of good qualifications, and had even traveled a little. It was now time for him to begin his career, and he quickly realized that the little Ukrainian village was not the place for it. So, he decided to go a few hundred miles east, crossing the border into Russia. Although it was technically another republic, there was no great difference. The internal borders between the fifteen republics that once made up the Soviet Union meant little in those days. Like the Ukraine, Rostov was mainly an agricultural region, which had suffered badly during the 1930s and had been ravaged by war. It, too, was beginning to recover some of its past prosperity. The landscape with its wide-open plains planted with corn reminded Chikatilo of home, as did the distinctive accent with which the locals spoke Russian.

Chikatilo found a job as a telephone engineer in a little town called Rodionovo-Nesvetayevski, about twenty miles north of the city of Rostov. Although he only had a single room in which to live, things were going well. As millions of other Russians were to find during the massive rural exodus of these years, town life, with such unheard of luxuries as indoor toilets, running water, and electricity, was vastly better than life on a farm. After a year there on his own, he persuaded his mother, father, and sister to join him.

At first they all lived together, squeezed into his little room. But things soon took a turn for the better. By 1962, his parents had saved enough money to buy a little house of their own, and they moved out. His sister, Tatyana, meanwhile fell in love with a local boy and got married.

The passing years did not cure Chikatilo of his chronic shyness, and his life gradually began to fill with episodes of unrequited love. He kept eyeing girls around him, either at work or during his leisure time, but often he did not even dare to talk to them, let alone to invite them out. After taking a fancy to a girl who worked at a local library, he used to go there almost every day on the pretext of taking out books, trying to summon up the courage to talk to her. She couldn't help noticing him and waited for him to make a move—but he never did. On another occasion, he was so much in awe of a girl at work that he found it easier to write an article in the local newspaper singing her praises as a model worker rather than actually dare to speak with her.

His sexual urge was still there, though, and in order to satisfy it he used to spend more and more time masturbating. He was ashamed of himself afterwards, however, and believed all the old wives' tales about it being bad for health. But that didn't stop him and when he got the urge to satisfy himself, he had to do so immediately—even if he was at work. It inevitably led to embarrassing situations.

One of the worst happened soon after he started his job. He was out with a gang of fellow telephone engineers repairing the lines at a point where they run through the woods near the village of Khotunok and, as usual, they stopped to eat their packed lunch outside in a clearing. As the others were resting, Andrei disappeared off into the woods, ostensibly to urinate. However, after walking a few yards away, he instead began masturbating. It was a serious mistake. When he returned a few minutes later, he found that his chronic shortsightedness had played a cruel trick on him.

Even though he had been unable to see his fellow workers, they quickly made clear that they had seen him perfectly. The group leader, a man named Vasily, was among them. "Andrei goes into the woods to masturbate," he shouted to the amusement of the others. Not for the first time in his life, Chikatilo almost died of embarrassment. He was not sure what was worse: the masturbating itself or being spotted by his colleagues. Either way, incidents like this only increased his feeling of isolation. "I always thought about this and suffered because I realized that I was different from everyone else," he told investigators decades later.

Sister Tatyana, too, was getting worried about him. People in Russia have traditionally married early and many have their first child by the age of eighteen or nineteen. But her brother was now twenty-seven and, despite all her best matchmaking efforts, he was showing no signs of finding the right woman. It was clear she would have to step up her efforts. And then, in 1963, she suddenly stumbled across a girl who somehow seemed perfect for him. It happened when she was in the nearby town of Novoshakhtinsk having her hair cut at a salon where a friend of hers worked.

Fayina—or Fenya for short—was three years younger than Chikatilo and had just finished school but had not yet found a job. Her father was a miner by profession, and her mother stayed at home and looked after the children. It was a full-time job, with all the cooking and shopping and washing. There were six children in all, and Fayina was the second oldest. She was no great beauty. But she was tall and pleasant looking and gave an impression of being capable and confident, two qualities that Chikatilo patently lacked. When she and Tatyana got talking, it was clear that Fayina was single and looking for a boyfriend—and perhaps a husband. Tatyana quickly formed a plan.

One summer day soon after, when Chikatilo had a day off work, his sister invited him to go with her to Novoshakhtinsk to visit her hairdresser friend. Unbeknownst to him, she had already invited Fayina along. The beginning was not particularly auspicious. Although Chikatilo clearly liked the appearance of the girl, he was overcome by his usual shyness and could not bring himself to look her in the eye. He could barely get out his own name. And he grew even more embarrassed when Tatyana and her friend slipped off for a few minutes in order to leave them alone. The idea of embracing or kissing Fayina crossed his mind, but he could not bring himself to do it.

His sister could see relief written on his face when they came back. But she was persistent. On the way home, she asked him if he had liked Fayina. He didn't answer and looked away, embarrassed. From his behavior, Tatyana understood that the girl had made an impression on him and he was too shy to talk about it. When she proposed further trips to Novoshakhtinsk, he didn't say no.

As Tatyana had hoped, the two of them gradually began to hit it off. At first, Fayina had been struck by Chikatilo's incredible shyness, but as the barriers began to break down between them, she came to like him. Tall, powerfully built, and well-educated, he was certainly a cut above the other young men around the place. Unlike most of his contemporaries, he had no great liking for alcohol, the traditional bane of a Russian woman's life. At most, he would drink just a glass or two, and that was only when there was something to celebrate.

The thing that particularly struck her about him, though, was his attitude to women, the kind of gentleness that was a product of his own chronic shyness and insecurity. She wouldn't have minded if he had kissed her, of course. In fact she began to wonder a little why he wouldn't. But on the other hand it made a nice change that he didn't seem obsessed with sex. While the other boys were forever trying to get her into bed, Chikatilo was happy to wait until after they were married. It was unusual, but also welcome— particularly in a country where a lack of contraception meant so many youthful sexual encounters ended for the woman in abortion. Later in 1963 they got married in a simple civil ceremony at the local registry office.

The blessing soon turned into a curse. When the couple went to bed for the first time on their wedding night, Fayina realized that he was chronically embarrassed. In fact, he was unable to get an erection at all. It was a week before Fayina could persuade him to try again and it took all her kindness and patience for them finally to succeed in having intercourse. At first she put it down to shyness or modesty. But it was more than a case of first-night nerves.

To the outside world, they were a normal, happy young couple, with their whole lives in front of them. Not rich, but not poor either. Like millions of others, they were scraping along on their meager state salaries and pinning their hopes on a better life sometime in the future. And they seemed as if they deserved it. Andrei was bright and ambitious and was determined to compensate for his failure to get into Moscow University. His latest plan was even more ambitious than before: to study for a degree in Russian language and literature through a correspondence course from Rostov University. He also dreamt of a political career. After joining the Communist Party during his military service, he became a keen and active member. Although he did not talk much about his faith at home with Fayina, he remained a convinced Communist, who genuinely believed in the official line about the superiority of the socialist system and the inevitability of world revolution.

Their friends did not know anything of the barrier that existed between them in the bedroom. Try as he might, Chikatilo could not find enthusiasm for sex with his wife. They were continuing to sleep with each other. Proof of that was the birth of a daughter, Lyudmila, in 1965 and a son, Yuri, four years later. For Chikatilo sex quickly became little more than an obligation, for the sake of conceiving children. He loved his children and felt that two were not enough. And, after all that struggle, he was livid when he found out that his wife had had an abortion. "How could you let a doctor kill my child?" he demanded of her afterward.

And then there were the fantasies that he was beginning to have. They had started off quite innocently; he had imagined himself as an all powerful, almost superman-type figure battling against evil. But gradually, it began to turn into little more than a worshipping of strength for its own sake. His desire to dominate sexually was getting stronger and stronger, and he didn't know whether to fight it or just to accept it. He also kept going back in his mind to the thrill he felt from the incident during his army days when the girl had tried to break from his clutches.

If he had been of another, more liberal generation in another, more liberal country, Chikatilo would probably have discussed this sadistic streak with his wife, if not with a psychiatrist. With help, maybe he could have found a way to integrate it into his normal sexual life and somehow neutralize it. But this was southern Russia—not southern California—and Chikatilo could not imagine how he could bring up such a delicate matter with his straight-laced wife. In a sense, she was the one dominating him, whether in bed or outside it, and he didn't dare discuss it with her.

And so it went on, the two of them suffering in silence, Fayina feeling more and more neglected and Chikatilo sinking further and further into his fantasy world. Sometimes, in the depths of his depression, he found himself asking whether he would ever be able to have a normal sex life. The answer, inevitably, was no. But at that stage neither he nor his wife could possibly realize how far he was to deviate from that norm—and how disastrous the results could be for those whose paths were to cross his.

4

All those long evenings spent poring over books finally paid off. In 1971, Chikatilo was awarded a degree in Russian philology and literature from Rostov University. It was more than a piece of paper to him—it was yet another way of proving himself. With her simple working-class background, Fayina was suitably proud to find herself now married to a man of higher education. For once in his life Chikatilo seemed to have passed the test that he had set himself. Everything now seemed to be on the way up.

The year before, he had left the telephone station and found a job as head of a local sports center. With his tall athletic frame, he was naturally attracted to sports, and he liked young people. As part of the job, much of his time was spent with teenagers, frequently traveling around with them to sports competitions. He and Fayina were better off, too. He had managed to get hold of an apartment—no mean feat in a country of chronic shortages—and his own motorcycle. But still, he did not seem to fit in. People who knew him at the time remember him as closed-up and introverted; none of his neighbors or work colleagues were close to him. As far as they could tell, he spent most of his time reading. If anyone asked, he would always claim that he was studying for a doctorate rather than a normal degree.

With his new qualification in his pocket, Chikatilo thought he could do better. After a search, he found a job as a Russian teacher in the town of Novoshakhtinsk. With a population of about 200,000 people, it is an unprepossessing place deep in the heart of the Rostov coal field. Together with its larger neighbor, Shakhti (the name means literally "mines"), Novoshakhtinsk was a strictly functional place. Both cities were built in the first place because of coal, and coal continued to be their raison d'être. Together with pits over the border in the Ukraine, these were among the country's oldest mines and the toughest; conditions underground were some of the most dangerous in the world. Even though they have always been among the better-paid workers, few miners live long enough to claim their old-age pension. The appalling accident rate means each million tons of coal costs one miner's life.

Above ground, the outlook in Novoshakhtinsk is not much better. The streets are winding, gutted with potholes, and badly kept. The housing is a mixture of jerry-built six-story apartment buildings from the 1950s and 60s and older bungalows with outside toilets, which freeze in the harsh winter and turn foul in the hot summer. For a young couple it was hardly an exciting place to settle. Compared with Rostov, two hours' train ride to the south, it was positively depressing. But it could have been worse, and the two of them didn't complain.

Chikatilo launched into his new job with enthusiasm, spending hours each evening planning and preparing his lessons. It was easy to see why the job had appealed to him. Although the salary was not high, a schoolmaster had some prestige in the local community, particularly if he had a university degree. The feeling of having a classful of children under his power strongly appealed to him.

The trouble was that he turned out to be hopeless at teaching. Although undoubtedly intelligent, his shy, introverted character made him completely unsuitable for the classroom. Maybe a better system of teacher training would have turned him into a more effective teacher—or even perhaps convinced him to drop the idea of a teaching career completely. But neither happened. The first day that he stood up in front of a class, he was mercilessly mocked by his pupils. And so it went. Try as hard as he could, he was unable to maintain any discipline in class. While he stood stiffly in front of them, the children would shout, run about, and openly smoke in front of him. It sometimes seemed that all of them, from the youngest to the oldest, were united in a conspiracy to make his life a misery. Sometimes he was so emotionally battered after a morning of teaching that he would almost faint when he came back to the staff room, and he used to lie awake at night trying to work out what he could do.

Years later, his former students all used the same words to describe their little-loved teacher; introverted, uninterested, and unpleasant. The only ones who had a good word to say about him were those who had no desire at all to study; he rarely bothered to discipline his pupils or, in fact, to disturb them in any way. He instead cut himself off, reducing all contacts to an absolute minimum and withdrawing even further into himself.

His fellow teachers, too, found Chikatilo sullen and morose. He was certainly not the kind of person to sit down with after work for a glass of tea or something stronger. The fact that he didn't touch vodka made him even more strange in the eyes of his colleagues. They didn't much care for his constant moaning, either. He was always trying to blame things on other people. Nor did they like the way in which he seemed to be forever complaining about them to the director.

He suffered from more than an inability to teach. Every school has its share of bad teachers. Far more serious were the first indications that his unhappy sex life and strange fantasy life were quickly beginning to spill over into his relationship with the children. It started with his desire to dominate. But quickly it began to turn into signs of an unhealthy interest in the children themselves. The little girls attracted him like a magnet.

The first signs were fairly minor. When his pupils were sitting in class doing written work, Chikatilo often sought out opportunities to sit down next to them, perhaps to point to a passage in a book or to correct a mistake. The pupils could sense him coming just that little bit too close, crossing over the line that marked their own private space. His hands, too, would begin to wander. But that was only the tip of the iceberg. Some of the pupils also boarded at the school, and that was where he really got his opportunity. To the horror of the girls, he soon took to appearing without knocking in their dormitory as they were getting ready for bed. The sight of them in their underwear and nightdresses sent him almost mad. Girls described afterward how they had clearly seen him standing there, masturbating through a pocket of his trousers.

Things soon began to escalate. In May 1973, during a school walking tour, Chikatilo went swimming in a river with his pupils. Suddenly, he swan over to Lyuba Terentayeva, an attractive fifteen-year-old, grabbed her around the hips and started fondling her breasts and her genitals. It wasn't an attempt to rape her. He explained it later as being inspired more by a feeling of curiosity. But it quickly became more than that. As he touched the girl, she began to scream, and strangely he found the screaming gave him sexual pleasure. So he kept on touching her to make her scream more and more, stopping only when a group of his other students swam over to see what was happening.

Chikatilo was not disciplined over the incident— nor for another even more serious case of child molesting back in the classroom later the same month. One afternoon after school he told fourteen-year-old Anya Nikolayeva to stay on for an extra tutorial session. She was a bad student, lazy and not very bright, and he felt a strong desire to punish her. Once they were alone in the classroom, he began to beat her on the small of the back with a ruler, getting more and more sexually aroused as he did so. Her attempts to get away from him only heightened his pleasure as he wrestled her back onto the chair, and he ejaculated in his trousers. Then, abruptly, he stood up and stormed out of the room, locking the door behind him. Since they were only on the ground floor, Anya simply jumped out of the window and ran home to her parents. She said years afterward in court that she had told them about what had happened but, inexplicably, no further action was taken against him.

Nor was it only happening at school. Whenever he went on buses or trams, he made a point of picking the most crowded part and trying to rub himself up against the female passengers, particularly the teenagers and little girls. While marital relations with Fayina were going from bad to worse, Chikatilo's search for other forms of sexual gratification was also invading his home life. The girls whom he had molested at school had both passed puberty. But he was aroused by younger ones, too. His wife's niece, Marina, then six years old, became the object of his attention in the late summer of 1973. While she was playing in the back garden, he approached her and slipped his hand into her underwear. Some five years later, while the same Marina was sleeping at Chikatilo's flat after playing with her cousins, he went into the bedroom completely naked in the middle of the night and began masturbating in front of her.

Fayina appears to have known about her husband's strange behavior. But she seems to have preferred to ignore it. When she heard the rumors about his activities at school, she laughed it off, with apparent understanding: "What do you know? He obviously wanted to try out someone younger."

One year after the incident they acted. In January 1974, the young teacher was summoned to the director and told that he should resign—or be fired. He resigned. But dismissal merely moved the problem elsewhere. His work record contained no mention of his activities, and officially he left of his own free will. Even worse, nothing was done to stop him from getting another job at another school and doing exactly the same thing again.

Maybe the director wanted to give Chikatilo another chance before ruining his career so soon after he had started. In any event, it was reflective of a dangerous weakness running through Russian society: the fear of authority and the desire, at all costs, for a quiet life. Given the likely consequences, it is easy to understand why the director behaved as he did. If he had reported Chikatilo to the police, then an investigation would have been ordered not just of Chikatilo but undoubtedly also of the rest of the school staff. Like a factory or an office, a school was a collective, with its own group targets and group assessments. If someone did something well, the whole collective could claim credit. But if someone did something wrong, they would all suffer—including the director, himself. If it became clear how long Chikatilo had been misbehaving, he would necessarily be criticized for not having dealt with him earlier.

In retrospect, it is also easy to understand why no protests were forthcoming from the parents of the children. The fact that Nikolayeva actually told her parents about her dramatic leap from the classroom window was remarkable, in itself. In the puritan Soviet society of the 1970s, when sex was brushed under the carpet with as much enthusiasm as in Victorian England, many teenagers would have been far too embarrassed or ashamed to talk about such an incident. It would have been equally painful for parents to try to take the matter further with the school or with the police. Children involved in such cases were routinely required to undergo a series of interviews and medical tests, which often left them with the feeling that they, rather than the offender, were the guilty ones. And then there would be the gossiping behind their backs by the other parents. Why had Chikatilo chosen that girl to molest? they would ask. What had she done to lead him on?

Understandable though their conduct may have been, it did not stop its effects from being disastrous. If Chikatilo had been punished there and then, it might well have stopped him in his tracks. And even if it didn't, it would have given him a police record for child molesting, making him a prime suspect if any further such crimes were committed. But the police never heard a thing about it. By merely asking him to resign, the school authorities had sent Chikatilo a dangerous signal: He could pursue his perverse activities and get away with them.

Chikatilo easily found another job, just around the corner in Novoshakhtinsk's technical school number 39. The shock of being found out—if not punished— seemed to have frightened him into controlling himself. The opportunities, too, were more limited; the youngest pupils there were aged fifteen, and he was too frightened to try anything with them. He preferred younger ones. In any case, though, he was as unpopular there both with his pupils and his fellow teachers as he had been at the previous school. And so, in September 1978, when there was a need to cut back on staff, Chikatilo was the obvious choice for a layoff. He quickly found a new job as a *vospitatel*—a kind of warden—in another technical school, in the nearby town of Shakhti. In a neat arrangement which should have allowed her to keep an eye on her husband, Fayina managed to get herself hired on the staff as well, and they were given a flat in the school.

About half an hour or so away by train, Shakhti is a little larger than Novoshakhtinsk and a little bit older. But otherwise there is not much difference between the two. The same mean streets and the same skyline of pit shafts, each topped with a red star in a celebration of Soviet labor. The job of the college was to train young men from the age of fifteen to nineteen to become skilled workers in the mining industry. It was an odd place for Chikatilo to end up. His degree was in philology and he had no experience in mining. But the director seemed to take a liking to him for some reason and, although the various department heads were skeptical, Chikatilo was taken onto the staff.

Chikatilo still taught a little in the new school, but his main responsibility was for the hostel in which the boys lived. They went there in the afternoon after lessons, and Chikatilo used to supervise their homework, recreation, and sport, as well as leading the inevitable political discussions. It was also his job to summon parents when their sons got particularly bad marks. Sometimes he worked with a colleague, but usually he was alone with the boys in the hostel, working a twenty-four-hour day shift one day in three. His responsibility was not so much academic as moral; it was his job to look after the boys' morals and character development. Given his own increasingly strange sexual preferences, it would have been difficult to think of a more unfortunate choice.

Chikatilo made an odd impression at Shakhti, just as he had done at his previous posts. Despite more than seven years of experience, he did not manage to win any more respect from the students, even when he threatened to hit them, as he sometimes did. Some of the worst fights used to go on in the hostel the evenings when he was on duty. As for the other teachers, they much preferred Fayina, who came across as much more pleasant and open. They had a nickname for him: "Goose," because of his tall, gangly build and protruding adam's apple. Whenever they went off for a few beers after work, he never joined them. Ivan Gulyak, another teacher who lived a floor above Chikatilo in the teachers' quarters, remembers him as a particularly unpleasant man who had little going for him as a neighbor. As his son, Yuri, grew up, Chikatilo also seemed to have as many problems controlling him as he did his students.

Despite all this, Chikatilo had the reputation as being polite, cultured, and well-educated—the kind of man you would never hear swearing, especially if there were women around. There was also his passion for politics. It was the one thing in which he was really interested and would talk about. Once he got started, it was difficult to stop him. Millions of people joined the Communist Party merely for the sake of their careers. But not Chikatilo—he was quite fanatical about it. The childhood job of reading and intepreting the party press for his classmates had turned into a habit. All he seemed to do in his spare time was read the newspapers, and he believed everything, accepting without challenge the division of the world into the capitalist bad and the Communist good. He continued to dream of a political career for himself.

But it was only a dream, and he did nothing to realize it.

To his colleagues, he came across as a person who was able to work the system, even though no one could understand exactly how he managed it. Other teachers at the school waited years for the local council to give them somewhere decent to live; yet soon after Chikatilo arrived in Shakhti, he and his wife were given what seemed to the others a palatial four-room apartment on the school grounds. In what also aroused great jealousy among his colleagues, Chikatilo obtained permission to build a garage on the grounds. Then there was the matter of his car, a sturdy Moskvitch—a luxury vehicle that few were wealthy or lucky enough to own. He had apparently bought it with the money he got from selling his former home in Novoshakhtinsk, but after a year or so he suddenly got rid of it. He sold it to a policeman— or at least that is what he told anyone who asked. There was a rumor going around that he had simply given it away, maybe to buy his silence over his misdemeanor with the children. One of the teachers tried to ask Fayina. But she wouldn't say anything.

It is easy to imagine the possibilities which work in the hostel opened up for Chikatilo, as well as the appalling use that he made of them. Again, many of his activities appear to have gone unnoticed. One, however, stands out. Those who studied in the school remember a particular incident in the autumn of 1978 when Chikatilo went into a dormitory where teenage boys were sleeping and approached the bed of a fifteen-year-old called Sherbakov. Leaning over him, Chikatilo pulled back the sheets and began to suck the boy's penis. When Sherbakov woke up, Chikatilo fled.

That wasn't all. A few days later, he came back with the obvious aim of trying again. But this time they were all waiting for him and drove him out. The incident quickly became the talk both of the pupils and the staff room, fueling speculation that Chikatilo was a homosexual, and further adding to his chronic isolation.

But again, the story did not seem to find its way to the director and, even if it did, it was again ignored. Far from being drummed out of teaching, Chikatilo was able to continue his outward pose as a good Communist and an upstanding member of society. In one of the great ironies of his life, he also began to write a column for the local newspaper *Znamya Shaktyora*—"The Miner's Banner." The articles must have made for grim reading—a kind of classic ham journalism of a type found only in the local papers of a Communist state: a mixture of stilted officialese and high-handed lecturing. Chikatilo wrote about the great achievements of local industry: five-year plans fulfilled and new, even more ambitious plans set. As a teacher, his speciality was the problem of bringing up young people as good Soviet citizens, and most ironically of all, teaching them morality.

Chikatilo's unsatisfactory sex life continued to overshadow everything. Taken together with the reports of his strange activities at school, Fayina was seriously wondering what kind of man she had married and despairing of what she could do with him. And so she had the idea of trying to persuade him to visit a psychiatrist or even one of the new sex therapists who were beginning to set up in the Russia of the 1970s. He refused, feeling deeply hurt. Russia is a typically macho society where men hold very clear ideas of their roles. And although Chikatilo was already prepared to admit to himself that he was not normal, he was not yet ready to go off broadcasting it to the world. Besides, by now he was also beginning to come to terms with his desires and fantasies in a different way.

5

Shortly after moving to Shakhti, Chikatilo bought a little house in Mezhevoi Pereulok, a narrow lane on the edge of the city. It cost him only a few hundred rubles, and he didn't tell Fayina and the children anything about it. Not that "house" is really the right word for the tumbledown dwelling at number 26. It was little more than a one-room hut with a bed and a few other bare sticks of furniture. Chikatilo's neighbors were unfortunate enough to live in theirs all the year round—squalid slums without running water, which were cold in winter and hot in summer. But Chikatilo hadn't bought his house to actually live in.

It was no longer enough for him merely to dream. He had already come too far for that; he had to translate his urge to dominate into reality. He convinced himself that it was the only way he could overcome his feeling of impotence. So, while still living with Fayina and maintaining the front of a normal marriage, he began to build an alternative, secret life in the little house on the edge of town. It was not only more convenient to have a place of his own, it was also a lot safer. The speed with which reports of the incident with Sherbakov had gotten around the school had convinced him of the need to be careful. His reputation was already bad enough, and he knew his teaching career could scarcely survive another such episode. If he was to indulge his strange desires, then he needed to do so away from the rest of the world.

And so it started. Taking advantage of the large amounts of time off which the shift system gave him, Chikatilo began to wander the city in search of people to bring back "home." Sometimes, it was grown women. He began to plunge ever deeper into the world of the down-and-outs, of the prostitutes and drunks who slept in the parks and the railway station. Desperate for the gratification which he knew he could no longer obtain from his wife, he lured them to the little house in return for promises of food and drink. Often he didn't succeed in having sex with them anymore than he succeeded with his own wife. Nevertheless, they would do things for him that he would never dare ask his wife to do.

But he got more pleasure from little girls. The overwhelming need he felt was to dominate, and the thing that aroused him most was a struggle and eventual victory. In a sense, the women were too easy. They would do anything, yet at the same time never really let him have the feeling that he was in control. With little children, though, it was different—and more dangerous. When he found his way into the toilets of one of the city's girls' schools, he was almost arrested. It was also much more difficult to pick them up. On one occasion, he lured two six-year-old girls back to his shack and assaulted them. But it was rare. When he ran into what he thought were likely candidates on the street, they would usually refuse his offers and run off home to their mothers. That was why he sensed an opportunity too good to miss when he ran into nine-year-old Lena Zakotnova in Sovyetskaya Street, the main road a few steps away from Mezhevoi Pereulok. The following is a description of their encounter from a confession Chikatilo gave to prosecutors, but later withdrew in court.

That evening, December 22, 1978, Chikatilo had finished work at school at about five P.M. and gone to the local *gastronom*, the closest Russia had to a supermarket, as much to look at the people as actually to buy food. Then, as he walked back along the road, he saw her. She looked straight out of a fairy tale, a pretty little girl with a red coat with a black furry collar, a rabbit hat, and felt boots. It was late for a child that age to be coming from school, and as he came close he asked her where she had been.

"I've been visiting a friend," the girl replied. She had gone to see her right after school, but had stayed on playing with her a little too long. Now she was hurrying home and was worried that her mother was going to be angry. As Chikatilo fell into step beside her, they continued talking, about her life, her family, friends, and hobbies. She liked the man. He was kind and he smiled a lot; he reminded her a little of her grandfather. But she also had a problem: she urgently had to go to the toilet, and she told him. But it was December and it was cold and she did not want to go outside.

"Don't be silly, of course you can't," said the man. "I live just around the corner from here. It's only a couple of minutes away. You can go to the toilet there."

And so she followed him. It took only a few minutes before the pair of them had left the main road and turned into Mezhevoi Lane. It was already dark as they walked down the narrow road, and the anticipation of what was to come was making Chikatilo tremble. It was always the same when he walked along this road. The house was simple and shabby and run-down and the last place on earth where he could imagine living. But he had never planned to live there. He had bought it for one thing and for one thing only: sex. This was to be the place where he could get away from his dominating wife and live out his fantasies. And little Lena was going to play her role in one. He felt an urge to caress her body, so small and so perfect, maybe even to have sex with her. He could feel himself getting more and more aroused as they neared the house.

The two of them walked from the street through the garden gate and up the path to the front door. There was no one else around. Chikatilo knew it because he had looked around carefully to check. Nor could any of the neighbors see them. There are houses along only one side of that road, and number 26 is sheltered from the others by trees and bushes. Chikatilo fumbled with the lock, opened the door and reached inside to put on the light. The girl felt a sense of relief. They had been walking far longer than she had expected, and she really wanted to go to the toilet. But she never got that far.

As the door clicked shut behind them, the kindly grandfather transformed himself into an animal. Flicking off the light, he flung himself on the little girl, pushing her to the floor of the cramped living room, just beside the small table. A tall powerful man, he must have weighed at least three times as much as she and was many times as strong. As he pushed his full weight down on her, the only thing that the tiny girl could do was scream. And even that did not last for long. Worried about the neighbors, he covered her mouth with his hand and began to strip off her clothes. Although she did all she could to resist, he finally ripped off her underwear and began to rub himself against her.

But still something was wrong. Maybe it was the horror of what he was doing or maybe it was purely physiological. He wanted to rape her but, not for the first time, his body refused to respond. The lethal combination of desire and inability to satisfy it made him mad. The frustration welled up inside him. Then it happened. In his attempt to put his still limp penis into her with his finger, he ruptured her hymen and a few drops of blood trickled out. He had always thought of himself in the past as squeamish. He used almost to faint at the sight of his own blood. But seeing her blood was different. Far from upsetting him, it caused him deep pleasure and he immediately had an orgasm which was the best and the most vivid and the strongest that he had ever had.

It was the most decisive moment of his life. Until then, he had felt only the need to hurt and to dominate. But it had been a matter only of pushing and squeezing and slapping. Now he understood that he needed much more: he needed blood. And, having made the discovery, he wasn't going to just leave it at that. He wanted to have another orgasm as good as the first, and for that he realized that he needed more blood.

Instinctively, he reached into his pocket and felt the small folding knife in there. He had been carrying it around for several weeks, ever since some of his pupils had surrounded him in a dark corner one evening and tried to beat him up. He was convinced that they would try again—in his nightmares he thought they might even try to kill him. Now he was going to put it to a different use. Just one little cut, he thought, as he pulled it out of his pocket. Just enough to make a few more drops of blood flow.

And so, as the girl lay screaming and struggling beneath him, he plunged the knife into her stomach. But any thought of moderation was quickly forgotten. For it was not just the blood that excited him, but also the stabbing and the agony that it caused her. Any last vestige of control that he may once have had over himself was gone now. But so too were the frustration and the impotence. He said afterward he felt that he had at last been freed from the shackles which had bound him. As he thrust the blade into her again and again, he lost himself in the pleasure, exploring her body with his hands. He had this terrible desire to touch everything, even if it meant tearing her apart. Then he put his hands around her thin throat and started to squeeze.

Minutes later, he came back down to earth with a jolt. As the ecstasy passed, he suddenly became aware of the full horror of what he had done. The girl's naked body was barely recognizable at all after the orgy of stab wounds. Blood was everywhere. And now she was dead. He was filled with horror and with remorse. He also began to panic. For the first time in his life he had killed someone, and he did not know what to do. Anyone could come in and find him there. And he couldn't even run away. The dead girl was lying on the floor of his house, and however far he ran she would still be there.

Gradually, though, he began to regain control. He needed to get the body out of there and get it out fast. A plan began to form in his mind. With some difficulty, he gathered up the clothes and tried to push them back over the bloodstained corpse. Picking the girl up under his arm, he put his head out of the door to see if anyone was watching. The coast was clear. So he walked outside, crossing the road to the wasteland beyond. It took only a few minutes before he reached the river, the Grushevka. It was dark and there was no one around. Swinging his arms back, he tossed the little girl's remains into the river and then threw in her bag as well. In the dark, he rather overestimated the width of the little stream. In fact, her bag ended up on the opposite bank. But the body tumbled into the water and began to be swept away by the current.

And then he quickly left. He was filled with an overwhelming desire to get away from the place as fast as possible, to get back to his room at the school and forget all about it. He was in luck. His wife had not come home yet, so he was able to clean himself up and make it look as if he had been there the whole time when she came in a little later. But in his hurry, he made two serious mistakes: Not only did he forget to turn the light off in his little house, but he also failed to notice a small drop of the little girl's blood which had fallen on to the snow on the opposite side of the road from his house as he had carried her past.

The little girl's body was found by police two days later, December 24, 1978, in the Grushevka River where it flows through the city of Shakhti. It was trussed up in a sack. Her school bag was found on the bank nearby. The river was fast flowing, but narrow. The girl's killer had obviously hoped that the current would have carried the body a long way out of the city. But it did not. In those days, the killing of a child was a horrible rarity, and a special investigative group was set up immediately.

There was little for police to go on. Zakotnova, described by her teacher as a helpful child of above-average intelligence, had last been seen leaving school on what since became clear was the afternoon of her death. But that was it. When she had still not come home a few hours later, her parents had sounded the alarm and the search began.

Officers started going door to door, concentrating their attention on Mezhevoi Lane, the closest road to the point where her body was found. They were particularly interested in number 26 and the man who owned it. Their attention had been drawn to him by one of the neighbors. Asked if she had seen anything strange on that evening, she said she had noticed the light burning all night in his house. Like most of the others in that part of the street she had long since guessed what Chikatilo was up to. All those women and girls going in and out over the last few months had been proof enough that he was using the place as some kind of squalid love nest. However, he generally never slept there. By evening, the place was usually dark and he had gone, presumably home to his wife. That night was different.

When police talked to Chikatilo, they quickly began to share her suspicions. There was certainly something strange about this man. The very fact that young girls had also been seen going with him into the house in the past added to their suspicions. There was also the case of his activities at work. Enquiries at his previous schools in Novoshakhtinsk revealed the circumstances under which he had left. They also began to hear some interesting stories from his new colleagues in Shakhti. In all, they must have questioned him some eight or nine times, but he appeared to have an alibi. His wife said he was at home that evening, and they never got around to checking his story completely.

Inexplicably, their attention suddenly shifted to twenty-five-year-old Aleksandr Kravchenko, who lived a few doors farther along the lane. He had already been convicted for a similar killing several years before, when he was living in the Crimea. He had been saved from the executioner's bullet by the fact that he was a few months short of his eighteenth birthday and was instead given a ten-year jail sentence. He was let out after six. Police did not have any direct evidence to tie him to the killing and they had no witnesses. But his record made him seem suspicious, and under pressure from their bosses to clear the case up they became convinced that he was the killer.

For the time being, though, they decided to wait: to see whether he would commit another crime. It did not take long. Shortly afterwards, Kravchenko tried to break into a house near his own and was virtually caught in the act. He was pulled in and charged not just with burglary but also with murder. After some intensive questioning, the man confessed, and the name of Chikatilo dropped quietly out of the investigation.

The police were convinced they had caught the right man. Some of them still believe it today. To back it up, there was even one theory developed according to which Kravchenko had deliberately bungled the burglary so that he would be caught and would then somehow be in the clear as far as the murder inquiry was concerned. If that had been so, he made a very serious miscalculation.

The case was complicated. By the time it came to court in the city of Rostov, Kravchenko was denying that he had killed the girl at all. He claimed police had beaten the confession out of him. But it was too late. The evidence was certainly thin, to say the least. All the prosecution really had were some fragments of grass of a type common both to Kravchenko's clothing and to that of Zakotnova. Besides that and his own— by now, withdrawn—confession, the only other thing they had to go on came from his wife. She said her husband had admitted to her that he had killed the girl. But her words, too, were suspect. At the time she was also being charged with involvement in Kravchenko's housebreaking.

The court found him guilty. However, perhaps as a sign of his doubts, the judge did not pass the widely expected death sentence. Kravchenko was instead given fifteen years in a labor camp, the next most serious punishment. In a country where people were still being routinely shot for petty corruption and black marketeering, the leniency of the sentence caused an outcry. Under Soviet law, the right of appeal is not confined to the defendant. The prosecution, too, can also demand a stiffer sentence. And so, after several years of going back and forth between the court in Rostov and the Supreme Court in Moscow, the death sentence that the public was clamoring for was finally pronounced. Still protesting his innocence, Kravchenko was out in front of the firing squad—but more than four years later, in 1984.

The case was a typical product of the times and of the Soviet Union's legal system. After all, what quality of justice could one expect in a country where millions of people had been sentenced to jail and death over the years for the crime of disagreeing with the system—or even simply to make up the numbers for some bureaucratic quota? By the late 1970s, the bloody purges of the Stalin era were already distant history. But the principles of the legal system remained unchanged. Dissidents, religious believers, and homosexuals, although no longer being executed, were still being jailed.

Law, like everything else from economics to culture, was subordinate to politics and to the will of the ruling Communist Party. And this was not confined to matters of high state interest. It could also apply to something as nonpolitical as the killing of a little girl in a provincial town. Just like mines and factories, the legal system had its plan to fulfill. Police *had* to catch the criminals, and once they were caught, the judge *had* to convict them. The very fact that they had been arrested was considered proof enough of their guilt. The rights of the accused carried little weight. Acquittal in those days was instead a messy process which would inevitably end up annoying many more people than it would please. In this case, there was also the question of public opinion. After having first led people to believe that the crime was solved and the killer caught, it would have been an extremely unpopular move for any judge to free him again.

Years later, after Chikatilo had claimed the killing as one of his own, investigators from the prosecutor's office who went back to look at the case where staggered at how flimsy the evidence was against the unfortunate Kravchenko even by the standards of Soviet justice. For them the biggest puzzle was why police did not pay more attention to a woman called Burenkova. She came toward and told police that, at about the time in question, she had seen a middle-aged man with glasses talking to a small girl who looked like Zakotnova at a bus stop near the beginning of Mezhevoi Pereulok. She had been standing about fifteen feet away from them, too far to hear what was being said. But the incident had still made an impression, because it had seemed to her that the two of them had not really known each other. The man, she said, seemed to have been trying to persuade the girl to do something. But then after a few minutes the two had walked off together along the lane, and the woman had thought no more about it.

Inexplicably, the woman was not called as a witness at Kravchenko's trial. If she had been, she would undoubtedly have denied that the young man before her had been the same one whom she had seen at the bus stop with Zakotnova. She would have instead described a man who was more than ten years older and closer in appearance to another suspect that the police had pulled in and then released.

"For years, I was afraid that this man would come and kill me," she said years later after Chikatilo was finally arrested.

Neither had the police paid much attention to the bloodstain in the snow opposite his house. One of the officers who mentioned it was told by a superior that it must have been the blood of an animal.

Chikatilo, too, was living in fear. The repeated questioning by the police had been alarming for him, and he was aware how close he had come to being arrested. The charging of Kravchenko and the loss of interest by police in him afterwards took a huge weight off his mind. Still, though, he could not just pretend nothing had happened. For weeks afterwards, he was haunted by the vision of what had happened that evening in the little house. And at first he did not dare to go out again, not back to the house and not to any other deserted place. But coupled with all the revulsion that he felt, was the memory of the intense satisfaction caused by the little girl's suffering—and above all by her blood. And he knew, to his horror, that if he ever found himself in the same situation, he would kill again.

Although Chikatilo was cleared of any involvement in the murder, his questioning by the police caused further consternation at school. Any school officials who knew about it must have found it difficult to justify not having done anything about his assault on Sherbakov. However, again the desire for a quiet life and the wish to avoid any embarrassing scenes could have overcome the obligation to do the right thing. The situation in the country was little different by the end of the 1970s from how it had been at the beginning. The motto was still to keep your head down. It was not until 1981, when Chikatilo had been teaching in Shakhti for almost three years, that the director of the school finally dealt with him. Taking advantage of orders from above to cut staff, he summoned Chikatilo to his office one day and suggested to him that he should leave voluntarily.

Again, those in the school system had failed, reacting to Chikatilo's misdemeanors by closing their eyes. The director could not be blamed for not knowing the truth about the killing of Zakotnova. The blame for that lay fairly and squarely on the police. But as director he might have been expected to have known of Chikatilo's other actions and, assuming he did, he would have had no excuse for not doing something. It would be nice to think that in one of the more open societies of the West, the first signs of such abnormal behavior would likely have been picked up. Later, if not sooner, Chikatilo would have been obliged to seek professional psychiatric help and leave teaching, and even be prosecuted. But in the Soviet Union, this simply did not happen. In retrospect, it seems almost nothing was done to prevent this twisted man sliding down the downhill slope which was to end in disaster.

If his past experience was anything to go by, Chikatilo could have still gone off and gotten yet another teaching job. But he didn't. Maybe he had become bored with it. Or maybe the taunts of his students and the disapproving looks of his colleagues had convinced him that he was no good at it—and never would be. Instead, in another of the bizarre twists which characterized his life, he decided to change profession completely. And so, in March 1981, the former teacher with a university education began work as a simple supply clerk in the Shakhti offices of Rostovnerud, a heavy industrial conglomerate.

The job of supply clerk was unique to the old Communist centrally planned economy. Begun under Stalin and developed by his successors, everything in the system was controlled and ordered by the government in Moscow. There were no wholesalers or markets of the type found in the West. The plan was king. Factories were told what to produce by their respective ministries and allocated the necessary materials with which to produce it, down to the smallest individual ball bearing. That, at least, was the theory. In practice, it was very different. Factories were forever failing to fulfill their plans or hoarding what they had produced, causing perennial shortages. With spare parts always in short supply, an unexpected breakdown, however small, could paralyse an entire factory.

Enter the supply clerk. It was his—or rarely her—job to travel around the country persuading factory managers to release the much needed supplies. Sometimes it was a matter merely of signing papers, sometimes even going with a dumper truck and driver and bringing back tons of metal, components, or building materials. It was a job that required a particular kind of person, above all one with strong powers of persuasion who got on easily with other people and was able to win their confidence—everything which Chikatilo, himself, was not.

For someone with a higher education, it was also something of a comedown, and he seems to have been aware of it. Significantly, even after starting work at Rostovnerud, Chikatilo continued telling the people he met that he was a teacher. It was partly a cover for his activities. But it also reflected his belief that his current job was below him. Partly to maintain his intellectual self-esteem, he went to evening classes in Marxism-Leninism and does not seem to have dropped his dream of a political career. In the room where he worked in Shakhti, on the second floor of 130B, Victory of the Revolution Avenue, the walls are now decorated with calendars with pictures of semi-naked women and Aloine scenery. For the three years he was there, he hung up posters with portraits of the members of the ruling Communist Party Politburo.

In a way, the job was also better suited to his character. Faced with large groups of children, he had been a disaster; they had walked right over him. As a supply clerk, he worked on his own much of the time. This also meant one other advantage: freedom. With the factory dependent on supplies from across the length and breadth of the Soviet Union, Chikatilo was to be forever away on business trips. Some were mere day trips, but others farther afield could last a week or ten days, giving him enormous flexibility in how to spend his time. Often, no one would know exactly where he was or, more importantly, exactly what he was doing. In that respect, he was to find it an ideal job.

6

With a population of more than a million people, Rostov is by far the largest city in southern Russia. Perched high on the right bank of the River Don, it is a major administrative and industrial center for one of the country's most important and populous regions—a region which in itself is equivalent in size and population to a small European country such as Switzerland or Denmark. The layout is unoriginal; the streets are almost all straight and cross each other at right angles. All seem to lead to one thoroughfare: a long straight tree-lined road running from one end of the city toward the other which, in Soviet days, used to be called Engels Street and which has since reverted to its prerevolutionary name of Bolshaya Sadovaya Street—Large Garden Street. Here on either side are the city's main buildings: the railway and bus stations, the police, prosecutors, and KGB headquarters, parks, hotels, and restaurants. Just off the street, too, is the courtroom where Chikatilo was to end up on trial almost a decade after moving to Shakhti.

The architecture is dull: a combination of crumbling prerevolutionary buildings and monstrosities of modern Soviet architecture—among them a giant new theater school which has been under construction for as long as anyone in the city can remember and is still not finished. The city's only redeeming feature is a church modeled on the magnificent Saviour Cathedral in Moscow, which Stalin knocked down in the 1930s at the height of his antireligious campaign. And even this is tucked away out of sight somewhere behind the city market.

Yet this dry description hardly does the city justice. Like the rest of the country it has, of course, seen better days. With its strategic location on the banks of the River Don it was for centuries a trading city and it prospered as a result. Look behind the grime which today covers most of the buildings in the city center and you will see the magnificent houses where once lived and worked merchants, traders, and bankers. Most date from the end of the last century when the trade was at its peak and the legendary *Kuptsi*—merchants—were helping make themselves and Russia rich.

Something of this air has remained about Rostov—if only because of its location on the crossroads not just between the plains of mighty Russia and the mountainous republics of the Caucasus but also between Europe and Asia, and between Christianity and Islam. The frontier is the road bridge over the River Don on the edge of town. Rostov's population is a melting pot which relects this location. Although predominantly Russian, its people's blood has been mixed by centuries of immigration by the ancient tribes that roamed the Caucasus Mountains and the lands beyond to the south. The first to come were the Armenians, fleeing north from the Turks. There were so many of them that one part of the city was even called Nakhichevan in honor of the region of modern-day Azerbaijan from which they had fled. Mingled in with them are the Azerbaijanis, Georgians, Chechens, and the other semiautomous peoples of the North Caucasus, who are bitterly divided from one another over territory and religion but united by hot tempers and a love of buying and selling. For them, Rostov is the nearest large city and has always been a mecca not just for trade but also for those studying or working in large scale industry—or just looking for the kind of adventure and entertainment that only a metropolis can provide.

The southerners are not the only ones to be drawn to Rostov. With its mild climate, the city has also long attracted people from the great Russian landmass to the north. Because of its rich farm land, the whole of southern Russia has always been more prosperous than the central region around Moscow. Compared to the grim industrial cities carved out of the taiga of Siberia it is little short of paradise. The first snow rarely falls before New Years and melts away by March or April. The summer, although hot, is not spoiled by swarms of insects. Even more importantly, in a country where food has long been in short supply, fruit and vegetables are plentiful and relatively cheap at the city's bazaars and markets.

Perhaps because it acts as such a magnet for the surrounding area, Rostov has always been a city with an extremely high criminal rate, in a long-standing rivalry with the nearby Ukrainian port of Odessa. With a mixture of pride and disapproval, locals like to recite to visitors the old Russian saying: "If Odessa is the mother of crime, then Rostov is the father." The dividing line between business and crime was always gray in the Soviet Union and has continued to be so in independent Russia. While many came to Rostov for honest trade, others came for black-market dealing, racketeering, and worse. The city's central position and the influx of people that this encouraged made it especially difficult for police to keep track of its citizens.

Together with the criminals, came a group, which even in a supposedly classless society, one could call an underclass: the lumpenproletariat of Marx and Engels, who drifted south to Rostov largely for want of anywhere else better to go. Often without homes or families, they were attracted to the region by the climate and the relatively low cost of living. In summer, there was plenty of casual work in the fields of the giant collective farms helping bring in the grain or potatoes. In winter things were tougher. The economic unheaval that the country went through at the end of the1980s dramatically increased their number. But even at the beginning of the decade, many of them could be seen sleeping in the railway station or in the parks. Many were young, perhaps in their teens, often the product of broken homes who had fled after being shunted backward and forward between mother, father, and grandmother. Many also brought with them a free and easy morality, which in the case of many of the women verged on prostitution. Their poverty, desperation, and a feeling that they somehow had nothing more to lose turned them into easy victims for those who tried to prey upon them. Seventeen-year-old Larisa Tkachenko was such a victim. The following is a decription of their encounter based on Chiketibs confession to prosecutors, although he later denied this killing.

They met on September 3, 1981, in the center of Rostov, just outside the public library at the place where Engels Street crosses Voroshilovsky Prospekt, another major thoroughfare. Chikatilo, a keen reader, had been there as usual to look at the newspapers. He used to drop in to read the local papers like *Molot*

(Hammer) and *Vecherny Rostov* (Evening Rostov), as well more highbrow Moscow-based papers, such as *Literaturnaya Gazeta* (Literary Gazette) and the government daily, *Izvestia*. Summer ends early in most of Russia. But down in Rostov the weather was still good. It was one of those balmy autumn evenings typical of the south, warm but not stifling. The kind of evening when even the interminable long wait for the buses didn't seem as bad as usual. Chikatilo's home in Shaknti was more than two hours away on the local train. But he was in no hurry to rush back to his wife and children. He wanted company and he felt like picking up a woman, or better still a young girl.

Tkachenko was an unlikely partner. At seventeen, she was almost thirty years younger than this man. But then she had always had a wild and unpredictable streak. It might have been because of separation from her parents. Although she spent a fairly normal childhood in the republic of Moldavia, on the Romanian border, she had been left with her grandmother in 1976 when her mother and father upped and left in search of work on a state farm in a district of the Rostov region called Tselinski. A lively twelve-year-old, she had at first missed her parents. But as she began to grow up, she began to relish the independence that her schoolmates did not have. Her grandmother was kind but not very strict. And although she moved back with her parents when she was fifteen, she had already tasted freedom and was pleased when they decided to send her off to a boarding school. School work was of little interest to her. Her classmates described her as a bad student who often skipped lessons and paid little attention even when she bothered to turn up. But she was outgoing and popular with the other girls—and, even more, with the boys. Defying the strict curfew in place in the school, she would climb out of the windows of the dormitory to spend her time with the conscripts from the nearby army base.

Not that she had been out with the soldiers for a few weeks now. It was harvesttime and in a tradition long observed in the Soviet Union, she had been sent together with her classmates to the local farm to help bring it in. The weather had begun to cool a little, and so after a few weeks work, they had all been allowed home for a couple of days to rest and collect warm clothes. It had been a long and complicated bus journey back from the farm where they were working to her parents' place. Now, five days later, she was back in Rostov, on her way to the school where a bus was waiting to take her and the other girls back to the farm.

Why she accepted Chikatilo's invitation to go for a walk when she met him at the bus stop is not clear. Maybe she was just bored and had time to kill. Or perhaps she was curious to see what it was like to go with an older man. In any case, she said yes. And she was not so naive as to think he was just inviting her to go off to admire the sunset. No, she expected something to eat, perhaps, certainly something to drink—and more. And so they walked off together, along the pavement on the main bridge over the River Don and down toward the road running parallel on the other, more deserted bank.

Chikatilo told her that they were going to a *baza otdykha*—literally a relaxation station: a concrete complex of restaurants, cafes, and recreational facilities typical of the Soviet idea of tourism. There, it was understood, they could find a quiet corner out of the way where they could lie down unnoticed. But they never got that far. As they left the main road and crossed onto a gravel track which led through the wood, something suddenly snapped inside Chikatilo's head.

For most middle-aged men, the idea of a sudden

liaison with an attractive young woman would have
been exciting enough. And there was no doubt in his
mind at this stage that she would agree to have sex
with him. But Chikatilo was no ordinary man and he
knew only too well that he was not able to get sexual
satisfaction from straight sex. He needed something
more. As he pushed her down onto the ground beside
the track, she caught a glimpse of a look in his eyes
which frightened her. She began to wonder what she
had let herself in for. Certainly, she knew she had
expected their meeting to end in sex, but she hadn't
expected such a show of passion from a man like that.
It was all going a lot faster than she wanted. Where
was the food he had promised her and where was the
drink? She began to remonstrate as he pulled off her
trousers and put his hands on her panties.

Chikatilo could not hear her anymore. For two years
he had struggled with himself and what he had done.
Now his fantasies were already beginning to take over,
transporting him into a kind of frenzy. This had nothing to do with the kind of sterile and unsatisfying sex
he had once practised with his wife in the security of
their bedroom at home. The girl lying pressed beneath
his body on the ground was no longer a human being
with rights and with feelings. She was little more
than an object now. He was a wild animal and she
was his prey. She belonged only to him. He could
dominate her. He could use her and abuse her in any
way he wanted. Her growing sense of alarm did not
deter him. It began to remind him of the fear he had
felt in the body of little Lena Zakotnova and this only
added to his arousal.

Then she started to fight back, her terror giving her
a last burst of energy. But it was hopeless. Compared
to her, he was a giant—taller and heavier and
stronger. He stifled her screams by pushing earth into
her mouth. Then he struck harder, stunning her momentarily by punching her in the head and closing his

thick powerful wrists around her neck. She was fading now, the life being slowly choked out of her. But with every blow, he was getting stronger. Every strangled cry only aroused him further. He didn't want to stop now, he couldn't. And so he pushed the violence to its terrible and inevitable end, ejaculating over her as she lay dying beneath him. The beast inside him took over completely as he bit off one of the nipples from her lifeless body.

But this time, there was no panic, no horror, no frantic attempt to run away. Despite the danger of being caught he did not try to flee the scene of the crime. Grabbing the dead girl's clothes, he began to run around her body, faster and faster, whooping with a kind of ecstacy as he went. He was feeling drunk now with emotion, with the overpowering of avenging all the wrongs and injustices that he had suffered in his life. It was as if he were floating in the air. The clothes flew out of his hands, some into the trees, the remainder on to the ground. At one point, he sank to his knees in front of the body as if to seek forgiveness, if only for a moment. Then he was back on his feet, running for all he was worth. If anyone had arrived at that moment, they would have thought that they had stumbled into some kind of strange ritual or else that he was simply mad.

"I felt like a partisan," he said years later. The violence had given him a sexual high which had driven him deeper into a fantasy which had its roots years back in his youth. Inspired by the combination of his own savagery and the peace and stillness of the woods, he felt himself to be like one of his wartime heroes from *Molodaya Gvardiya* fighting the Nazi occupiers.

But if it was madness, then it was only temporary. Some time later, maybe after twenty or thirty minutes, his mood began to change. He calmed down. His rational side took over and he began to contemplate what he had done. It is difficult to know whether he felt remorse as he looked at the naked body lying below him. Even if he did, he was not about to go and confess. His overwhelming drive was now one of self-preservation. He had to do everything to make sure that there was no evidence. Walking quickly around the clearing, he gathered a handful of leaves and branches and covered the body. Then he took the pieces of clothing, pushed them together into a ball and hid them in a thick part of the undergrowth. After one more look to make sure that nothing had fallen out of his pockets during the struggle, he left almost as calmly as he had come.

As Chikatilo walked away, he knew that he would never be the same again. His shock after the killing of little Lena Zakotnova had been terrible; but this time, he felt almost nothing. He had known in advance what would give him satisfaction, he had sought it out and he had found it. He tried to justify the whole thing in his mind. As he saw it, Tkachenko had brought her death on herself. She was depraved. If not, why had she consented to go off with a stranger for sex in the woods?

He knew, too, that he would not stop at that. He finally understood that this was where things had been leading all his life. From the first moment that he had gone to school and mixed with the other children, he had realized that he was different. He was an outcast. And so it had gone on, from the pain of trying to establish his first relationships with girls to the frustration he felt in married life to his growing attraction to his own students at school. Now, at the age of forty-five, he realized what it all meant.

He was like a drug addict who started with marijuana and ended up on heroin. At first, it was enough to look and to touch. But as time went on, he needed to hurt and destroy. Some sex offenders have a particular fetish—maybe a kind of clothes or a certain hair color. Chikatilo's requirements were simpler. He needed only suffering. He wanted to see the pain of his victims, to hear them cry out in agony. That was how he got his kicks. He was no rapist in the ordinary sense of the term. Knowing that failure was almost preordained, he often made no attempt to have intercourse. Instead, merely masturbated over their bodies. As if desperately trying to convince himself of his own adequacy, he then tried to push his sperm into them with his hands. His satisfaction came from the thrust of his knife and blows from his fist. It was no coincidence, either, that he chose to kill in the woods. Here, of all places, he felt secure and at home.

There is also little doubt about the premeditated nature of his attacks. At his trial. Chikatilo was to claim that he had not set out to kill. He said he intended merely to have intercourse, consensual in the case of most of the adults, and rape in the case of the children. If he had stopped at Tkachenko, then it might have been possible to defend such a theory. The attack need not have been premeditated. When the two of them set out together from the bus stop, he might well have intended nothing more than sex. Yet the theory became less and less plausible with every killing that he carried out. However determined his denials, it was clear that several had been carefully planned, sometimes hours, sometimes days in advance.

For all the gradualness of his descent into depravity, it was clear that the first murder had been a huge step. This, his second, was just that little bit easier. And, so it would go on, until killing became for him as natural and routine as it was for another man to have sex.

Even so, for the next nine months, Chikatilo managed to contain his urges, at least according to police records. Then, on June 12, 1982, thirteen-year-old Lyuba

Biryuk became his next victim. She was young, clever, and well-behaved, the antithesis of Tkachenko. But that didn't save her.

The morning of that day before leaving for work, Lyuba's mother asked her to go to the nearby village of Donskoi Posyulok to buy some food. She was happy to go. The sun was shining and the weather was warm. All she was wearing was a thin blue-and-white floral dress and a pair of light sandals. Piecing together what little evidence there is of the last few hours of her life, the girl arrived at the Voskhod food store as planned and did her shopping; a boy later reported having seen her at the bus stop. But after leaving the shop, she apparently decided not to take the bus home. She walked instead. And it was then, at around midday, that she met Chikatilo.

He had been planning to travel by bus himself, but the bus never came and so he, too, set off on foot. There was something about the girl that caught his attention as soon as he saw her. He fell into step beside her and they began to talk. He asked the usual questions: what her name was, what she was doing, and where she was going. He was so attracted to her that he had to hold himself back to avoid pouncing on her then and there. The talking may have been frustrating, but it served one purpose: to keep with her until the time was right.

A few minutes later that time came. After crossing over the road, they began to walk along a path set back a little behind the bushes. It was a lot quieter there. There was no one ahead of them. Still talking, Chikatilo turned his head around to ensure that there was no one behind either. There was not. Even so, he waited a few seconds more for a final check. Then he seized his chance. The animal inside him took control and he jumped on the terrified girl, forcing her down on the ground. Ripping off her clothes, he tried to have sex with her. But, just as had been the case on the riverbank with Tkachenko, he failed. His body was letting him down.

This time, he had come prepared. He produced a knife out of his pocket and began to stab and cut her in different parts of the body. The combination of the flowing of the blood and her muffled cries of agony gave him the satisfaction that he wanted so badly. But it cost the girl her life. There was no time, though, for the ritual he had performed over Tkachenko. He was too close to the street. Aware that he could be caught at any moment, he covered the corpse, took her clothes and shopping bag and threw them into the woods. Her body, by then little more than a skeleton, was found just under two weeks later.

After Biryuk's killings, the floodgates were open. Before the end of 1982, Chiaktilo was to have killed another six people. Lyuba Volobuyeva, fourteen, was the next to die, savagely killed by Chikatilo on July 25 that year during his business trip to the southern region of Krasnodar. Nine-year-old Oleg Pozhidayev died on August 13 during another business trip, this time in the nearby Adygey district. Back in the Rostov region, he killed sixteen-year-old Olya Kuprina three days later. Another two victims followed in September: Ira Karabelnikova and Sergei Kuzmin, within nine days and a mile of each other, just outside Shakhti. Then, in December 1982, he killed ten-year-old Olya Stalmachenok, although he later recanted his confession of this murder in court.

The killings marked the beginning of a police operation that was to be known as *Lesopolosa*—forest path—taking its name from the place where almost all of the first bodies were found. Despite Rostov's high murder rate, it was clear from the start that these were no ordinary killings. A special group was formed within the police and they began to investigate. For the time being, though, they decided to tell the public nothing. To do so, they believed, would only cause panic and, in the last days of Leonid Brezhnev, the media were still rigidly controlled and did as they were told.

This was even more the case because of the very cruelty of these killings. It was not the quantity of knife wounds—even though in some cases there were as many as thirty of them. It was also their nature. It quickly became clear that this was not just someone who wanted his victim dead; a couple of well-aimed blows would have been enough for that. No, he was deliberately prolonging the killing for the simple reason that he derived pleasure from it. Many of the bodies, too, were horribly mutilated: stomachs were ripped open and sexual organs sliced off. In some cases the forensic evidence suggested that this horrific surgery had taken place while the victim was still alive and possibly even conscious.

There was another feature of the killings, which was almost like the murderer's signature: virtually every body they found had stab wounds around the eyes. As a phenomenon, it was extremely rare. Later, when other bodies were found hundreds of miles from Rostov, it was these bizarre eye wounds that would help police to identify the victims as part of the pattern. Explaining the wounds was not so easy. According to one theory, the murderer believed that a dead person's retina is somehow marked by the last image which they see before they die—in this case the face of their killer. Another more likely one was that the killer was so ashamed of what he was doing and so unwilling to come to terms with it, that he tried to avoid the gaze of the victims. Blinding, or at the very least blindfolding, them was the only way.

But if they were alike in death, then in life the victims had been very different. They were a strange mixture of age, social background, and of sex. Like Biryuk before him, Pozhidayev had been an innocent child who had just been unlucky enough to cross Chikatilo's path. But most of the others fitted into the mold of Tkachenko. They were victims of broken homes, who had drifted out of conventional society into extreme promiscuity and thence into prostitution.

This was certainly true of Karabelnikova, an eighteen-year-old who had been killed after going off willingly for sex with Chikatilo. The product of a broken marriage, she had lived first with her coal miner father. But then, after falling out with him, she had gone off to her mother. However, she quarreled with her as well and went to live instead in a hostel. An affair with a soldier offered a way out, but their wedding plans fell through and she was caught in the middle, with no one to confide in besides a grandmother. Given the variety of places where she lived, it took days before her disappearance was even noticed. As for her body, it lay unnoticed for a full two weeks before it was found.

It was precisely this problem which made it so difficult for police to solve many of the murders. Normally, the solving of a murder begins with identification of the victim. However, if the police do not even know the name of the dead man or woman, then it is difficult to move to the next stage: where they lived, where they worked, where they spent their time, and who their friends were—in short, all the kind of information that is needed to reconstruct the last few hours and days of their lives and ultimately to track down the killer.

With many of Chikatilo's early victims, it was the step of identification that was the difficult part. Many of the women he killed in the first few years were people whom nobody cared about. Some were teenage girls caught between their mother and father in a broken home. Others were mentally disturbed women from hostels, or else tramps, alcoholics, and prostitutes. In comparison with large Western cities like London or New York, Rostov had few such people. Yet, however much the Soviet authorities tried to pretend that they did not exist, they formed a perceptible social group not just in Rostov but also in many other sizable Russian cities.

For all the Communist state's pretentions to equality and compassion, it did very little for those at the bottom of society. Social services were badly developed and there were virtually no social workers of the type found in the West. With unemployment officially deemed nonexistent, those without jobs were treated as parasites and threatened with jail rather than given help and welfare money. Alcoholism and homelessness, too, were traditionally treated merely as public order problems rather than social ones. Every evening, the police would appear at the railway station, round up the tramps and either put them overnight in drying-out stations or else in the cells. The ranks of the down-and-outs were also swollen by former prison inmates, who often returned to society to find themselves without home or job or any kind of counseling on how to build a new life. Life was particularly hard for former residents of Moscow, Leningrad, and other cities with strict residence requirements, who were often forced into a kind of hopeless nomadic life because authorities withdrew their much prized right to live in their home town.

It was no coincidence that Chikatilo chose this particular kind of victim. Without a *propiska*—the formal registration of residence—a person was a mere name, not an individual let alone someone with rights, and had no place in the system. They were treated as little better than a stray dog. The police were not the only ones to be aware of the problems of tracing such people. A cool and calculating killer, Chikatilo must also have realized the clear advantages of murdering someone whose disappearance could go unnoticed for weeks, months, or even years.

But there was also a strong bond between murderer and victim, a mixture both of attraction and of hatred. Even if it did not seem so on the surface, they had a lot in common. Certainly, he had things that they did not, like a home, a good job, and some money. Despite his increasingly horrific crimes, he was still in society and they had dropped out of it into the limbo below. Yet, like them, he also felt a sense of rejection, of being a misfit who was forever misunderstood and not properly appreciated by his fellow men. There was some very powerful affinity which drew him to them.

He was at once drawn to and repelled by that world where the barriers of decency and morality had long since fallen. The more time he spent hanging out in the railway station, the more he was appalled by the side of humanity he saw there. He despised the women for their drunkenness and the way they were ready to go off for sex with a man for a glass of vodka or a few crumbs to eat. And he hated them even more for the way that they would go off with him.

"They followed me like dogs," he told his captors later, the choice of words expressing the depth of his disgust at the ease with which they had submitted to his will. The thinking behind the remark was obvious. If only *they* had behaved according to higher moral standards, then they would still have been alive. Yet they had come with him and by so doing had demonstrated that they had no right to live. In all likelihood, such reasoning was little more than a weak attempt to justify his actions to himself after the event. It also suggests that Chikatilo's motives may not have been exclusively sexual. He put himself in the role of an exterminator of those he considered little more than vermin. In his perverted way, he began to see himself not as a killer, but somehow as a cleanser of society.

Yet it would be difficult to apply that argument to the death of Olga Stalmachenok, who disappeared in Novoshakhtinsk on December 11, 1982. A well-brought-up girl from a caring family, she set off home on the bus that afternoon from music school as she always used to do every day. But in a cruel twist of fate, the bus broke down. All the passengers had to get off at the railway station to wait for a replacement. It was in that moment, at about five o'clock in the afternoon, that Chikatilo arrived and made contact with her.

As it turned out years later, there were several people who saw the little girl leave on that last fateful bus ride. There was even one who saw her walk off with her killer and could even have identified him—if anyone had bothered to ask. Maria Sobivchak watched the two of them walk past as she went out onto the street to fetch in her own child that evening. The man was leading the girl very firmly by the hand, as if he were her father or grandfather who had just told her off for something. "Why is he being so harsh with her?" she thought at the time. The incident, itself, seemed like nothing to her.

However, it stuck in her mind because of the face of the man. She felt that she knew him from somewhere. It was only years afterwards, when police came around the neighborhood with a photograph of Chikatilo that she put two and two together. Not only had this been the man, but she also remembered where she had seen him before: Chikatilo had taught her son when he was working in the school in Novoshakhtinsk. She had even met him once when she went there for a parents' evening. It turned out that a bus conductor had also noticed the girl. She remembered her getting off the bus when it broke down at the station, but then disappearing during the few minutes it took for the replacement to arrive. A red car had been standing nearby and she assumed that Stalmachenok had gone off in it. But she was not so sure, realizing only later that she had been one of the last people to see the little girl alive. The police, however, never made contact with either of the women. They were pursuing another, more bizarre line of questioning.

At that time, a postcard arrived at the main post office. By the afternoon it was already on a desk at police headquarters. The postcard was addressed simply to "Parents of the Missing Child." Its text was short and cruel. "Greetings, parents. Don't get upset. She is not the first and not the last. Before New Year we need another 10. If you want to find her, then search among the leaves on the Vdarovski Posadki." It was signed "Sadist—Black Cat."

Having so far enjoyed no success in solving any of the murders, police threw everything into their attempt to identify the author. Viktor Burakov, chief of the section for serious sexual crimes in the Rostov CID, was convinced the card was written by someone who knew the area well. For, as he pointed out, the term Vdarovski was one used only by the locals. As the investigation gathered pace, dozens of police officers were dispatched to local post offices. The desk clerks were questioned over whether they had seen anyone posting the card—or even asking to borrow a pen in order to write it.

That was only a part of it. Breaking new ground, experts from the local branch of the KGB were called in to analyse the handwriting for clues to the identity of the author. Using the individual letters which made up the text, they devised a key which was then applied to thousands of other letters and documents written by employees of factories, offices, and other institutions in the region. The letter was also carefully compared with other anonymous ones reported in the past to police. To many of those taking part, the operation looked like a fruitless search for a needle in a haystack. But it was merely a foretaste of the huge operations which were to be launched in the next few years in response to a particular theory or piece of evidence.

Their bosses thought it was worth it. In the past, the same technique had been applied successfully to track down another killer from the city of Vitebsk who was convicted of killing thirty-six women. This time, though, it drew a blank. A search of Vdarovski Posadki failed to turn up the body. The remains of the girl were not found until four months after she died and then, only by chance and some distance away.

Nevertheless, the police never entirely gave up the idea of a connection. They even revived the theory briefly some four years later. But again, it was to get them nowhere. And, when Chikatilo was finally arrested, he denied all knowledge of it. The police were already facing enough problems tracking down the killer. Now, it seemed they had to contend with a hoaxer as well. Black Cat turned out to be a red herring.

By summer 1983, the Soviet Union was going through a minor earthquake. Nothing to compare with the turmoil that was to come at the end of that decade, but dramatic nonetheless. After just over eighteen years in power, the aging Leonid Brezhnev had finally died and was replaced by Yuri Andropov, the former KGB chief. His successor was barely younger and certainly not much fitter, but he was determined to inject new life into the moribund Soviet economy. And the way he wanted to do it was by improving discipline. Towards the end of the Brezhnev era, the whole attitude to work had been summed up by the old saying: "We pretend to work and they pretend to pay us." But no more.

The pay was not getting any better but Andropov was determined that the work would be. In order to achieve his goal he was ready to resort to the strong-arm methods that had served so well in his previous job. Employees long used to slipping out to shops, the barber, or the cafe during working hours were hauled

unceremoniously back to their bosses. Punishments
meted out to these so-called violators of "labor discipline" varied from cuts in salaries and bonuses to
demotion to the bottom of the waiting list for state
housing. Trying to turn the whole country into a giant
gulag was never going to save the Soviet economy. It
was already locked into a deep, long-term decline that
no amount of tinkering could change. Yet it might still
have succeeded in slowing the slide if only it had been
continued for a little longer.

By all accounts, Chikatilo survived the new harsh
regime relatively unscathed. As he found time and
time again, the great advantage of work as a supply
clerk was the independence. Andropov or no Andropov, he remained his own master. His working hours
were flexible and his trips away from his office in
Shakhti were frequent. If he wanted to spend hours
just hanging around at the railway station or walking
the street, then he was free to do so—and no one
would know about it.

That was about the only thing that *was* going well.
He was quickly beginning to realize that he was almost as bad a supply clerk as he had been a teacher.
Colleagues found him cold and unfriendly and wondered why he behaved so oddly the whole time. His
superiors thought him incompetent and wasted no
time in telling him so.

"As a man there was something strange about him.
I cannot say that anyone particularly liked him,"
recalled one woman who worked with him as head of
the warehouse where he had to bring his supplies.
Others used to watch in fascination as he sat at his
desk writing in a little exercise book. He was so
absorbed in what he was doing that sometimes he did
not even seem to hear when people were talking to
him. He used to keep his distance from the men, too,
never joining them when they went out drinking after

work and walking straight past when they stood in the corridor talking and smoking.

By now, his obsession was also beginning to have an effect on his work. The so-called *planyorki*, the planning meetings held early every morning, inevitably saw Chikatilo receiving a sharp dressing down from his bosses. Any job in the supply division was inevitably a thankless one. Shortages and breakdowns were a permanent feature of the old planned economy, with things always running out or turning out to have been of poor quality. And always the poor supply clerk seemed to get the blame. It was one of the hazards of the job.

Even so, Chikatilo seemed to get told off more than most. Pyotr Evrafov, the deputy director of the plant who chaired the meetings, began to loathe his employee so intensely that he would make him leave in the middle, just like a teacher sending out a naughty pupil. The former teacher accepted meekly, without putting up any kind of protest. But the air of indifference that he cultivated was only a front. Underneath, he was suffering. Despite the criticism, he was convinced that he was doing his job properly. Evgrafov and the others simply didn't like him, just like his bosses at the school hadn't liked him. And because of that, they would pick on him and deliberately do so in front of as many people as possible.

"God, it would be better if I went away on a trip again," he told Nina Dovgan, a brassy blonde who worked as a bookkeeper in the material supplies department. "At least when I am on the road, there is no one always there telling me off." She was about the only one in the place who didn't have only bad words to say for him. Whenever he came back from a trip, it was her job to book in the materials that he had brought back.

Despite all the stories about Chikatilo being a bad worker, Dovgan was more struck by his incredible memory. If she could not find anything that he was meant to have brought back, he could tell her immediately where he had put it in the warehouse, down to the last shelf or cupboard. She was also one of the few people ever to have sat down and had a drink with him. Sometimes he would flirt a little with her and a couple of the other secretaries, even inviting them to join him on summer picnics to celebrate their birthdays or other special occasions. He was good fun as well. He liked jokes. But that was all. He never made a pass at her nor, as far as she could tell, at the other women.

As for everyone else, they were struck by what seemed to be Chikatilo's increasingly odd behavior which was, in itself, a product of his other secret life which he was finding difficult to keep separate. As part of his job, for example, he would often go off by truck with a driver to pick up supplies in Rostov or other nearby cities. But then when the job was done, he would stay on, sending the driver back to Shakhti on his own. "I've just got some business to attend to here," he would say. "I'll find my own way back later." Even if the driver offered to wait for him, he would refuse. It seemed strange, particularly since it took a good two hours to get back on the train. From early evening onward, they also began to be infrequent.

And there was the matter of the bag he had with him the whole time. The women in the office were always curious about it and one day they couldn't resist any longer; waiting until he had left the room for a few minutes, one of them quickly opened it. After all that buildup, what they saw in the end was rather disappointing. Inside they found nothing more exciting than a change of clothing, a pair of white underpants, and a T-shirt. Nevertheless, it did not stop them from playing a trick on him. Before closing the bag, they popped a brick into it as a joke. He did not say anything at the time. Despite the extra weight, he just picked up the bag when it was time to go home and took it with him. He probably did not want to open it in front of them. The next morning when he came to work he told off his colleagues for not acting their ages.

However strange Chikatilo's behavior, none of his colleagues would have believed him capable of murder. After his arrest, several were still insisting there must have been a mistake. One woman, though, recalled peering over his shoulder one day when he was writing in his usual exercise book. What she saw on the blank pages were row after row of little crosses. Suddenly, all those years later, she understood what they meant.

The police were not doing any better in guessing what Chikatilo was up to. During the course of 1982, he had committed some seven murders and police appeared no closer to catching him then they had been a year before. The evidence was virtually nonexistent and, as far as they were concerned, it was difficult to be sure that the killings were really a series. Despite the similarity of the bizarre eye injuries, the very different character and background of the victims were throwing them off. Even more problematic was the time that it took before they were able to locate the remains of some of the first victims. The four months that it had taken them to find Stalmachenok was long—but not the longest. The body of Sergei Kuzmin, killed three months before her, had lain undiscovered for six. That of nine-year-old Oleg Pozhidayev, killed in August 1982, was never found at all.

This inevitably made things more complicated. Whenever children were involved, it was always difficult for police to know whether they were dealing with an actual murder or just with a boy or girl who had run away from home. They could only be one hundred percent sure once they had found the body.

In many cases, too, they were found without clothes, further adding to the problems of identification. Even if the clothes were found, they were often some distance away and picked up only later.

The Rostov police were not the only ones exasperated by the lack of progress. In Moscow, too, there was consternation about the murders. So, in summer 1983, a joint group including representatives of the police and the Public Prosecutor's Office was sent down to the region to find out what was happening. One of the leading members from the prosecutor's side was an articulate, intelligent man called Vladimir Kazakov. Boasting extensive experience in fighting serious crime, he was a natural choice for the team.

During a month that he spent in the region, Kazakov had a chance to study the investigation, and he was not happy with it. Given the region's high murder rate, he accepted the difficulty faced by the local police in working out which murders were linked and which were not. But after a few days spent studying piles of dossiers in the local prosecutor's office in Rostov, Kazakov came to the conclusion that at least six of the murders should be linked and attributed to the same killer. Partly it was because they were all children and partly because of the geographical location. More important still were the eye injuries.

But if this were true, then it required immediate changes in the way the investigation was being run. Until now, each murder had been the work of the individual district in which it had been committed. If they were linked, then they would automatically be passed to the next higher level, the regional prosecutor's office in Rostov. And that would be a good thing in itself, anyway. As far as he could tell from the records, most of the district agencies had showed a deplorably low level of competence in dealing with the crimes. Moving the investigation to the next level above could put the whole thing into the hands of more professional investigators. There was no more time to be wasted. A monster was out there and the police were getting nowhere.

When he arrived back in Moscow. Kazakov wrote a report to his boss, Boris Namestnikov, the deputy prosecutor of the Russian Federation. In it, he spelled out his criticism of the way the investigation had been going and argued that there was overwhelming evidence to suggest that six of the murders had been committed by the same murderer for sexual motives. His recommendations were swiftly followed.

On September 6, 1983, Namestnikov signed a resolution formally uniting Kazakov's six. Biryuk was among them, as was Stalmachenok. So too were the two tramps, Karapelnikova and Kuprina, even though a year after their killings their identities had still to be established. Number five and six were two new murders which had just happened that summer. Both the latest were in Aviators' Park, a large deserted stretch of woodland on the edge of Rostov near the airport: Ira Dunenkova, a thirteen-year-old girl whom Chikatilo later confessed to having murdered in July, and seven-year-old Igor Gudkov, who was slaughtered the following month.

Young Dunenkova was not his first murder of 1983. Less than a month before, he had killed a fifteen-year-old Armenian girl, Laura Sarkisyan. But her body was never found. The police learned of the case only when Chikatilo confessed years later. In retrospect, though, the killing of thirteen-year-old Ira Dunenkova stands out. In almost every other case, Chikatilo's victims had been unknown people whom he had met at railroad stations or on the street. Little Ira, however, knew her murderer and had even been to his house. Her older sister, Tatyana, had been one of the girls whom Chikatilo had taken back several times to his hovel in Mezhevoi Pereulok in Shakhti. Sometimes, Ira had come along too.

They were an unfortunate pair. Their parents had died a few years before and although Tatyana was old enough to live on her own, Ira was not. She was also slightly mentally handicapped and so had been sent to a children's home. Chikatilo's affair with Tatyana had been short and not particularly sweet. As with his other lovers, he had been terrified that his wife would find out, so he insisted that they should never be seen together. If she came to see him, then she would do so on her own. If they met somehow by accident in town, then he told her to act as if they were complete strangers.

Throwing caution to the wind, though, Tatyana once decided to bring her sister along. To her surprise, Chikatilo had not objected. On the contrary, he seemed rather pleased. The little girl was pretty and neatly turned out, and although he did not try to molest her, it was clear to her elder sister that he was fascinated by her. It was a meeting that he put to good use when he ran into Ira again by chance one afternoon that July.

It had been more than a year since they had seen each other. But with his memory for faces, he recognized the little girl immediately when he saw her hanging about at the railway station. She was shabbily dressed now, her hair was unkempt, and she looked as if she hadn't washed for several days. In her dirty palm, she was clutching a few coins with which she was planning to buy a pie from a stand. From talking to her before, he knew that she would be easy prey for him. All he had to do was tell her to come with him and she would obey. And sure enough, he turned out to have been right. Once he had led her to a secluded spot in Aviators' Park, he attempted to have sex with her and, when he failed, he got out his

terrible knife and killed her, too. Her mangled body
was found in the park a month later.

Other murders followed soon after. The victims
were either prostitutes or girls who went willingly
with Chikatilo in the anticipation that their meeting
would end in sex—rather than in death. Lyuda Kut-
syuba, twenty-four, a tramp, was killed near a small
railway stop just outside Shakhti later in July—although it took more than nine months to find her
body. Two others, Valya Chuchulina, twenty-two, and
another woman were killed late that summer. In the
investigators' records she appears only as "N": the
first letter of the Russian word for unknown. They
were able to say only that she was probably between
eighteen and twenty-five and had type B blood.

All this time, the police had not been idle. Yet the
path on which they embarked turned out later to have
been spectacularly wrong. The very horror of the
killings had convinced them that they were the work
of someone who was mentally handicapped. And so,
acting on this hunch, they pulled in their first suspects, a couple of young men called Kalenik and
Shaburov. Residents of a special hostel for the handicapped, they were formally arrested for trying to steal
a car. What happened next, though, formed the basis
of an action formally accusing the police of "infringe-
ment of legality" in the handling of the investigation.

After he pulled the two in, the officer working on
their case believed police had reason to suspect them
of more than just the theft charge. And during questioning, they obtained what they had hoped for: Besides stealing the car, the two confessed to having also
raped and killed several women and children. Kalenik's confession was dated September 10, Shaburov's
soon after. Because of Kazakov's theory of a single
murderer, the police were in doubt about the validity
of their statements. Although the men were both mentally subnormal, they apparently identified with great

accuracy the places where the victims' bodies had been found and described convincingly how they had killed them. In fact, to some their very sub-normality seemed further confirmation of their guilt. As one policeman put it, they were simply not intelligent enough to have made up a story that fitted the facts so neatly.

But there was a catch: The killings were continuing. While Kalenik and Shaburov were being interrogated, the police were presented with two more corpses: Vera Shevkun, a nineteen-year-old prostitute killed on October 27 on the edge of Shakhti and fourteen-year-old schoolboy Sergei Markov, killed exactly two months later on a piece of wasteland about a mile north of the nearby town of Novorherkassk, but this was little more than a hiccup. Police quickly found new suspects for the new crimes. Another two young men named Tyapkin and Ponomarev, both from the same hostel as Kalenik and Snaburov, were pulled in, and they, too, quickly confessed. Although police claimed they were acting perfectly correctly in the way they extracted the confessions, again there were doubts.

And so it went on. The new year bought more killings—and the arrest of another suspect. On January 10, workers in Aviators' Park found the body of a seventeen-year-old girl called Natalya Shalapinina. It was in a terrible state, covered with stab wounds. To their horror, they saw that the nose and upper lip had been cut off—as had one of the fingers of her left hand.

According to information put together by police, Shalapinina had been a tramp and an alcoholic who neither worked nor studied. Like many of the previous victims, she had been the unhappy product of a broken marriage; her father had left her mother while she was still at school and then remarried, and she was effectively shunted back and forth between the two. Often she lived with neither, instead staying with one of several casual boyfriends. She was also found to have been suffering from a number of sexually transmitted diseases.

Things were going badly for Chikatilo. His colleagues were virtually ignoring him, while his bosses were finding fault with his work. Although he clearly believed he was still doing his job properly, it was very difficult to see how he could have been. In the three years since he had begun working at the factory, he had been drawn more and more deeply into his secret life.

His life at that time was divided into three parts which he strove to keep separate from one another: home, work, and the hunt for victims. So far he had managed to keep his obsession secret, from the police, from his wife, from everyone. But it was like a cancer, squeezing out the first two, ruining his career, and destroyed what was left of his private life. Although he was still trying to keep up the pretense for outsiders of being a happily married man, it was increasingly difficult to do so. By now, he was rarely at home anymore, with the excuse of business trips—some genuine and some invented—he was spending more and more evenings and nights in search of prey, seeking out the places where the vagrants hung out and trying to infiltrate their world. And he was also rarely at work.

Despite all this, he somehow managed to convince himself that his bosses were wrong and that he was being unfairly treated. But what could he do? He never had the courage to answer them back to their faces. Instead, he would go back to his office and sit quietly writing letters of complaint about them to their superiors and to the local Communist Party. The letters did his position no good whatsoever. If anything, they made things much worse, only increasing his reputation as a moaner and a tale-teller. But for him, it was a way of getting anger out of his system, like chopping wood or other heavy physical work.

Strangely, the emotion which he put into it had an effect of monetarily calming the sexual frustration which was taking over his life. While he was venting his spleen on paper, he managed to forget his obsession with sex and with his own inadequacy. The sense of relief wore off quickly, and soon he was out again on the streets looking for victims.

Once work in the factory started again following the New Year holiday. Chikatilo set off by truck for Moscow with one of the drivers from the factory in Shakhti. It was a routine trip. Rostovnerud needed supplies from some factories in the capital, so the two of them drove the 600 miles or so north to collect them. The whole thing was expected to take a few days.

The driver hadn't been looking forward to it. It was bad enough having to go to Moscow, but doing so with Chikatilo made it worse. He did not like the man any more than his other colleagues did, and the thought of being stuck with him for hours on end in the cab was positively depressing. Yet nothing that he had seen of Chikatilo at work had prepared him for what he was to witness in Moscow. After they had finished their work on the first day, Chikatilo sent him back to the factory hostel where they were staying and told him he would return on his own later. The driver didn't see him until the morning. He had no idea where Chikatilo had stayed and presumed that he must have found a woman somewhere. But he did the same thing again the next evening, and the one after.

However, in the end it was not Chikatilo's bizarre nightlife which got him into trouble. When they got back to Shakhti, they dropped off the rolls of linoleum and other material they had collected in Moscow and went home. It was only when the bookkeeper checked it all in later that she found that there were about 70

meters less of it than the paperwork said there should
have been.

The fact of something being missing was not
strange in itself. Pilfering was almost an integral part
of the old Communist system where, in theory, everything belonged to everyone but in practice it belonged
to no one. Despite stringent penalties—up to the death
sentence—for theft of state property, the practice was
virtually unstoppable. Even in post-Communist Russia, it continues on a massive scale. There were stories, not althogether apocryphal, of workers in car
factories stealing enough parts day by day eventually
to build a car of their own. But if theft was a charac-
teristic of the system, then so too was paperwork.
And, whichever way you looked at it, the two rolls of
linoleum were not there and had to be accounted for.

Determined to avoid being blamed herself, the
woman rang her boss over at headquarters where
Chikatilo worked and explained the problem with the
shipment. He immediately called Chikatilo and told
him to track down the missing linoelum and take it in
immediately.

"All right, I'll bring it in," Chikatilo replied. But he
didn't. He was convinced that he had delivered the
right amount and had no idea what had happened. At
a loss for what to do, he simply stayed away from
work for a couple of weeks.

If it had been any other employee, it might well
have been left at that. Chikatilo, however, was different. Evgrafov was not the only one of his superiors
who disliked him. The way he behaved had not en-
deared him to any of them. And he was not very good
at the job, either. In fact, they had been trying to find
some way of getting rid of him for a long time. There
had already been one occasion shortly before when
they had suspected him of stealing a car battery. But
there had been no evidence and one person claimed

that he had actually paid for it. This time, though, they seemed to have a much more cast-iron case.

Although he could have seen it coming, the whole thing had a dramatic effect on Chikatilo. His anger and frustration were growing now. Often he would go to places like the railway station or the park where he knew he could find tramps and other down-and-outs ripe for the picking, preferring to sleep there on the benches with them, his suit contrasting with their own shabby clothes. At first he had been sickened by the stinking corridors and the dirty benches, but the instinct to hunt and to kill helped him overcome his revulsion. They were not the only victims he was after. By now, wherever he went, he was on the lookout, forever alert and searching for someone to pick up.

To the surprise of Chikatilo's colleagues, his wife Fayina turned up at the factory and began trying to remonstrate with his bosses. She insisted that her husband was innocent, only too shy to speak up for himself, and begged them to drop the whole thing. But they did not listen to her pleading. The case was passed to the local police and on February 22, 1984, formal charges were made against him for theft of state property. Although they could not actually fire him until the case came to court, it was suggested in no uncertain terms to Chikatilo that it would be a good idea if he found himself a new job.

That very night the body of a forty-four-year-old woman, later identified as Marta Ryabyenko, was found in Aviators' Park—virtually in the same place where Natalya Shalapinina had been slaughtered a month before. Like the eighteen-year-old girl, she was a tramp seeking oblivion in sex and alcohol. Once happily married, Ryabyenko had broken up with her husband and had begun walking the streets. Vodka, hunger, and venereal disease made her look desperate and much older than her age.

On February 27, five days after her killing, police arrested a man not far from the scene of the crime. Although a little older than the other suspects pulled in over the previous few months, he was also slightly mentally slow. He was detained after allegedly raping a tramp in the woods nearby. Again, solid evidence was lacking. But the coincidence appeared to have been too great for police. He was charged with the two killings and he, too, confessed. Like the others, he also withdrew his claim insisting that it had been obtained under duress. But it was too late. He was already in jail.

Just over a month later came another killing and with it what should have been the first piece of evidence to lead police to Chikatilo. On March 27, in a housing estate on the edge of Novoshaktinsk known by the initials ATX, was found the body of a ten-year-old boy called Dima Ptashnikov. He had been a gifted child who loved stamp collecting, archaeology, and poetry; a complete contrast to Shalapinina and Ryabyenko. Nevertheless, his body had the all-too-familiar stab wounds—a horrifying fifty-four in all—that should have immediately characterized it as having been one in the series. Not far from the body in a piece of muddy ground was found a footprint. Police and investigators were convinced that it had been made by his murderer. The print was incomplete and not a lot to go on. All they could tell from it was that the killer had large feet. But given the absence of any other real evidence, it seemed at the time like a major breakthrough.

There was also another piece of evidence: Soon after Ptashnikov's body was found, one of his neighbors came forward to say that she had seen the boy walking with an unknown man just before the time he was believed to have died. Although she had seen the man only from behind, she reckoned that he was somewhere between fifty and fifty-five years old, and from five foot ten inches to six feet tall. He was wearing glasses and carrying a bag. A final detail she had noticed was that he was walking strangely: He had a slight limp and was dragging one of his legs behind him.

In retrospect, there seems little doubt that the man she saw was Chikatilo. It was even established later that he had been suffering a problem with the blood vessels in his leg at the time and for that reason had some problems walking. But even if she had known his name, it would barely have helped police. Although Ptashnikov was the twenthieth person he had killed, Chikatilo was still completely unknown to them.

8

The railway station in the town of Shakhti is a nondescript, green one-story building at the end of Yury Gagarin Street. Far from the city center, it is a sleepy place: four platforms, a few wooden benches, and a buffet full of gray salami and sad-looking hard-boiled eggs. The calm is disturbed only by the roar of the express trains which pass through on their way from Moscow down to Rostov and beyond. There in May 1984, during a pause in his search for work, Chikatilo met Tanya Petrosyan.

In fact, the two of them went back a long way. They had first met in 1978. Then, as now, it had been at the station. Tanya, a plain-looking young woman with short straight black hair, had been working in the station buffet, selling pies. Chikatilo went in there one day to get a bite to eat and they started talking. Then aged twenty-six, the woman had been impressed by this smooth-talking man who was almost twenty years her senior. Certainly, you couldn't call him striking. But he was smartly dressed and had a pleasant manner. Other men who came in were so rude. They barked out their orders without so much as a please or thank you and treated her as if she were nothing. He was well-mannered and polite—charming even. Soon they began to hit it off. He invited her out and, although she was married, she accepted.

After that first chance meeting at the buffet, the two of them had become lovers, if you could really use the word. Chikatilo had always taken her to the house in Mezhevoi Pereulok. She was not very clever, maybe a little simple. Police would later describe her as having been slightly mentally subnormal. Chikatilo liked his women that way. It made them easier to manipulate. Tanya used to slip out to meet him there whenever her husband was away, leaving her young daughter, Sveta, with the girl's grandmother.

Even so, the whole thing did not last long. Chikatilo's sexual powers had already deteriorated to the point where he was unable to achieve full intercourse. She soon lost interest and after a few clandestine meetings they did not see each other again. Neither spouse found out.

But all that had changed by the time they met again, quite by chance, on that sunny spring afternoon in Shakhti. Chikatilo had not been Tanya's only lover and her husband had found out. After a huge fight, he had left home, leaving her alone with her daughter and mother. Now, all that time later, she was back at the station. She had just been with little Sveta to visit her ex-husband and collect her alimony payments, and was on her way back home.

They recognized each other immediately. It had been six years, but neither had changed much. For Petrosyan, it was a pleasant reminder of the past. Although Chikatilo had been fairly hopeless in bed, he had been nice to her. Now, lonely and single again, she would have been happy to resume where they had left off. Chikatilo, too, was keen to resume the ac-

quaintance. It had been more than a month since he
had killed Ptashnikov and he was beginning to feel
the terrible hunger again.

As they stood there chatting at the station, he began
to analyze the situation. From what he remembered
about his old girlfriend, taking her off to one of his
favorite spots in the woods would be easy. All he had
to do was propose a small, preferably alcoholic, picnic
and she would follow. There was also the bonus of her
daughter; he had last seen Sveta as a small child. Now
she was eleven years old and also, perhaps, beginning
to be interesting.

There was a problem. Tanya did not seem interested
in coming with him now. If he wanted her, then they
would have to arrange to meet again and that would
be dangerous. Chikatilo knew how intensively the
police were looking for the killer. He knew, too, that it
was the care with which he picked his victims that
had prevented them from realizing that he was the
killer. No one knew who he was as he chatted with the
women and children at railway stations or on trains;
no one noticed as he led them off to their death in the
woods. The only exception had been little Ira Dunenkova, and she had been a child.

However, Petrosyan knew him. If they went out
together again, there was a danger that she might tell
one of her friends or even her mother in advance. If
she didn't come back, then it could be extremely
dangerous for him. In any case, he decided to keep his
options open. He took her new address and said he
would come around and visit her one day. But he
insisted that she shouldn't tell a soul about him—and
with good reason. After all, he was still married.
Shakhti was a small town and he did not want news
of their little liaison to get back to his wife.

Despite his fears, Chikatilo did not resist for long.
The thought of a new conquest was too much for him.
He didn't have to kill her, after all. So, a few days

later, he was back on the train, riding towards Petrosyan's new home in the village of Donskol. The place
held memories for him. As he walked out of the station
he passed within a few yards of the stretch of woodland where he had killed Lyuba Biryuk almost two
years before. Still he remembered it all as if it had
been just yesterday: the way he had ripped off her
little blue-and-white floral dress and the expression
of agony on her face as he had begun to stab her. It
was only now, all that time later, that he appreciated
quite how dangerous the killing had been. It had been
broad daylight and he had been far too near the road.
As he saw it, it was one of those opportunities in life
that present themselves, and he had seized it. This
time would be different, though. With Petrosyan, he
could name the meeting place and she would follow
him there. He began to get excited at the thought of
it.

When he arrived at the house, he was dismayed to
see that Petrosyan's mother was at home. But she was
old, and like her daughter, she didn't seem to be
entirely there. He greeted her without introducing
himself and immediately went off with Tanya into
another room to talk. He didn't stay long. Chikatilo
was no lover of conversation for its own sake and even
if he had been, Petrosyan was not the kind of partner
he would have chosen. He wanted her for another
purpose. They set a meeting for a few days later, again
at the railway station in Shakhti. After seeing Sveta
playing there, he suggested to Petrosyan she might
like to bring her daughter along as well, and promised
to bring her a doll.

A little voice in the back of his head was still telling
him to be careful. Again, he made Petrosyan promise
that she would not tell anything to her mother or to
anyone else. Even if she had, though, there was little
that she could actually have told. Although they had
met often back in 1978, she had never asked his

surname. She knew only that he was married and was a teacher. As far as she knew, he was still one. After receiving her word, Chikatilo slipped quietly out of the flat and got the train back home to his wife.

The meeting was set for a few days later, and it went like clockwork. Chikatilo had already selected the stretch of woods where he was going to take Petrosyan. It was a matter only of leading her there and making sure that as few people as possible saw them on the way. They met as planned at Shakhti. She was already on the train and he quickly found her compartment. They traveled together for just ten minutes as far as a little stop called Sady—which literally means gardens. It was hardly an appropriate name. At this point, the wood through which the railway line runs is at its densest and most impenetrable.

Petrosyan feared nothing as they climbed out. It was an ideal secluded place for a romantic picnic on a sunny spring day. She might have been wary about going there alone with a complete stranger. But she had known Chikatilo for years. And anyway, her daughter was with her. Sveta often came along, even on romantic outings like this one. By now the girl was used to it. She had learned when was the time to make herself scarce and to go off and play with her doll.

Anyone who watched this threesome as they sat together on the train could be forgiven for being puzzled. What was the relationship between the man and the woman? Was he her husband or her father? They would also have noticed that the woman was already drunk and unsteady on her feet. The man, by contrast, was calm and sober. But no one seemed to have noticed anything. If anyone did see them getting out at the little country railway station, then it made little impression.

They walked for only about ten minutes after getting out of the train. Chikatilo knew that they did not have to go farther. The station itself was unmanned;

like most of the other minor stops on the line, it was
little more than a raised concrete platform, which
sprung only briefly to life whenever the train came in
and then quickly emptied. He knew the next train
would not pass for more than an hour.

And anyway, he couldn't wait. As Petrosyan giggled
drunkenly, he persuaded her to lie down. Sveta had
already got the message and was already walking
away. She didn't mind. Her mother's new friend was
being kind to her and, best of all, had actually brought
along the doll that he had promised. Taking it eagerly,
she went off a few hundred yards into the woods. She
was out of view of her mother, but as she began to
play she could still hear her laughing.

Petrosyan took off her underwear and Chikatilo lay
down beside her. He had oral sex with her and then
tried to have intercourse. It was then that the woman
made her fatal mistake. While they were sitting on
the train coming out, she had been thinking about
Chikatilo's problems with sex in the past and had
wondered if time had cured him. But when she saw
that it hadn't, her drunkenness got the better of her.
Like others who had fallen victim to him before, she
began mocking his impotence.

"Call yourself a real man?" she jeered.

Inevitably, it was more than Chikatilo could bear.
All his feelings of isolation and inadequacy welled up
as this pathetic, drunken woman began haranguing
him. He had to silence her. But even more he had to
prove her wrong. He had to show her that he was a
man in all senses of the word. And he knew how to do
it. Reaching into his bag, he produced a long sharp
kitchen knife and before Petrosyan knew what was
happening, he plunged it into the side of her head.
The whole forest shook with her scream. But he didn't
stop. As the blood and her suffering finally gave him
the sexual satisfaction that he craved, he began hitting her with a hammer. Petrosyan died almost im-

mediately. Compared with many of the other murders, it was all over quickly. But then there was the problem of Sveta.

Her mother's first blood-curdling scream had shattered her play. Dropping the doll, the girl ran back toward the place where she had left them, unable to imagine what could have happened. She had little time to find out. There was no sign of the kindly uncle with whom she had been riding on the train. In his place was a wild animal. In a scene straight out of a horror movie, he was running, stark naked, through the forest toward her with a knife in his hand. The girl turned and began to run for her life, but to no avail. He was stronger and he was faster and before she could take more than a few steps, he was on her. He felled her with the bloodstained knife just as he had felled her mother minutes before. If the first blow did not kill her outright, then she lived only a few seconds more, as he sent a shower of hammer blows down on her.

It was the first—and indeed last—time that the ever cautious Chikatilo had killed in front of a witness. And even though she was only a child, she could not be allowed to live. Nor was he interested in the kind of slow painful death that he normally needed to achieve satisfaction. He was already aroused. Admittedly, killing Sveta heightened his pleasure. But more than anything, he saw it as a matter of self-protection. If he had not killed her, then the state would have killed him.

The defense was successful. Petrosyan's mother waited several days before reporting her daughter's disappearance. As she told police later, she didn't think anything of it when her daughter did not come home that evening. It was quite normal for her to stay out one or even several nights. Nor could she tell them much about the man she had gone to meet. Petrosyan had been casual enough about sex even while she was married; and after her marriage broke up, she had been even more so. There were so many men friends, it was difficult for her mother to keep track of them all.

Nothing that the woman said ultimately helped police find either Petrosyan or her daughter. She was old and confused. She had a vague idea that the two of them might have gone off with the teacher who had come around that day. But she did not know his name and could not really remember what he looked like. All she could be sure about was that her daughter had talked about spending a day at the dacha with someone. But she did not know where they were due to meet. Maybe it was Shakhti or else the nearby town of Novocherkassk.

In fact, it was not until July 5th that police found the first body, almost by chance, and that was of the young Sveta. Nor did they immediately realize the scale of the horrors perpetrated by Chikatilo that spring day. The undergrowth was so dense that her mother's body did not turn up for another three weeks. And then it was only because people picnicking in the area had started complaining about an unpleasant smell. Even when they found the bodies, it took some time to identify them because they had been lying there for so long.

There was also one other, horrific detail: Sveta's head had been completely severed and lay in the undergrowth some five yards away from her body.

9

Valentina Lysytskaya, head of the wages department of a factory with the unpronounceable name of Sevkavenergoavtomatika, was at her desk in Rostov on August 1, 1984, when a tall, powerful man with thick glasses walked in. Every new employee had to report to her office on the second floor to fill in the multitude of forms Soviet bureaucracy required. The latest addition to the payroll scarcely made an impression. He introduced himself a little stiffly as Chikatilo, Andrei Romanovich, sat down, took the form and filled it out. He didn't pause as he crossed out the section asking for details of a possible criminal record. News of the incident with the linoleum had clearly not filtered its way from Shakhti to Rostov, and he certainly wasn't going to tell them. Lysytskaya did not have any questions and neither did he. He completed the formalities and went to work. A nondescript man who made neither a positive nor a negative impression was how she remembered their first meeting years later.

It had taken Chikatilo months of searching to get the job. Situated in a quiet part of Rostov just behind Engels Street, the factory was like thousands of others across the Soviet Union: a plant making heavy industrial machinery and a series of small administrative offices. Years later, following the end of Communism and the breakup of the Soviet Union, Sevkavenergoavtomatika was forced to the brink of bankruptcy by the collapse of the old command economy. But back in summer 1984, things were still going fine. The death of the unloved Andropov in February of that year and his replacement by the stolid, ailing Konstantin Chernenko had left old-style Communism in full swing. The Soviet Union was sliding back to the comfortable stagnation of the Brezhnev years and no one had started talking about strange words like profit, efficiency, or unemployment.

Yet even the general indifference to work which characterized those days didn't stop Chikatilo's colleagues from wondering why their bosses had taken him on—especially since he was no longer a mere supply clerk but actually head of the department, with a team of five other people working under him. Again, it was not just his distant, unfriendly manner which counted against him. Just as in Shakhti, he showed very quickly that he was no good at his job nor at winning the respect of his subordinates. On one occasion, a big order came in and Chikatilo could not find the forklift truck in the warehouse. But instead of looking for it, he unloaded everything by hand—while all his clerks just stood around and watched. "To do this job well, you need contacts," said Olga Kudelina, one of his deputies. "And he had none. He was hopeless. He simply wasn't up to the job."

The only thing that he did seem able to do well was to crawl to his bosses. Whenever the telephone rang, he visibly stiffened. To the amusement of his team, he would almost stand at attention as he listened to orders. But this was more than a man keen to do his best. He was also a man with secrets and a guilty conscience who feared his superiors could call any moment to tell him a policeman was waiting in their office to ask him a few questions.

Even if Chikatilo did have a conscience, he certainly was not listening to it. Tatya Petrosyan and her daughter had not been his only victims that spring. In the weeks that followed their death, his list of victims had swelled to twenty-five with the addition of another two women, Yelena Bakulina, twenty-two, Anna Lemesheva, nineteen, and a thirteen-year-old boy called Dima Illarionov. The bizarre linoleum case had been hanging over him in those months and the feeling of injustice it created was fueling his anger and his determination to strike back at society. The prospect of a brush with the courts over the issue may also have encouraged him to make use of what he feared could be his last few months of liberty.

If this was so, then the sense of achievement at finding a new job should have calmed Chikatilo's appetite a little, especially because of the promotion which went with it. But it didn't. The temptations presented by work in a big city like Rostov with more than a million inhabitants were just too great. The main railway station, where he had already spent many a sleepless night in search of victims, was now only a few stops away by bus from his office. So was Aviators' Park, where he had already killed four of them. And everywhere there were streets teeming with people. The crowds also gave him a feeling of security. The very way in which he picked up and then killed his victims required the kind of anonymity that only a big city could provide. He knew that every yard he walked with them was fraught with danger. All he needed was one person to see him and remember his face, and when the manhunt started he would be easily caught. In Shakhti, a city where he had worked for the last ten years, that could happen only too easily. In Rostov, the dangers were far less.

It was therefore no surprise that the two short months Chikatilo spent in Rostov during the summer of 1984 saw his most intensive periods of killings. Ten people fell victim to his horrific collection of knives during that August and September, more than one a week, far more than any time before or after. He had turned into little more than a killing machine.

There was another reason, too. Despite the carnage that Chikatilo had caused over the previous six years, the police were still no closer to catching him—and he was as aware of the fact as they were. All the checks, controls, and investigations had yielded nothing except for a group of mentally subnormal young men whose confessions looked anything but convincing. Chikatilo certainly wasn't lowering his guard. He knew that it was his own caution as much as the incompetence of police which had allowed him to stay at large. Yet he could still allow himself a certain feeling of invincibility as he performed his macabre war dance around his victims in the forest. He was forty-eight years now, and no longer young. But he was still as strong as ever. Sometimes it seemed to him that he would be able to go on killing until long after he had drawn his pension.

Most remarkable in those two bloody months was Chikatilo's ability to lure to their deaths young people who would not normally have dreamed of going off with a strange man. In contrast to prostitutes like Petrosyan, Ryabyenko, or Shalapinina, they certainly had no intention of having sex with him. Yet despite this, he still managed to catch them like a spider catches a fly, tying them up in a deadly web of compliments, platitudes, and proferred advice. The tactic was always the same, although the precise formula was tailored for each. Approaching them as a complete stranger, Chikatilo played on his harmless exterior in order to win over their confidence, talking to them about the weather or holidays or other such neutral subjects. And most times it went no further than that. The intended victim would walk away after a few minutes, oblivious of the true intentions of the man to whom they had been talking and of how close they had come to death. There must have been thousands of such cases during his twelve-year reign of terror. Chikatilo didn't care. For just a few times he struck lucky and the victim agreed to go off with him.

One such victim was sixteen-year-old Natasha Golosovskaya. They met on the evening of August 2 at the bus stop near Rostov Airport after Chikatilo had finished work for the day. She was young, fairly well-dressed, but disoriented. A girl from out of town who was rarely in the big city, she was planning to go to Novoshakhtinsk to visit her sister but didn't know how best to get there. Plus it was beginning to drizzle and the bus wasn't coming. There wasn't anyone else at the bus stop and so the two of them inevitably fell into conversation. Chikatilo had spent several years living in Novoshakhtinsk and so he knew well how to get there. She, in turn, was pleased to listen to his advice.

"I'm going to Shakhti, myself," said Chikatilo. "We'll never catch a bus from here. Let me show you a shortcut."

And so off they walked, the middle-aged man with the gray suit and his black bag and the naive girl from the country. At first, she suspected nothing as he led her off through the thick woods which surround the airport. Although the lamps beside the path were not lit, it was not quite dark and there were buildings nearby. She knew nothing untoward could happen to her there. So did Chikatilo. That was why, claiming to know an even better shortcut, he led her off the asphalt path to a narrower, gravel track running even deeper into the forest.

They were the last steps she took. Minutes later, Chikatilo threw himself on her, ripping off her clothes, and cutting her with the knife he pulled from his bag. Unusual for him, he did not stay around long after she died. As the passion subsided and he began to look around, he realized how busy the place was. There was a school only a hundred yards or so away and despite the late hour, he could hear voices from there. And this meant that someone could well have heard Golosovskaya's cries. In fact, they had. Fifteen-year-old Nikolai Vedrintsev had been playing basketball with his friends in the yard outside the building when they heard what sounded to them like a woman's screams. They stopped briefly to have a better listen. But everything went quiet again and they didn't think any more about it. The park was full of drunks and people having fun.

They found out the truth the next day when a horrified park keeper spotted a hand poking out from underneath a pile of leaves. But by then, Chikatilo was already far away.

Another girl from out of town was seventeen-year-old Lyuda Alekseyeva. Like Golosovskaya, she knew little of Rostov and after waiting a long time at a bus stop, she, too, was happy to meet a stranger whom she thought could help. Chikatilo was even happier. He was immediately attracted to this well-brought-up girl, with her skirt just that little bit too short and her blouse cut just a little bit too low. It was already eight P.M. and she was trying to get to the town of Azov, about forty minutes away, to visit relatives. Again promising a shortcut to another better-placed bus stop, Chikatilo led the girl off across the city's Voroshilovsky Bridge and down through a wooded path on the deserted left bank of the river. He walked ahead, and she followed meekly behind.

Alekseyeva's death was particularly grisly, even by the ghastly standards set by Chikatilo. He got so much pleasure from her suffering that he prolonged it as much as possible, planting his knife at points in her body where it would not kill her. But eventually, too, her nightmare was over. Chikatilo covered up the body, put the knife back in his briefcase and left for home. The body was found three days later. But by then, Chikatilo was no longer in Rostov. The next morning he left on a business trip to Uzbekistan, several thousands miles to the east in Soviet Central Asia. The evening he killed Alekseyeva, he already had the air ticket in his pocket.

The trip to Tashkent, the Uzbek capital, was a routine one for someone in Chikatilo's job. His factory needed switches for the equipment it was making, and the only factory which made the necessary ones was in Uzbekistan. No one questioned quite why it was necessary to go such a long way for supplies. It was just the way the Soviet economy worked. Following the Stalinist motto of "Big is Beautiful," the entire production of many items was concentrated in just one or two huge plants. It was meant to be cheaper and more efficient that way. Thus, nuts were produced in one end of the country, bolts in the other end, and the two put together somewhere in the middle. The "socialist division of labor" they used to call it. It was not only a matter of misguided economics but also a neat way of holding together the fifteen very diverse Soviet republics. By creating interdependence, the country's rulers thought (as it turned out wrongly) that the Union would go on forever.

Like the other Central Asian capitals, Tashkent is a dull place, an old Russian garrison town of straight streets crossing each other at right angles. Although more than 1,500 miles from Moscow, its architecture shows the signs of decades of domination, first under the tsars, and then under the commisars. It was the Russians who came and built the first industry a century ago, and it was their descendants after the 1917 revolution who led the drive to turn Tashkent into a large Soviet city like any other. While life in the countryside in the 1980s still continued much as it always had done, things in the capital were very different. The local branch of the Communist Party was firmly in control and running things just as the Kremlin dictated. Uzbeks in badly made Soviet suits worked alongside Russians and other nationalities in the city's factories and offices.

Not that any of that made any difference to Chikatilo. Trips away from home always had the same effect on him, particularly when they were to a city which he did not know. On the one hand, he felt anxious, cut off from his roots in alien territory. Yet when he started to look around, he quickly began to relish the freedom given to him by all those days away from his wife and factory. He knew well enough that he stood little chance with the Moslem Uzbek women, with their bright head scarves and modest clothing. They didn't have anything like the free and easy manner of Russians. But the city was mixed, and there were plenty of other opportunities.

One of the first things he did after his plane landed at Tashkent airport was to go to an ironmonger's shop and buy a knife. He quickly found a use for it. He was in the city for just one week, from August 8th until the 15th. But in that time he managed to kill two women.

The first died shortly after he arrived. After finishing his business for the day at the factory at lunchtime, he boarded a bus and went toward a river beach, where he got to know a woman who had sought refuge from the intense summer heat. Not until the 16th, the day after Chikatilo had left for Rostov, was her body found—minus the head. That was not found until October 7. The Uzbek police could not establish the identity of the woman, let alone of her killer. From the body itself, they could tell only that she was aged something between twenty and twenty-five years. So on November 26, they closed the case for lack of evidence. More than eight years later, they have still not yet found out her name.

They fared only slightly better with the second, whom Chikatilo killed on the 13th. They established that the body was that of Akmaral Seidalieva, a twelve-year-old girl who had run away from her home in Alma-Ata, capital of the neighboring republic of Kazakhstan, and somehow ended up 600 miles to the west in Uzbekistan. But again they found no clues to the identity of the killer.

Yet the clues were there if they had known what to look for. The bodies, which were still in a fairly good condition when they were found, both bore the trade-mark knife strokes of Chikatilo. But Rostov was far away, and no one made the connection. It was yet another major lost opportunity. If only they had been able to link them, then it would have given the Rostov investigators a major lead in tracking down their killer. After all, how many people from the Rostov area would have been in Tashkent at that time? Given the huge distance involved, the killer would inevitably have traveled there by airplane. The number of flights a week between the two cities could have been counted on the fingers of one hand. Compared with the massive probes and checks which police were to carry out over the subsequent few years, it would have been like child's play to go through the passenger lists.

It was not to be. Like several of the other murders, investigators only learned of the "Uzbek Connection" more than six years later when Chikatilo claimed them as his own and even led them to the precise spot where they had died.

Back in Rostov, Chikatilo reported to work, bringing with him the two large packets of switches which he had picked up in Tashkent. By now, his subordinates had largely grown used to their boss. But this did not mean that they did not find him strange. If anything, he seemed to be reacting more and more oddly whenever the telephone rang. For someone in a responsible position, he was also beginning to turn up for work looking unkempt, as if he had been sleeping in his clothes. As Lysytskaya found out one morning, sometimes that was precisely what he did.

A busy woman, she prided herself on being the first person into the office in the morning. Although work started at eight A.M., she was often at her desk as early as seven-thirty A.M. One morning, though, she was surprised to see a light already burning in one of the other offices when she came in. When she opened the door, she saw Chikatilo sleeping, his head slumped over his desk. It was strange, but maybe not that strange, she thought, particularly since she knew he lived some way from Rostov. "He's probably just been away on a business trip and got back late," she thought, as she tiptoed out of the office.

There was also the matter of the bag that Chikatilo always carried with him. His Rostov colleagues were just as fascinated by it as their predecessors in Shakhti, and one day they too could not resist a look. But again, the same disappointment. When one of the women tiptoed over and peeked inside all she found was a towel and some soap. It was all perfectly normal for a man whose job required him to spend much of his working time out on the road.

A few days later, Chikatilo was out walking on Rostov's Voroshilovsky Prospekt, not far from the point where he had met Alekseyeva, the seventeen-year-old girl whom he had killed the day before flying off to Tashkent. He had set out after work with the aim of going shopping. But as usual, there was nothing in the stores and his mind began to wander. And again it was the slowness and unreliability of the city's public transport system which gave him the opportunity to act. This time there was a knife in his bag.

Sasha Chepel was eleven years old, bright and healthy and obedient. His parents said he rarely even played outside on the street. Certainly he was not the kind of boy to go off with strange men. But like many of the other victims he was momentarily disorientated. As they fell into conversation at the bus stop, Chikatilo quickly worked out how to take advantage of it. Sasha's parents had recently moved out of their old home in the center of Rostov into a bigger, newly built one in the so-called Northern Mikrorayon, one of the complexes of skyscrapers springing up on the outskirts of the city. For a boy of his age the move had been hard, and he missed his friends from the old courtyard. But since it was still summer holidays, he had gone off for the day to play with them. His father was away on a business trip, but his mother let him go—in return for a promise that he would not stay out late.

Now it was already eight P.M. and the boy was late. His friends had come with him to the bus stop, but they too had homes with anxious mothers to go back to and they did not wait. He stood there getting more and more worried as the buses went past one by one, so full that their drivers did not even bother to stop. The middle-aged man who was also standing at the stop was equally fed up. But at least he had an idea.

"Why don't we go over to the central market," the man suggested. "It's the beginning of the route. We must be able to get on one there."

Chepel's shortcut ended just as tragically as had those of Golosovskaya and Alekseyeva. Rather than leading the boy to the market, Chikatilo took him across the bridge over the Don and onto the beach on the secluded left bank. As they walked, they went within yards of the point where police had found Alekseyeva's body just over two weeks before. But to Chikatilo's relief there was no reminder of what had happened, no sign left of the ferocious struggle that he had had with her. It was as if nothing had happened at all. More importantly, there was no police guard. They clearly did not believe lightning could strike twice in the same place.

Lightning was precisely what he was like as he threw himself on the hapless boy. The attack was fast and ferocious, the body so badly mutilated that Sasha's father fainted when he saw it five days later in the morgue with the eyes literally gouged out. He could not believe a man could have been so cruel. He was so convinced that a bird had done it after his son's death that he even consulted a couple of zoologists, to ask whether the crows would really have plucked out Sasha's eyes as he lay there. Maybe they could have. But this time they had not been to blame.

Chikatilo, too, found it difficult to explain why a child like Chepel would have gone off with a man like him, especially at a time when he was dirty and unkempt. "I thought about it," he said at his trial. "Even I could not understand it. I think I must have had a kind of magnetism."

Despite the intensity of the police operation now underway, the local newspapers had been strangely silent. In some cases, the disappearance of a victim or the discovery of body earned a few inches tucked away at the bottom of the page. But beyond that, there was nothing. Chikatilo had already killed more than thirty people, yet there was no indication in the media that a serial killer was out there; no warnings to young women to take care nor to parents to keep a closer eye than usual on their children. It was typical of the way the Soviet press was still working in the last days before the arrival in 1985 of Mikhail Gorbachev and his policy of *glasnost*, a result not just of censorship from above but also of self-censorship on the part of journalists and editors, who already knew what could be printed and what could not.

"Bad news," such as air crashes, mining disasters, and the illnesses of politicians—in short, the stuff of which Western newspapers and news reports are made—were ignored. Their place was taken instead by interminable speeches by Communist politicians, printed verbatim, reports on the fulfillment and over-fulfillment of the economic five-year plans and praise of the heroic achievements of individual workers and peasants.

The category of "bad news" clearly included murders, especially when they were as numerous and terrible as Chikatilo's. Yet the Communist authorities were mistaken if they thought that by not reporting the killings, they could keep the problem to themselves. Censorship inevitably brings with it rumor. Knowing that they cannot believe what they read—or don't read—in the papers, people begin to rely more and more on the information they pass among themselves by word of mouth. And this was especially the case with these murders. Starting from the parents, friends, and neighbors of the victim, the word would gradually spread like the ripples from a stone hitting the water. Officially the people of Rostov had been told nothing about the killings, but already, thanks to the rumor mill, many of them knew a lot.

The killing of Sasha Chepel sent it spinning at full speed. It may have been because of the victim's age. At eleven years of age, he was young and innocent, and every parent that heard what had happened to him quickly imagined how easily it could have been their own child. It was also the circumstances of his disappearance from the middle of Rostov virtually in broad daylight. In the days afterward, wild stories began to circulate and panic began to spread. Some were true, some pure fiction. One of the most bizarre maintained that Chepel had been whisked away by a black official limousine with the registration letters SSO—the initials for the Russian words "Death to Soviet Children."

It was a sign of the strength of these rumors that local officialdom at last felt itself obliged to confirm what was happening, although it was done in a typically roundabout Soviet way. A few days after the boy's death a long, rambling article appeared in the local Communist Party daily, *Molot* (Hammer), signed by General Alexei Konovalov, a high official in the Interior Ministry of the Rostov region. Its theme was the usual one: praising the work of the official organs and describing how the advent of "developed socialism" was cutting the crime rate. Buried in the middle of it, though, was for the first time a mention of one of the murders. "The savage killing of the boy Sasha Chepel has taken place." Konovalov wrote. "We assure the population that the killer will be found in the near future."

By the standards of the Western press it was nothing. But for those used to reading between the lines, it was a clear acknowledgment by authorities that they could not keep the truth from the people of Rostov.

If Chepel was young and naive, Irina Luchinskaya was not. Aged twenty-four, she still lived at home with her parents. Like most other girls of her age, she had no alternative. In Rostov, as in almost every other Soviet city, there was a chronic shortage of apartments and a waiting list that stretched for years. But she didn't let it cramp her free and easy lifestyle; although it often ended in arguments with her mother who worried every time that she didn't come home at night. Tall and slender with a good figure and shiny black hair, Irina was a hit with the boys and took full advantage of it. People who last worked with her in the archive department of a local institute, said she was never interested in her job—her seventh in almost as many years. Her interests seemed to lie elsewhere. Often she just did not bother to turn up in the archives at all, never saying why she had been away or where she had been.

Luchinskaya often gave the impression she was suffering from some kind of deep inner tragedy. She once told a friend that she wished she had been born a man. As if to underline the fact, she invariably dressed in jeans and T-shirts rather than dresses or skirts. More than anything else, though, it was men's sexual freedom that she envied. According to Vladimir Pomogayev, a onetime boyfriend who had been at school with her, she had a reputation among the young men who knew her as an easy lay. "She never said no to a man who asked her," he told police years later.

The evening of September 6, 1984, proved no exception. Irina had gone to work that morning but told her mother that she would be home late because she was going with friends to the *banya*, the traditional Russian steam bath. Like saunas in Scandinavian countries, the *banya* is more a place for going out with friends and having fun than for getting clean. Any therapeutic effects are usually outweighed by the large quantities of beer or vodka inevitably consumed during the course of the evening. It was, of course, also a place to meet men.

But she didn't make it there. Maybe she had lied to her mother and never actually intended to go. In any case, as dusk approached she was standing at the bus stop near the airport and fell into conversation with a man also standing there. Although he was almost twenty-five years older than she was, she found him strangely attractive and did not say no when he suggested they go off together into the nearby woods to "relax"—a Russian euphemism for sex. As with Chikatilo's many other encounters with consenting women, it simply did not turn out like that. As they lay down together on the ground, he tried to have intercourse with her, but failed. She was not used to men who could not fulfill their promises and like others before her began to shout at him, telling him he was hopeless and pathetic. It was more than Chikatilo could stand. He punched her hard and, as she paused to take breath, drew his knife from the bag and began to stab her. Only then as the blood began to flow did he finally begin to feel a real man. But for Luchinskaya it was too late. She was already lying dead below him.

Chikatilo did not go home that evening. By the time he had finished disposing of the girl's body it was already late and he didn't want to go all the way back to Shakhti to face his wife. As was often the case after he killed, he was also in a kind of trance, as if he were drunk or on drugs. When he finally made it back to the main road, it took all his concentration to avoid stumbling in front of a truck. The driver braked and swerved at the last moment, cursing as he drove off. Chikatilo made it a few more steps to the bus stop and went back to his office to sleep. It was one of the last times that he was to do so. Shortly afterwards, he simply disappeared.

Most people would have found it difficult to keep such a secret life from their wife. When Chikatilo was arrested years later, investigators were initially sceptical at Fayina's claims that she had known nothing about her husband's Jekyll and Hyde existence. After questioning both of them further, they began to believe her. It was not that she was stupid. Rather, Chikatilo was clever. And through a combination of skill and luck he managed to deceive her just as he did everyone else who knew him.

Part of it was due to the job itself. If he had been working in a normal nine-to-five job, or indeed still as a teacher, then it would have been much more difficult. Chikatilo needed time for his killing. It wasn't his style to lurk in deserted places and pick off passersby. He was a hunter in the urban jungle. And this meant he often needed to wander around for hours before finding a suitable victim. His job, with its frequent business trips, was to provide the perfect cover. He certainly also made the best of it, often planning ahead when he was going out hunting and warning his wife in advance that he would not be coming home.

In most cases, as with the murder of Luchinskaya, he also made a point of waiting at least several days before returning to the family home. In part, it was because he wanted to savor what he had done, away from his wife and the other domestic associations which would have only diluted the pleasure. It also gave him time to clean up, and above all to wash his clothes, so she would find nothing unusual when he finally returned home. The whole situation with respect to accommodation helped him: Sometimes he could seek refuge in the various company flats and rooms to which he occasionally had access. And, although he eventually sold the little house in Mezhevoi Pereulok, a series of complicated apartment swaps, sometimes involving his daughter, meant there were also short periods when he had an empty apartment of his own to use.

Chikatilo even had a ready excuse for the deep scratches that his victims often made on his face and body during the struggle before he finally killed them. He used to tell Fayina that he got them while he was helping his workers load metal and other heavy materials off the truck. She wasn't happy about it. It was bad enough that her husband, who had a university degree, had such a lowly job in the supply department rather than something more worthy of his qualifications. It was even worse that he was doing heavy lifting with his bare hands. However angry it made her, it still had the intended effect of pulling the wool over her eyes.

But there was one thing that he could not fool her over, and that was his lack of interest in sex. Even at the beginning of their marriage, there had never been any real passion between them. In retrospect, it seems that the marriage itself may have been little more than a front, as far as he was concerned. It could have been an attempt to convince not just the outside world, but also himself, that he was a normal, well-adjusted heterosexual. The two of them had slept together rarely and without much enthusiasm. As for the two children, they had been the product of little more than a sense of duty on his side.

But things had got worse and worse throughout the 1980s as Chikatilo sank further and further into his murderous other life. From making love just once every two or even three months, they almost stopped completely. Part of the problem was that he was almost never at home. It was a two-hour commute from their flat in Shakhti to his job in Rostov, and on top of that there were the business trips, whether genuine or phony. But that was only a part of it. More important was that he had simply lost interest. By 1984, the killings had almost become to him what a normal sex life was to any other man. It was out in the woods, with a knife in his hand and a screaming victim beneath him, that he got his satisfaction and his orgasms. Not in his bedroom with his straight-laced wife. If he was obtaining any real sexual pleasure at home by now, it was only while on his own, masturbating, while he lost himself in his sadistic fantasies.

Fayina did her best to snap him out it, alternately telling him off and pleading with him. Even so, she apparently never contemplated leaving him. Nor did she have any lovers.

"I'm a healthy woman with normal healthy needs," she shouted at her husband once during a fit of depression. "What am I doing stuck with a useless man like you?"

Chikatilo was livid. "You're just obsessed with one thing," he hit back. "Try thinking about something else for a change."

That summer, though, she scored a partial success in her struggle to make him at least acknowledge the problem. After much nagging, she persuaded him to go to a psychiatrist to get treated for what she believed was his lack of sexual drive. The fact that he actually agreed to go there was a step forward. But it didn't help. Although the doctor's diagnosis has been lost in the years that passed, it seems he merely saw him, gave him a few tranquilizers and sent him on his way. An incident on the way out of the hospital also ensured that he would not go back. Who should he run into as he left the waiting room but one of the policemen who had already dealt with him over the linoleum incident.

"What are you here for, then, Chikatilo?" he asked with a sneer as they passed. "Getting treated for a drinking problem?"

Back at Sevkavenergoavtomatika, Chikatilo's subordinates were beginning to wonder quite what had happened. It had been several weeks since they had last seen him, and his work record for the period showed a row of "Ns," bureaucratic shorthand for "Absent. Reason unknown." Even so, they didn't make much of an effort to find him. Absenteeism was a way of life not just in Chikatilo's factory but also right across the whole Soviet economy. Whatever little progress Andropov had made in stamping it out was long since forgotten now that Chernenko was back in the Kremlin.

In September, though, Lysytskaya suddenly had

reason to remember her weird colleague. Early one morning, before the rest of the staff had arrived, two policemen appeared at the office building and came to her office.

"I believe you have an employee here named Andrei Romanovich," one of the officers said. "We have come to check his things and we need a civilian witness."

As the woman stood and watched, the officers broke open the flimsy padlock on his locker and began putting the contents into a transparent bag: a towel, a T-shirt, some shoes, soap, and a few other bits and pieces. They noted them all on an official piece of paper and she put her signature at the place marked "witness." They didn't tell her what had happened to Chikatilo and she did not ask.

The Faces of Evil: Chikatilo in his courtroom cage.

Viktor Burakov (seated), one of the few detectives involved in the case from the beginning, consults with colleagues.

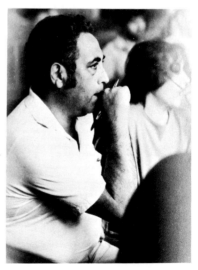

Aleksandr Bukhanovsky, the Rostov psychiatrist who drew up a psychological portrait of Chikatilo during the search and later helped during the interrogation.

A collection of knives found in Chikatilo's apartment.

Mug shots of Chikatilo after his arrest.

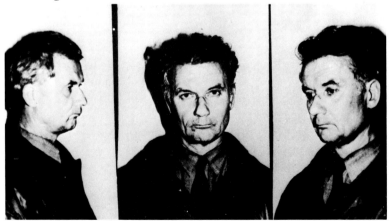

Chikatilo at the scene of one of his killings,
describing the crime to investigators.

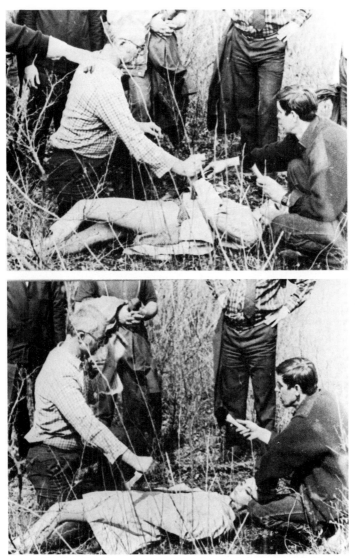

Chikatilo demonstrates to investigators with the help of a dummy how he killed one of his victims.

Sveta Korostik, Chikatilo's last victim, killed on November 6, 1990, in the woods near Donleskhov Station.

Relatives of the victims break down in the courtroom.

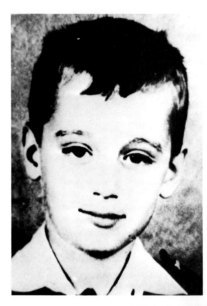

Vanya Fomin, eleven, killed in Novocherkassk in August 1990.

Yelena Varga, twenty-two, killed in August 1989.

A police composite sketch of Chikatilo used during the search.

The Red Ripper being led into court.

10

There was something about Rostov. Dislike it as he did, Kazakov of the Russian Public Prosecutor's Office could not seem to keep away. So it was no surprise when, in July 1984, his bosses sent him back down there again, this time to Morozovsk, a little town about 70 miles northeast of Shakhti on the way to Volgograd. It was a matter of murder, again several particularly brutal ones, which had been committed just outside the town. No one believed that there was any link between them and the "Forest Path" murders. But even so, Kazakov had a feeling in the back of his mind that it would be impossible for him to go to the region and not get sucked back into the whole desperate affair again.

On his way back to Moscow, he drove through Shakhti to see his colleagues in the prosecutor's office. The place was abuzz. As chance would have it, the police had just picked up another body close to a small railway station barely outside the city which was called simply "1130 km." The victim, a nineteen-year-old girl later identified as Anna Lemesheva, had been killed six days before, on the 19th.

She had been typical of the group of prostitutes and other down-and-outs who formed such a large proportion of Chikatilo's victims. The unhappy product of divorced parents, she had married early in search of stability. And, inevitably, her marriage had gone wrong as well. Alone, bored, and unloved, she had accepted Chikatilo's offer to go off swimming with him. It was one of the days before he started work in Rostov and he too, had time on his hands. He proposed sex and she agreed. Then he attacked her. As the blows rained down, she tried to frighten him. She said her husband would come around and straighten out Chikatilo when he found out how he had mistreated her. But Chikatilo did not have the intention of letting her tell anyone anything, and he killed her, just as he had killed all the others before her.

Kazakov did not find out any of this until later. All he had to go on for the moment was the horrible wounds: the stabs and slashes and the uterus which had been chopped out and thrown into the nearby bushes. But it was enough to convince him that the killer had struck yet again. It was also only the beginning. When he traveled farther to Rostov, he found there had been more murders not just there but also in other parts of the region, which were also clearly part of the series.

The year before, he had taken the investigation the first major step foward by having six of the first murders united into one case. But that clearly was not enough; the killer was still at large. When he got back to Moscow, he wrote another note to Namestnikov, the Deputy Public Prosecutor of Russia. In it he said he strongly believed that the murders had been committed by one person. To be absolutely sure, it was necessary to analyze them all, to link them together into one major case and entrust it not just to the local police, but to the serious crimes department of the Public Prosecutor's Office.

Namestnikov studied Kazakov's report. He, too, was alarmed at what was going on in Rostov and believed there was a need to shake things up a little. But at that time, no one with the experience and seniority needed was free to tackle the case. He came up with a temporary solution, instead: Kazakov should go back down south at the head of a group of specialists and spend a month looking more thoroughly into the murders and at the way in which they were being handled. Then and only then would Namestnikov, himself, join him and decide on further action.

And so, in September 1984, Kazakov was back. His job was essentially to look at the work being done by the local prosecutors. The activities of the police were to be supervised by Ivan Krapov, a top Moscow-based official in the central department of the Interior Ministry's Criminal Investigation Department. With a battery of experts from a number of different scientific disciplines, they were determined to make up for the slowness and downright incompetence which had characterized the earlier part of the operation. They did not dare to realize what a huge job they would have on their hands.

Installed in the dingy headquarters of the local prosecutor's office in Bolshaya Sadovaya Street, Kazakov began to study all the recent unsolved crimes in the area, particularly those with any kind of sexual basis or involving children or young people. The more he looked at the files, the more he became convinced of his initial hunch that a large group of them was the work of one man. He came up with a total of twenty-three that he believed should be linked into one case. His list started with Lyuba Biryuk, the thirteen-year-old girl whose body had been found by the side of the road in the little village of Donskoi back in June 1982.

Convincing himself was the easy part. He also had the
bigger task of persuading the police.

The relationship between police and prosecutors
was often a sensitive one in the Soviet system. On
paper, at least, the division should be clear. The job
of the police is to find the criminal. They are the ones
out on the streets, whether on foot or in cars, doing
the groundwork, staking out buildings and handling
informers. The Public Prosecutor's Department, or
rather its investigative branch, has no part in all that.
Its men come into play only when the suspect is
hauled in, questioning him or her and organizing the
forensic and other scientific analysis. They are also
parts of two separate bureaucracies which answer
ultimately to different masters in Moscow: the police
to the Interior Ministry and the prosecutors to the
Prosecutor General.

In practice, there are often tensions. The prosecutors, most of whom have had university education,
are frequently critical of the police, often complaining
of them as being poorly educated, badly paid, and
inefficient. For their part, the police feel misunderstood and claim no one appreciates the difficulties
and frustrations of their own work. The more important the case and the longer it drags on, the greater
those tensions are likely to be.

It should not be forgotten that this was a particularly difficult case. Despite all the murders, the real
evidence was extremely thin. The bodies, too, were
also often badly decomposed by the time they were
found. Of Kazakov's twenty-three, some thirteen were
virtual skeletons by the time they made their way to
the morgue. In Rostov, the summer temperature can
often soar to the mid-nineties or more. In that kind of
heat, a body can turn to a skeleton in as little as ten
days. And there were some bodies which had been
undetected for five to six months.

The police already had Tyapkin and the other inmates of the psychiatric hostel under investigation. Each of them was charged with several murders and, what is more, each of them had confessed. Although their cases had not yet come to trial, there was little doubt that a court would convict them. If the authorities accepted Kazakov's theory of a single killer, then, by so doing, they would also be admitting the men in their cells were innocent. It would have been extremely embarrassing for all involved—from those on the ground who had arrested the accused and taken their confessions to those higher up in the police hierarchy who had put confidence in their subordinates and accepted their hypothesis at face value.

It would be unfair to say, though, that it was merely a matter of pride. The police did not share Kazakov's doubts about the reliability of the men's confessions. They seemed genuine enough to them. In their defense, they also pointed out that both Tyapkin and Ponomarev had been able to identify with some accuracy the places where they had supposedly carried out their killings. The fact that the two were mentally subnormal made this more, rather than less, reliable, they maintained. As they saw it, neither of the men seemed capable of inventing a story like that.

Kazakov's theory also seemed to go against all the basic assumptions that the Soviet police made about murderers. In their book, a killer normally either attacked men or he attacked women. In fact, some of the earlier male victims had even been identified as having been women, such was the conviction that the victims would have to be of a single sex. But now they were being confronted with a kaleidoscope of different ages, sexes, and backgrounds. It was extremely difficult for them to cope with the idea of a killer like Chikatilo who seemed indifferent to the nature and sex of his victim.

It was difficult for Kazakov, too. Yet he was prepared to suspend his disbelief in the face of the facts.

For him, the most important thing was the manner in which the victims had been killed. Mutilation of bodies was rare enough, in itself. Even rarer were the kinds of injuries they kept finding, particularly the stab wounds around the eyes and the amputated nipples and sexual organs. It would be too much of a coincidence for two or more killers, acting independently, to have this same trademark. He was also swayed by the distribution of the bodies, most of which were found on a line somewhere between Rostov and Shakhti.

Kazakov's hunch was also backed by the forensic evidence. One of his biggest complaints about the case had been the almost casual way in which police had handled the clothing of the victims and other objects picked up at the scene of the crime. Some of what could have been vital evidence had simply disappeared. And the bulk of what they still had in their hands had not been properly analyzed and key tests not carried out.

Among the group who had come down from Moscow was Svetlana Gurtova, head of the Criminal Biological Department of the Russian Ministry of Health. A ferocious worker, she literally locked herself away for ten days and nights in a laboratory in Rostov with local experts and went through the often ripped, bloodstained clothing with a fine-tooth comb. Every fiber, every strand was subjected to the kind of painstaking examination that should have been carried out from the very start. For the first time, she also began to look for traces of sperm—a search which, inexplicably, had not been carried out before. It quickly yielded results. She found signs of it on the clothing of nine of the victims and believed that it must belong to their killer. Like blood, sperm is divided into distinct groups. In what constituted a major breakthrough, Gurtova found that they all belonged to the same group: AB.

Kazakov already had almost all he wanted. But then he came up with the coup de grace, the vital element to demolish a case which had been built almost entirely on confessions. Even if there was no evidence that Tyapkin and the rest had been physically mistreated, he did not exclude the possibility that strong psychological pressure had been put on them in order to make them confess. He also feared that, given their mental weakness, they did not really understand the gravity of the charges which they were admitting. As he had suspected, when he went to question them himself, they told him straight out they had not carried out these crimes at all—in direct contradiction of what they had told police. So why had they confessed in the first place? The way he saw it, they were so unable to understand what was happening that they would have confessed to anything. And so it turned out. While going through the cases, Kazakov found that the eleven crimes admitted by the unfortunate Kalenik included the killing of Valya Chuchulina, the mentally subnormal twenty-two-year-old woman whose body was found outside the town of Shakhti late in September 1983. There was only one problem: Kalenik was already sitting in jail at the time the girl was killed.

It was enough for Kazakov and it was enough for his bosses, too. When Namestnikov saw his findings, he agreed to his proposal to unite his list of twenty-three into one case and to create a special joint police and prosecutors' group to which the locals from both branches would all be subordinated. Given the seriousness of the case and the sheer volume of material, the Rostov region was divided into two: The murders in the city of Rostov were put under control of Rashid Aliyev, a prosecutor from the neighboring north Caucasian republic of Dagestan, while a man named Ustinikov, an investigator from the Rostov region's prosecutors office and a specialist in serious crimes, was put in charge of the rest of the area, based in Shakhti. To his belief, Kazakov himself was allowed to fly home to Moscow.

The next week, Namestnikov's decision was given formal basis. On October 8, 1984, Yuri Velikanov, head of the criminal department of the Russian Public Prosecutor's Office, signed the necessary order to link the cases and dropped murder charges against the existing suspects. They didn't all walk free, though. Several of them had also been charged with various homosexual acts, still illegal under Soviet law, as well as other public-order offenses, so they served a few more months in jail.

Although pleased that they had finally won their case, Kazakov and his colleagues in the Public Prosecutor's Office were understandably angry about the way the whole investigation had been handled. The police had been so convinced of the guilt of the men they were holding in custody that they had neglected other ultimately more fruitful lines of inquiry. And this was at a time when the real killer, who was clearly still at large, had been at his most active, adding eight murders to his grisly tally in July and August alone. Even Major-General Mikhail Fetisov, the current head of Rostov police and a staunch defender of police conduct during this difficult period, admitted subsequently that the whole investigation had reached a dead end by the summer of 1984.

All these years later, it is still difficult to understand how the police could have spent so much time on what was patently the wrong track. Was it an isolated case of sloppy work on their part or was it merely a symptom of the way the whole system of criminal investigation worked under the Communists? The performance of police the world over is judged largely on the percentage of solved and unsolved crimes. But in the Soviet Union, this was particularly so. As the case of Kravchenko had shown five years earlier, the main thing was to have a suspect. It mattered less that it was sometimes the wrong man.

The questions are more than purely academic ones. For Velikanov's decree did not simply drop the charges against the innocent men. Acting in response to evidence collected by Kazakov, the Public Prosecutor's Office also opened its own probe into what had gone wrong with the police investigation and the so-called "contraventions of legality" committed along the way. Eight years later, the case was still open, a source of continuing tension between police and the prosecutors. Until Chikatilo himself was convicted, the whole procedure was in limbo. But once he was confirmed as guilty for the killings wrongly attributed to the others, the way was open to move forward. As for the results, only time will tell.

With the passing of the resolution, the investigation should have been back on track. It wasn't. Part of the reason was that many in the police remained unconvinced by the new theory that had been imposed on them by faraway Moscow. Angry at the way they appeared to have been overruled, they clung to their version of events—even well after Kalenik and the other initial suspects had been released.

Among the experts who had come down to Rostov with Kazakov were some psychiatrists from Moscow's Serbsky Institute who were trying to draw up a psychological portrait of the killer. A local psychiatrist, Aleksandr Bukhanovsky, had already come up with a description which, although necessarily vague, turned out in retrospect to have been a fairly good likeness. In particular, he had stressed correctly that the mystery killer was likely to be an apparently normal, probably married man with a regular job rather than the crazed, mentally deranged maniac many expected. The experts from the Serbsky agreed. Like Bukhanovsky, they were also convinced that the killer would not be able to stop his activities. Yet this was exactly what was happening.

In fact, after the carnage of summer 1984, things had grown suspiciously quiet in the Rostov region. Of course, people were still getting murdered. There was such a high crime rate there that one could not expect anything else. But none of the bodies had the telltale injuries which would mark them as the work of "their" killer. The last two bodies had been found in September in Aviators' Park: that of Irina Luchinskaya, a mentally subnormal twenty-four-year-old, on the seventh; and that of a twenty-year-old prostitute named Sveta Tsana, two days later. But several months had passed since then, and there had been nothing more. As the prosecutors saw it, something had clearly happened to the killer.

The theories were numerous, each one plunging them into what was to be a huge and ultimately fruitless investigation. The first and most obvious explanation was that the killer had died. But how? Suicide was one possibility or maybe an accident of some sort, perhaps a car crash. The investigators checked both accident and suicide records but did not come up with anyone who might have fitted the bill. There was also the possibility that he was alive and well, and simply committing crimes elsewhere in the Soviet Union. For this reason, they began to step up contacts with police forces in other regions in the hope of finding similar murders. But here, too, they drew a blank.

There was also a third possibility, although no one put much faith in it: The killer had been arrested for some other crime and was actually, unbeknownst to them, already in jail. It did not seem very plausible, but it still had to be checked. So they began the enormous task of checking through the prison population for likely suspects. It was such a massive job, that they allowed themselves to narrow the field.

According to the research on the sperm samples done by Gurtova, the killer had AB blood, so they restricted their search to those prisoners who had that type.

When Major Gennady Bondarenko, deputy head of the police in the Pervomaiski district of Rostov, came to work on September 14, 1984, a report was already waiting on his desk. He immediately began to study it. In the early hours of that morning, one of his most experienced men, Inspector Aleksandr Zanasovski, had detained a man behaving suspiciously at the city's central market. According to the officer's report he had been watching him for more than nine hours since late the previous evening, during which time the man had traveled across the city and made several attempts to pick up women. Most interesting, though, was what Zanasovski had found in the man's bag: knives and some lengths of rope.

Even in normal times, all this would have been reason for investigation. But these were not normal times. There was a serial killer on the loose. So, Bondarenko went down to the interview room and had the man brought in. Like Zanasovski, he had to agree that he seemed an unlikely sex offender on the face of it: married with two children, Communist Party member, responsible job at Sevkavenergoavtomatika, and so on. Nor did the man's name, Andrei Romanovich Chikatilo, mean anything more to him than it had to Zanasovski.

But the more Bondarenko talked to him, the odder Chikatilo seemed. As they sat there, face to face across the little wooden table, Bondarenko ran through his officer's report aloud, describing to his suspect how his nocturnal journey back and forth across Rostov had been observed and recorded in its entirety from the moment he first started trying to pick up women in the station. When he had finished, he asked Chikatilo to explain his strange conduct.

Chikatilo said merely that he had missed the local train home and since the bus station was closed overnight, had gone to the mainline station to spend the night there. But he didn't explain why he had kept crisscrossing the city, nor what he had been planning to do with the knives or rope.

Bondarenko realized there was obviously a need to take a closer look at Chikatilo. So, in order to keep his suspect in custody, he sent him over to the equivalent of the local magistrate's court where he was charged with minor hooliganism—the usual charge for harassing women—and given ten days. To his regret, that was as far as Bondarenko could go. Under the rules established by the investigative team, anyone suspected of involvement in the Forest Path killings had to be handed over to them. From then on, it was out of his hands.

When the investigators to whom Chikatilo had been passed began to check on their suspect, they quickly turned up an interesting fact, namely, that he had been questioned several times back in 1978 in Shakhti over the killing of Lena Zakotnova, the little girl whose body had been found tossed into the Grushevka River. During the course of questioning, Chikatilo also revealed how he had been forced out of teaching because of the series of misdemeanors involving his pupils. Combined with his strange behavior and the suspicious contents of his bag, it was enough for the investigators. They began to think he might be the killer.

In particular, they suspected a link with the murder of Dima Ptashnikov, the eleven-year-old boy who had been killed six months before—and the only case for which they had any real clues, including a footprint. Although the evidence was thin, Chikatilo had the same shoe size. He also seemed to fit the rough description that they obtained from a witness who had seen a man going off with the boy.

Although he had been knocked off balance by his arrest, Chikatilo had recovered his composure and told them their theory was rubbish. He knew the evidence that police had against him was flimsy and was determined that he was not going to confess to the murder of Ptashnikov—anymore than he would admit his more than twenty other killings that they weren't accusing him of. Taking the offensive, he started insisting on his rights and demanded he be released immediately. They ignored him. Armed with the hooliganism charge, they could still hold him for a few more days, and, in the meantime they took a sample of blood with the aim of trying to match it with the traces of sperm found on the boy's clothing.

It was then that came one of the decisive moments in the case. When the result of Chikatilo's blood test came back from the laboratory, he turned out to be group A. The sperm on Ptashnikov's shirt had been AB. The samples were checked and double-checked, but again the same result. The police were dumbfounded. Before the test, everything had seemed to fit so neatly. Now, they were being forced to think again.

However, they were not yet ready to give in. And for one of the rare moments in the investigation, luck seemed to be on their side. Among the information gleaned by the routine checks on Chikatilo in his hometown of Shakhti was the case of the stolen linoleum, still pending from February that year. Normally, such a minor charge would have earned the culprit little more than a warning or fine. This time was different. However minor, it was enough to give police the justification needed to hold Chikatilo beyond the initial ten days and run more checks. In the meantime, they hoped to gather enough evidence to be able to nail him for the murders.

But it was not to be. As the months went on, the investigators failed to find anything incriminating him. In retrospect, it is easy to criticize the police, particularly for the excessive faith they appeared to have had in the forensic evidence. Chikatilo's appearance on the list of suspects for the Zakotnova murder should have sounded the alarm; so should his self-confessed record of molesting children.

Yet it should not be forgotten that Chikatilo was only one among dozens of potential suspects picked up during the period. Police had already had their knuckles rapped over Tyapkin and his associates; they had little enthusiasm for pursuing another suspect who seemed excluded from the running from the start because he had the wrong blood type. In the meantime, other suspects were being picked up and other leads followed.

On December 12, 1984, Chikatilo appeared in the People's Court of the Leninsk Region of the city of Shakhti charged with theft. He was found guilty and given a sentence of one year of corrective labor. However, taking into account the three months he had already spent in custody, the judge decided to set Chikatilo free immediately. He could see no good reason for him to be detained any longer, and the prosecution did not attempt to give him one.

For three short months, a man since revealed as probably the world's worst serial killer had been sitting behind bars. Unknown to police, he had already killed thirty-one people. And now he was at large again, it was not just an indictment of the police force and of the Communist society in which it operated. It was also a testimony to a ruthless murderer, so cool and calculating that he could fool police and prosecutors by killing and killing again, without leaving the tiniest scrap of evidence.

11

About 25 miles north of Rostov lies Novocherkassk. In a region dominated by coal mining and heavy industry, the city remains a cut above its neighbors. Compared with Shakhti and Novoshakhtinsk, the streets seem wider and the potholes smaller, while the buildings which lie along them have a little more style. Coming into the city from below, visitors by road pass through a lavish archway celebrating the Russian army's victory over Napoleon during the war of 1812–14. The other end of the center is dominated by a massive cathedral which seems on too grand a scale for a city of 300,000 people. In front stands a huge statue to Yermak, the hero who captured much of Siberia for the tsars in the 16th century and somehow managed to remain on his pedestal through seventy years of Soviet rule.

Novocherkassk is a city with history, but the history is more tragic than glorious. For centuries, this was the center of the Don Cossacks, the legendary warrior peasants of old. The name means "free warrior," and the Cossacks have lived up to it. Slavic by nationality and Orthodox by religion, they fled serfdom in Muscovy to settle in the south of Russia along the River Don, forming a first line of defense for the Christian lands of the north against the Turks and the other Moslems of the south. Tough, volatile, and jealous of their freedom, they developed into a forceful people who were great fighters on horseback and practioners of their own unique form of direct democracy under the local *ataman*, or headman.

However, as the newly emerging Russian state grew stronger, their independence was gradually snuffed out. Although the Cossacks were permitted to continue living as free men on their old lands, they were forced to perform military service in the armies of the tsar. However, this was nothing compared with the fate they were to suffer following the 1917 revolution. After taking the side of the anti-Communist Whites during the Civil War, the Cossacks were massacred when the Reds finally triumphed. Tens of thousands of them were killed, tens of thousands more driven into exile. By any standards, it was genocide. For decades after, any expression of Cossack identity was banned by order of the Communist regime. At the height of the Stalinist terror of the 1930s, even mention of the word was enough to bring persecution.

Maybe it was this deep-set and enduring love of freedom which contributed to another bloody event which shook the city and the Soviet Union in June 1962. In the worst outburst of popular discontent of the Khrushchev years, thousands of workers joined a demonstration in the city that summer to denounce a decision by bosses to cut their wages at the same time as prices were being raised. The protest, which drew more and more people over the course of its two days, began peacefully enough. To show they were not out to challenge the state, many of the workers even marched under banners of Lenin.

The authorities' reaction was far from peaceful. Soldiers, reinforced by prison guards from local labor camps, sealed off the city and began firing point blank at the crowds, killing dozens. Many more were arrested, several of them later executed for their part in organizing the protest. The carnage not only colored the streets of Novocherkassk with blood, it also sent shock waves to the capital—and beyond.

Despite extensive evidence accumulated by Soviet experts in the West, the Kremlin refused for more than twenty-five years to admit that anything had happened that fateful June, and the full shameful truth emerged only following the rise to power in 1985 of Mikhail Gorbachev. All those years later, it was also revealed for the first time that Khrushchev had been so alarmed by the incident that there had even been talk during a meeting of the ruling Politburo of evacuating the entire city and splitting its population across the Soviet Union.

With its bloody history, Novocherkassk was an appropriate site for Chikatilo. And it was here that he found work after leaving jail. Prison had been an unpleasant experience. For a man who always considered himself a cut above the rest, it had been humiliating to be cooped up with common criminals. It rankled even more that the whole thing had been based on a charge he was convinced had been trumped up by his former bosses. It could have been worse, of course. If it hadn't been for the blood test, he may well have been convicted for murder. However much he thought about it afterward, he could still not work out how he had got away with it.

Now he was free. Certainly, he had a police record. But it was a minor thing. Even though he had not served the full term, it was over. Not for him any arduous suspended sentence. Nor would there be any probation officer probing into his affairs and looking for signs of suspicious behavior. Such a practice did not exist in the Soviet Union. In fact, there was a sense in which the period in jail would actually help him to go on killing with impunity. He had been arrested, checked and then released. It was the nearest to a clean bill of health that he could possibly have hoped for.

Nor did the conviction seem to harm his work prospects. The job he got was only as a simple engineer. For a former head of the supply department, it was a bit of a comedown. But it was better than nothing. There was regular pay and his family had something to live on. Like everything else in life, he managed to blame his prison term on the unfairness of his bosses.

Even Fayina agreed. Often her husband's constant moaning about other people got on her nerves, but this time he seemed to have a point. She remembered how unhelpful they had been when she went to the factory in Shakhti to try and get them to drop the charges. Naturally, though, Chikatilo never told his wife the real reason police had held him so long, namely, that they suspected him not just of theft but also of the murder of Dima Ptashnikov.

For more than six months after his release, Chikatilo did not commit a single murder. When psychiatrists were to insist years later that he was sane, this pause was a powerful piece of evidence on their side. The very fact that Chikatilo was able to stop killing, apparently at will, seemed to confirm that he was no crazed psychopath unable to control his basic urges. Self-preservation required him to bide his time, so he acted accordingly. However deep his urge—or even need—to kill, he could exercise a conscious choice as to both the time and place in which he satisfied it. They saw him as a calculating killer, who planned his attacks hours and maybe even days in advance, selecting the precise point to which he would lead his unfortunate victims.

Although it was not immediately obvious at the time, the Soviet Union was beginning to embark on a series of changes in 1985 which would change it for ever. In March of that year, after a long illness, Chernenko had died and been replaced by Mikhail Gorbachev. The standard-bearer of a new generation which had grown up entirely under the Soviet system, Gorbachev had already made a positive impression before coming to power when he made a short trip to Britain at the end of 1984. A contrast to the old, gray man who went before him, Gorbachev was described by ardent anti-Communist Margaret Thatcher as a man that she could do business with. However, it was not just the man, himself, who made headlines during the short trip; the newspapers also focused on his smart, almost Western-looking wife, Raisa.

Nevertheless, Gorbachev did not move immediately to reveal the extent of the path on which he was to embark. His caution was partly dictated by his initial dependence on support from the vestiges of the Communist old guard who had loyally served Brezhnev. When it had come to the crucial Politburo vote which brought him to power, Gorbachev had won over his main rival, the elderly Moscow party boss Viktor Grishin, and squeezed through by just one vote. He knew that the majority could try to remove him at any time, just as Brezhnev had pushed out Khrushchev twenty years before. For this reason, the new leader spent his first months in office just as his predecessors had done before him: maneuvering his supporters into positions of power and influence and gradually eliminating those who had opposed him.

But there is also little reason to believe that Gorbachev actually had any idea of the scope of changes that he was going to initiate. More than six years later, in 1991, after the abortive hard-line coup which speeded his ultimate downfall, he was still professing loyalty to what he called the Communist ideal, and expressing his belief in the ability of the ruling party to reform itself. And that was after his ideas had already developed a long way. Back in 1985, he appeared to envisage little more than a degree of "humanization" of the Communist system and a coming to terms with its past, as well as, even more important, an improvement in its planned economy.

It was about this time Chikatilo felt bold enough to kill again, although not on his home territory. Jail was not the only thing that had scared him. So, too, had the apparent stepping up of the whole Forest Path operation. Moscow, however, was a different matter, especially when the whole city was in turmoil because of the Goodwill Games, the Ted Turner-sponsored sporting extravaganza intended to bring together U.S. and Soviet athletes for the first time in nine years after two Olympic boycotts. The chance came when he was sent by his new employers on a business trip to the Moskabel factory.

His victim, eighteen-year-old Natalia Pokhlistova, was typical of the kind of girl he had sought out and killed in Rostov. So, tragically, was her death, right down to their meeting point on a train. He ran into her near Domodyedovo, the long-haul airport from which planes fly east to Central Asia and Siberia. What she was doing there is not clear. As soon as he caught sight of her, Chikatilo realized she was a potential victim. With her shabby green raincoat, she looked older than her age. She was smoking. And as Chikatilo stood there, it was she who approached him, asking if he had something to smoke or drink.

Chikatilo replied that he had money and could buy some drink and also give her some food if she agreed to get off the train and have sex with him. The girl agreed and a couple of stops before the airport, at a stop called Aviatsonnaya, they both got out. Chikatilo led her into the woods. They didn't talk much as they walked, but it was enough for Chikatilo to realize that she was mentally subnormal. When they got to what he considered a suitable place, she was happy to take off her clothes for him. Chikatilo, too, removed his trousers.

Years later, after his arrest, he told police that he had not wanted to kill her, but just to have sex with her. Maybe if he had succeeded, that would have been that. But inevitably he could not, and as he again failed what he saw as the test of his manhood, he got out his knife, stabbing her thirty-eight times before strangling her. When he had finished, he covered her body with the green raincoat and left it in the woods. It was found the next day by a man out picking mushrooms.

Ironically, Kazakov, too, was back in Moscow. He had returned several days before, happy to be in his office in the capital again and to have gotten away from the whole nightmare of the Forest Path investigation. As soon as he received the call, he rushed to the morgue where the body had been taken. The stab wounds gave it away. It was immediately clear to him this was part of the Rostov series.

For investigators, there were two obvious things to check: how the killer had managed to get to Moscow, and where he had stayed once he was there. The first was relatively straightforward, all the more so since the killing had been committed near the airport. Despite its often haphazard operating methods, the Soviet airline Aeroflot demanded that passengers on its internal flights show their passports and kept passenger lists afterward. Nor should it have been difficult to have worked out the hotel in which the killer stayed; here, too, thanks to the all-pervasive bureaucracy, passports would be taken and records kept. So again the police machine ground into action and hundreds, even thousands of names were checked. Once more, though, they drew a blank.

In fact, Chikatilo had planned to fly to Moscow but, probably because of the games, all seats were already booked. He had gone instead by rail—and on the train there are no passport checks. The search through hotel records did not prove much more helpful either. Like most of the city's big factories, Moskabel had its own special hostel. And naturally, Chikatilo had stayed there.

Chikatilo killed just once more that year, on August 27. The body was found the next day. And it was strangely close to home. Maybe he had grown bold again or perhaps the opportunity was just too good to waste. This latest victim, Irina Gulyayeva was in many ways like Pokhlistova, the girl he had just killed in Moscow. Aged just one month younger, she too was mentally subnormal and a vagrant, with no real friends and no place to stay. When they met at the bus station in Shakhti and Chikatilo offered her the chance to stay at his cottage, she jumped at it and went off willingly with him into woods. The cottage, of course, did not exist. And a few minutes later, Chikatilo killed her, leaving her naked body about 500 yards from the bus stop.

The murder, Chikatilo's thirty-fourth, according to prosecutors' later accounts, marked a turning point in the investigation. When news of it reached Moscow, Kazakov was sent down again to investigate. This time, though, he was accompanied by Issa Kostoyev, deputy head of the investigative branch of the Public Prosecutor's Office. When the two of them returned to report their findings, their bosses decided that enough was enough. The killings couldn't be allowed to go on any longer. The operation had to be beefed up substantially and put in the hands of the country's best men.

Kostoyev, a native of the North Caucasus with a

well-deserved reputation as one of Russia's top detectives, was put in charge; Kazakov was to be his deputy, with special responsibility for the Shakhti part of the operation. Forceful and determined and at the peak of his powers, Kostoyev was not the kind of man to give up. He had cut his spurs on some of the most serious crimes the Soviet Union could offer. But he was to meet his match in Chikatilo. Nothing that he had seen over the past twenty years in fighting crime was to prepare him for the struggle that lay ahead.

12

Age *from twenty-five to fifty-five, tall, well developed physically. Blood group: fourth (AB). Shoe size 43 or more. Wears dark glasses, well turned out. Carries with him an attaché case or briefcase, in which he carries sharp knives. He suffers from mental disorder on the basis of sexual perversion (onanism, paedolphilia, necrophilia, homosexuality, and sadism). It is possible that he suffers from impotence. He also has some knowledge of human anatomy. Most likely place of initial contact with his victims—on the local train, at the railroad station, and at bus stations. Inventive in the way he carries out his criminal acts. His job allows him to move about freely within the area of the towns of Rostov, Shakhti, Novoshakhtinsk and Kamenolomni.*

By collecting the few clues which they had acquired to date, Kostoyev and his team were able to put together what was in retrospect an accurate, if not very detailed portrait of their killer. The shoe size and dark glasses came from the evidence gathered in connection with the murder of Dima Ptashnikov, the eleven-year-old boy about whom Chikatilo had been questioned when he was detained in 1984. The remaining elements in it were little more than common sense observations from the killings as a whole.

The portrait was still alarmingly vague. It is one thing to look back today and compare Chikatilo with the portrait. It was quite another to try and catch someone on the basis of it or of other, even more detailed ones, drawn up by Rostov-based psychiatrist Bukhanovsky and his colleagues from Moscow. If the police had arrested everyone who fitted the above description they would have ended up with tens, maybe hundreds of thousands of men. And even a dragnet of that size would not have brought in Chikatilo. The fact that his blood type was A rather than AB would have eliminated him from the beginning.

As it turned out, though, the operation which Kostoyev launched when he took charge was only slightly smaller in scope. In a pure policing sense, this meant a dramatic stepping up in patrols and surveillance. The handful of investigators allocated to the two divisional headquarters—Rostov and Shakhti—were supplemented by dozens of police. Some were attached permanently to Forest Path, others drafted in after being freed for a week or so from their normal work. They were the foot soldiers of the campaign. It was their job to provide the manpower needed for almost blanket coverage of the places where the killer might show up: bus and train stations were obvious places; so too were parks and the public places where large groups of people gathered.

Together with Viktor Burakov, one of the few senior policemen to be involved all the way through the 1980s, Kostoyev set up an index into which anyone even remotely suspected of involvement in one of the killings was entered. A card index, that is. While the serious crimes departments of most Western police forces were long since computerized by this time, their Soviet colleagues could often dream only of a humble typewriter. Data was entered by hand onto the cards. And what a job that was. The index, which still stands in Burakov's shabby corner office in police headquarters on Bolshaya Sadovaya Street was eventually to hold some 25,600 cards.

Anyone looking at card number nine would find an entry beginning: "Chikatilo, Andrei Romanovich," dating back to his first arrest in September 1984. They would also find a note excluding him from further investigation on account of his blood type.

It was more than just a case of watching and waiting. Investigators were also trying to identify what were, in effect, a series of "high risk" groups, within one of which they hoped to find the killer. The rationale behind some of the groups they established was obvious: given the clear sexual motivation behind the killings, anyone deviating in any way from the norms of society was suspect. As Kazakov put it later, no one capable of normal heterosexual relations would need to commit this kind of crime.

To start with, this meant looking at people with past convictions for sex-related crimes as well as those who had been charged and then acquitted due to insufficient evidence. This included crimes committed outside the Rostov region in other parts of the Soviet Union. They also took note of patients registered at psychiatric institutions for treatment of sexual and other related problems, as well as those undergoing counseling at clinics.

The apparent indifference of the killer towards the sex of his victims meant homosexuals, too, were prime targets for the police probe. One of the most repressive features of Soviet society was intolerance towards deviations from the norm. This included homosexuality. Even under Gorbachev (as, indeed now), homosexual acts, including those between consenting adults, remained a punishable offence. Convictions were far lower than in the more repressive years of Stalin, Khrushchev, or Brezhnev. Yet the gay community, to the extent to which it existed as a distinct group, remained marginalized and criminalized. Falling outside what was seen as normal behavior, homosexuals were considered by many as capable of anything, even of murder.

Another line of inquiry was prompted by the geography of the killings: The bodies of the victims were found spread over a fairly wide area of the Rostov region, often some way from the nearest bus or train stop. Furthermore, most of them lay 10 or more miles from the point from which they were presumed to have disappeared; in one case, more than 75 miles. Since these places were all accessible by road, it seemed a good bet that the murderer either owned a car of his own or else had access to one at work. Perhaps he was a taxi driver or a chauffeur working for an official organization. If someone had told police that the killer actually persuaded his victims to travel hours with him on the train followed by more than a mile or so on foot, they would hardly have believed it.

And so the theory was pursued. In the West, where car ownership is high, this would barely have narrowed the field. But this was not the case in the Soviet Union of the 1980s, where a car was strictly for the rich or lucky. For this reason, investigators began systematic checks of all the people in the area with access to cars. The number was to pass 150,000 before they finally abandoned the line of inquiry in 1988.

Investigators were not just interested in *how* the victims traveled to their death; they were also interested in *why*. For that, too, could contain an important clue to the identity of the killer. They became convinced that there must also have been something either about his character or maybe even his job which persuaded the victims to follow him.

The large percentage of tramps along the victims suggested that the killer might have been a down-and-out. Yet this would not explain his apparent ability also to lure away children. The reverse was true of an alternative hypothesis which pinned the blame on a teacher or someone who worked in a sports club or other such institution frequented by children and young people. One theory which coped with the diversity of the victims was that the killer was a member of the police—or at least someone who had pretended to be one and had some kind of identification. So they began to investigate current officers, as well as former ones, particularly those who had been forced to resign over misdemeanors of any sort. Alarmingly, a few of those actually still in the force were convicted of sex-related crimes as a result of the probe. However, none turned out to be the man they were looking for.

There were other more bizarre proposals: Owners of video salons or video equipment were questioned, as were those people who spent a lot of time in the salons. In a chilling tribute to the professionalism with which Chikatilo hacked up the bodies of his victims, so were workers from the local slaughterhouses.

The sheer numbers of those checked in the course of the investigation are sufficient to understand the scale of the search: 5,845 men with previous convictions, 10,000 potentially dangerous mentally ill people, 419 homosexuals, 163,000 drivers. Eventually, they were to check some half a million people, a staggering figure equivalent to some 10 percent of the population of the whole Rostov region. As a result of their effort, they managed to clear up some 1,062 crimes, including 95 murders, 245 rapes, 140 cases of serious bodily harm (105 men were also punished for homosexual acts). The figures were impressive, except in one respect: They did not produce a killer.

At first, the new job in Novocherkassk seemed to be going a little better than those in Shakhti and Rostov. Although Chikatilo started off as a simple engineer, the departure of his boss to Germany in 1988 meant he was promoted to be head of the ferrous metals department of the supplies section. Again he had several people working under him—among them, his daughter, Lyudmila. However, it would be an exaggeration to say he was actually a success. Colleagues said later that he was only promoted because no one else wanted what was inevitably a thankless job, and criticism of his work soon started. It was to get stronger when the director who had hired Chikatilo retired and was replaced by another.

The early morning planning sessions were the worst. Every one in the supply department used to hate them. It was bad enough starting at seven-thirty A.M., but worse to be immediately subjected to the third degree from the boss, particularly when the shortcomings were not your fault. They were the fault of the whole absurd Soviet economic system which, by the early Gorbachev years, was already beginning to fall apart. One by one, the various department heads would be told off by the deputy director for failing to get the materials the factory needed; and one by one they would try to defend themselves and point the blame somewhere else. All of them, that is, except Chikatilo. He would just sit there like a sponge, soaking up the complaints in silence.

Nor did he even seem to mind that young Lyudmila was sitting there listening as he was dressed down. Alexander Gubernatorov, a rough but good-humored man who worked at the next desk away from Chikatilo for more than five years was staggered by the whole thing. He used to ask Chikatilo how he could stand it. "How could you have got your daughter a job here if you knew you were going to be told off all the time in front of her?" he asked Chikatilo once. "If I were you, I would have resigned years ago."

In the end it was Lyudmila who went. She was divorced from her husband, an artist who had earned his living as a window dresser for state-owned department stores. After living a short time at her parents' flat in Novocherkassk, she went off with her small son to start a new life with another man in Kharkov, just over the border in the Ukraine.

As for Chikatilo, he hung on in the factory in Novocherkassk for almost five years. He was so used to the criticism that he didn't react much anymore. Whenever the deputy director had gone out, all the rest of his colleagues would be swearing among themselves and joking about who had come off worst. But not Chikatilo. He remained calm. They thought he must have nerves of steel or simply did not care. Neither was true. Every complaint added to the bitterness and feeling of injustice within him. As at his former jobs, he was convinced that his bosses did not respect him as a person or appreciate his work. Maybe they were even jealous of his higher education, he told himself. Little had changed and he was still seeing faults everywhere except in himself.

It was worth putting up with the criticism for the sake of the other advantages of the job, particularly the freedom. He was his own master. Although he was obliged to be at the planning meetings every morning, the rest of the day was more or less his to arrange as he wished. If he wanted to slip out for a few hours or go home early, then no one would stop him. And then there were the business trips. Most people hated them. All that time on trains or planes and overnight stays in seedy factory hostels. But they were ideal for him. They gave him the time he needed. Sometimes he would be away as long as ten days, maybe even for two weeks.

Once he was offered another job in the factory at

the same pay without all the traveling. He turned it down, and his colleagues couldn't understand why. He had his reasons, but he wasn't going to tell them. In fact, there was a lot they didn't understand about him. As before, he rarely confided in any of them. None of his fellow workers knew exactly where he lived or had met his family.

Yelena Surikova, who worked in the bookkeeping department, couldn't fathom him at all. It was her job to match up the goods he had collected with the bills as they came in. It was complicated enough to start with. But whenever it was one of Chikatilo's orders, the whole bureaucratic process turned into a virtual nightmare. She had never seen such chaos. Even Gubernatorov, who knew Chikatilo best of all, pitied him more than really liked him. All in all, he wasn't a particularly likeable figure. True he was polite; he was also cold, distant, and always complaining about something or other. His colleagues never heard him laugh. The most they ever got was a smile. But what a smile! It used to remind Gubernatorov of a crocodile.

Most Russians feel they have never got to know someone until they have got drunk with them. During all those years in which they shared an office, Gubernatorov only sat down for a drink with Chikatilo once, and that was almost by accident. It was New Year's Eve, and he and another colleague had come back to the office after the working day was over to get some bottles of champagne they had left there. Who should be at his desk but Chikatilo. He was sitting there alone, staring out of the window. They had no idea why he was there or what he was doing. Somehow, though, they persuaded him to join them, and the three of them managed to polish off a couple of bottles. Not bad going, but then it was holiday time. It never happened again.

As memory of jail faded, Chikatilo was becoming bolder. Three more murders were recorded in 1987, all of them outside the Rostov area—one in the Urals, just outside the industrial city of Ekaterinburg, then known as Sverdlovsk; another in the Ukrainian town of Zaporozhye; and the third on the outskirts of Leningrad.

The decision to strike far from home appears to have been deliberate, serving as further proof of the premeditated nature of Chikatilo's killings and of his constant striving to reduce the risk of capture. His murder of the eighteen-year-old tramp, Natalya Pokhlistova, on his trip to Moscow during the Goodwill Games in 1985, was virtually the only killing he had committed outside the Rostov region that had been immediately linked with him—and then it was only because, by coincidence, Kazakov from the Public Prosecutor's Department, had just arrived back in the capital from Rostov.

On other occasions it was very difficult for local police, hundreds or thousands of miles away, to realize the body found in their locality was part of the Rostov connection. As with the two murders which Chikatilo had committed in Uzbekistan in 1984, none of these three new killings was added to the series until he confessed to them after his arrest years later. There was one drawback, though—which Chikatilo probably did not realize at the time: All his business trips were recorded with his employer. This was ultimately to make it extremely easy for investigators looking back to determine whether he had been in a certain city at the time a murder was committed there.

Chikatilo's victim in Zaporozhye was an twelve-year-old named Ivan Bilovetski. Although he initially confessed to this murder, he later denied it in court. A good-looking child, Ivan had a reputation as one of the best-behaved boys in the neighborhood. Friends used to ask his mother, Nina, how she managed to spend all day away at work and still do such a good job with him and his younger brother and sister. Before going out, Ivan would always tell her where he was going and ask permission. He was certainly not the kind of boy to hang out on the street at night, let alone to go off with a strange man. On July 29, 1987, all that changed.

Nina went to work early that morning. Her husband was away on a business trip, but she wasn't worried. A girl friend had slept at her place that night and had promised to look after the children for her. Her own day at work was routine, but the journey home wasn't. As so often happened, the intensive summer heat gave way to thunderstorms and it was pouring rain. Then to cap it all, the bus broke down. As she walked into her apartment block, her watch showed eight forty-five P.M.—more than two hours later than usual.

When her key turned in the lock, her youngest two came to greet her. But no Ivan. Her girl friend was still there and she asked her where he had gone.

"He's just went out," the friend said.

"Went out? Where?"

"One of his friends came by, they listened to some music for a little and then he said he was going out. But not for long."

Nina waited a few more minutes, maybe an hour, but there was still no sign of Ivan. At about ten P.M. she went outside. It was still light, but even so, she was worried. He had never done anything like this before. He had never been out anything like so late.

She went to the friend's house. But no Ivan. The little boy hadn't seen her son for hours. By the time she got back home it was midnight and there was still no news. It was just possible that he had gone to see his grandmother. Not that he had ever done so before, at least not without telling her. But it was still a hope to cling to. And it would last her through the night.

Her mother didn't have a telephone and it was too far to go on foot.

Nina found plenty to fill those hours. She must have called all her relatives, but none of them had heard anything. So, at four-thirty A.M. she took the first bus and went to her mother's. When she rang the doorbell and the woman came to the door, she already knew the answer.

The police were calm and told her not to worry when she went to the local station. When she got home from her mother's she had called them and they had told her to come in to bring a photo and make a statement.

"He'll turn up," said one policeman. "Kids are always disappearing like that."

But not Ivan, she thought.

Later that morning, her husband came back and they set out, together with her sister, to try and find him. They spent much of the rest of the day searching in the cellars which lie under most of the houses in Zaporozhye. A year before, a young girl had been raped and killed in one of the cellars. But again, no Ivan.

The next morning, Nina's husband and her sister went out again, this time to search the forest path which runs beside the railroad, just a few minutes from their home. Nina, herself, was feeling tired and stayed at home. But they were only away for twenty minutes, much less than she had expected. When she saw the expression on their faces, she realized at once that they had found him—and that he was dead. She tried to run there but they stopped her. They wanted to spare her the sight of her son's mangled body.

Now aged forty-seven, Nina looks more like sixty, her white hair a sharp contrast to the black clothes that she was worn every day since her son's death.

"The day I buried my son, I gave him my word that I would try to live long enough to see his killer with my own eyes," she was to declare as she broke down giving evidence during Chikatilo's trial several years later.

"I wanted to see this man who could rip open my son's stomach and then stuff mud in his mouth so that he would not cry out. I wanted to know what he looked like, to know which mother could bear such an animal.

"And now I see him."

The next year, 1988, that animal crept back across the border, and again, he killed three times. On April 6, police found the body of an unknown woman who appeared to have been killed two to five days before. On May 14, he killed nine-year-old Lyosha Voronko and then, exactly two months later, fifteen-year-old Zhenya Muratov.

For the police, it was the resumption of a nightmare. If the lull in the killings had left them puzzled and preoccupied, then their sudden resumption made life far worse. It was back to the bruising routine at twelve- and fifteen-hour days and long evenings at work with nothing to keep them going but cigarettes and glasses of strong, black tea. And again the telephone call which would summon them to a piece of deserted woodland to see the body of a child ripped and slashed almost beyond recognition.

As time went on, those beastly wounds were also changing. Chikatilo was becoming more skilled as far as his killing was concerned. The objects of his attention were the same—the tips of tongues, nipples, and genitals. But while in the early years he used to slice off huge chunks of flesh, by the late 1980s he was becoming more precise. By his own admission, later, he was also getting more skilled in dodging the spurts of blood as he stabbed and slashed. He was changing from a crazed butcher into a cool, calculating surgeon.

None of which, of course, made the process any less terrifying for his victims. In some cases, the most horrible "surgery" was done on the victims while they were still alive. In other cases it was once they were dead, or even some hours after—a detail that gave the investigators one more piece of information about the man they were seeking, namely, that he often hung around at the scene of the crime. It was all part of the ritual that he had followed, almost religiously, for each murder. It was not just the suffering and the killing which gave him the pleasure. It was what he did with the bodies afterward. Even the act of ripping off the victims' clothes and taking them from one place to the other seemed to give him pleasure. There was a special way in which he had to do it.

The killer still held many mysteries for police, especially as far as his younger victims were concerned. It was not difficult to fathom why the prostitutes and tramps would go off with him. Many of them were so desperate that they would have gone off with anyone. The behavior of the teenage boys, particularly those from happy, well-adjusted homes, was more difficult to understand.

If they had been homosexual, then it might have been easier to explain. But there was no evidence that any of them were. What strange powers did this man exercise in order to lure them to their death? What did he say? Did he order them to follow or did he beg them? And if he promised something, then what was it?

There was no single answer. Chikatilo's deadly success lay rather in the extent to which he had a different approach ready for every one of his victims, the children and young people included. In some cases, the victims, themselves, would make first contact even if it was only a matter of asking directions or requesting change for a vending machine. In those cases, it was relatively simple for him to begin a conversation.

And if he learned in the course of the conversation that they had run away from home or were otherwise unhappy or troubled, then it was not difficult for him to go further. Maybe they were hungry or thirsty? he would ask. If so, he could offer them something to eat or drink at his house, which was nearby. And even if they were happy and well-fed, then he knew how to lure them with the offer of a chance to watch some videos or to look at rare stamps.

Regardless of how the initial approach was made, Chikatilo also took advantage of other factors, in particular his appearance: It was difficult for any of his victims to believe that this educated, well-dressed man could be a killer. In a way, this was his secret weapon. Children who would not have dreamed of going off with a younger, more threatening looking man simply lowered their guard when they came into contact with this soft-spoken uncle- or grandfather-type figure.

Equally important was the naivety of his victims, which was itself again a product of society. Years of trying to sweep crime, particularly of a violent and sexual nature, under the carpet had made its mark. Certainly, Soviet parents used to warn their children against the danger of going off with strangers, just as their Western counterparts did. But there was rarely the same intensity about it, for the simple reason that the risks seemed smaller. Chikatilo could also play on a certain sense of solidarity between strangers, found not just in the Soviet Union but also elsewhere in the former Eastern bloc.

The very way Soviet society was organized—or not organized—also presented a wealth of opportunities to make contact with strangers. The country did not have a monopoly on lines for buses, but in the Soviet Union they were often longer and slower moving. To them should also be added the inevitable lines in shops, cafes, and other public buildings. On any line, there is a feeling of comradeship. People who would not talk to each other if they met by chance in any other circumstances behave very differently if they find themselves standing one behind the other waiting for a bus or a loaf of bread.

The extent of this willingness, especially on the part of children, to go off with complete strangers, was graphically demonstrated after Chikatilo's capture by an experiment carried out by the Rostov psychiatrist Bukhanovsky. A solidly built, middle-aged man, he cruised the streets of Rostov in his car one evening, trying to pick up children with promises of food and drink. To his surprise—and horror—he found many accepted apparently without fear, climbing into the passenger seat and happily going off with him to an unknown destination. In fact, the only place he took them was the local police station, where they were given a ticking off by police for their lack of caution. Such children made easy victims.

A fifteen-year-old boy called Zhenya Muratov who went off with Chikatilo on July 14, 1988, appears to have been one of them, although investigators spent a long time afterward trying to work out why. The boy's case was a puzzle to them. In retrospect, he seemed too bright to be tricked by a man like Chikatilo. Unlike many of the other young victims, he was not a runaway or a hooligan, nor was he too young to know what this kindly uncle wanted. At the top of his class and a keen chess player, he was also extremely strong and fit; his parents recalled years later in court an occasion when he had run more than 10 miles home after missing a train. He seemed to have everything going for him. It then all went terribly wrong.

His parents had last seen him the day before, when he set off early in the morning on the train to Rostov. He had passed the entrance exams to one of the city's institutes but had to go back to give a blood sample for his medical exam. It was not clear how long the whole thing was going to take. But he had an aunt in Rostov and it was agreed that he would stay with her overnight if he wasn't going to be able to get back in time. That he made it to his aunt's is certain. According to her, he arrived late in the evening after staying to watch a football match. When he left her the next morning, he said that he had some more things to do in connection with his exams and would then get the train home. It was on that train home that he must have met Chikatilo.

What Chikatilo said to him to persuade him to leave the train remains unclear. The murderer's initial version after his arrest was that the boy had accepted an offer to go off to eat and drink with him at his dacha. His parents rejected the theory out of hand. He was not that kind of boy, they insisted. Nor would there have been much logic to it. Judging by where his body was found, he had already been traveling more than an hour before getting off the train just a few steps from home. If he had been driven purely by hunger or thirst, then he would have been able to wait just a few minutes more. Nor do they think it likely that he succumbed to the other kinds of offers of stamps or coins with which Chikatilo used to try to tempt his young victims.

An alternate version, mentioned by Chikatilo later, during his trial, seemed more probable. He said that he had fallen into conversation with the boy after sitting down next to him on the train, and had asked him to get off the train with him at a deserted station called Lesastep, north of Shakhti, to help him carry his things to his cottage. According to Muratov's parents, only such an appeal for help could have persuaded their son to alter his plans in that way. Nevertheless, doubts still remained over the last few hours of Muratov's life. Nor was any more light shed by the discovery by children, playing in the woods, of his

body more than eight months later. By then, it was
little more than bones.

Towards the end of 1988, the Public Prosecutor's Office
in Rostov received a note from Moscow in the internal
mail. It was a standard document, sent out to investigating magistrates all over the country. Quoting what
it claimed was the latest Japanese research, the circular described a scientific breakthrough which it
said could have very important implications for the
fight against crime—albeit in a tiny minority of cases.

Until, then it had been assumed that a person's
blood and sperm were always of the same group. For
this reason, even when traces of sperm were found, for
example, on a corpse, it was thought enough to give a
suspect a simple blood test to determine if there could
be a link. His sperm would necessarily be of the same
group as his blood. However, the Japanese scientists
had apparently found that this was not always the
case. In extremely rare cases, they said, perhaps one
in ten thousand, or even one in a million, the two
could be of a different group.

The circular was handed around, without generat-
ing much interest and then put away in the files.

13

or anyone who lived through it, the spring of 1989 was an almost unreal time. Historians will look back on it not only as the high point of Gorbachev's *perestroika* but inevitably as the beginning of its end. It was the point at which the controlled "revolution from above" gave way to a spontaneous and far more powerful "revolution from below." Certainly, the consequences were not felt immediately. From then on, it was possible to trace a series of events which were to culminate two and a half years later not just in the fall of Communism and of Gorbachev but also in the dissolution of the Soviet empire.

Since coming to power in 1985, the former Communist Party boss from the provinces had already made enough changes to earn himself a place in the history books. Initially, it was largely a question of telling the truth about the past and debunking the myths and lies on which the Soviet Union had been built. Stalin, virtually deified by Gorbachev's predecessors, was at last revealed in his true colors as a monster who killed millions in his pursuit of power. One by one, the victims of his purges were rehabilitated and lessons drawn about the damage caused by the so-called "Cult of Personality."

Gorbachev's revolution was not only about the past. He was also interested in the present. At home, he began experiments in the economy, giving the green light to the formation of so-called cooperatives, in reality private companies in everything but name. Abroad, he agreed with the United States to deep arms cuts and began to loosen the stranglehold on the former satellites of Eastern Europe in a process culminating in the tearing down of the Berlin Wall.

Yet it was an uphill struggle. Although Gorbachev, himself, seemed uncertain at times about how fast or how far he wanted to go with his reforms, it was all too much for many of his more conservative colleagues. One by one they were removed in reshuffles. Yet the speed of changes was so great that many of the seemingly more enlightened men who took their places soon found that they, too, were out of step with the increasingly liberal mood.

Nor was society, as a whole, ready for the shock. While the young generally welcomed change, many of the older generation remained Communists, who were proud of the achievements of the past, from the defeat of Nazi Germany to the space program. What little they had seen of *perestroika* did not suit them at all. Despite Gorbachev's rhetoric, food stores were getting emptier not fuller. More alarming was the perceived growth in lawlessness. No sooner had authorities conceded openly for the first time that serious crime existed, than they had to admit that the situation was getting worse. This was particularly the case in Rostov, whose position in the south of Russia made it easy prey for the organized "mafia" groups run out of Georgia, Armenia, and the other republics of the Caucasus. Many ordinary people had had enough. They wanted the clock turned back.

Instead it went forward. In March 1989, for the first time in more than 70 years, the country went to the polls to choose a parliament in genuine, contested elections. True, the procedure was far from flawless in a Western sense: in order to ensure that the Communists remained on top, they and their allies were guaranteed a substantial slice of the seats as a right. There were also numerous abuses on the ground, particularly in outlying areas, where the Party barons were unwilling to lose their grip on power. Yet, the change had come. Enough progressive-minded people had broken through the obstacles put up against them to ensure that the first Congress of People's Deputies turned into an incredible spectacle when it met a few months later. To realize how far the country had come it was necessary only to watch former dissident Andrei Sakharov crossing swords with Gorbachev, the man who had freed him from internal exile in Gorky more than two years before.

It was as if the people had suddenly found a tongue after decades of enforced silence. And these were not battles fought out behind closed doors. The deliberations of the new parliament were watched by more than 100 million people on live television and listened to by tens of millions more on radio. Industrial production plunged by as much as a fifth as workers stayed away from their factories to follow proceedings. The sound of the debate echoed in shops, hotels, restaurants, and even taxi cabs.

It was against this backdrop that Chikatilo killed again. It had been more than seven months since he had murdered Muratov, but the boy's body still lay undetected under the snow. It was not to be found until April. By that time, Chikatilo had already met Tatyana Ryzhova.

As a girl, Tanya had been the kind of daughter every mother would dream of having: clever, a good helper at home, and one of the best students in class. Her mother Vera, a plump good-natured woman who worked as a milkmaid on a collective farm, was justifiably proud. But then things began to go wrong. To her mother's alarm, Tanya began to drink and she began to smoke. Inevitably, she was found out. But it was only one of the sources of tension that began to emerge at home. More and more, she began to argue with her mother and fight with her brother. Things were also going badly at the vocational boarding school where she was studying. Her grades were getting worse and she was arguing with the teachers and answering them back. Then, on January 11, 1989, the girl left home and never came back.

Not that her mother realized it immediately. She assumed that her daughter was at school in the nearby town of Kamensk. But then, a couple of days later, she received a telegram from the head teacher saying that she had disappeared from there, too. Vera Ryzhova was worried. Although her daughter was headstrong, she had never behaved like that before. The next day she hurried to Kamensk. After talking to teachers, she set off to visit Tanya's friends, as well as her grandmother to see if she was there. Then on January 15, in despair, she went to the local police. They did a few checks with local hospitals, but when they turned up nothing, they told her to look for herself. "If you find anything, then give us a call," said one in a matter-of-fact way as she walked out of the police station.

The months that followed were a period of terrible uncertainty for her. She tried to get information about Tanya through her daughter's friends, but it was difficult. The girl had never really been close to anyone. Even those she called friends were little more than acquaintances. Nor did Tanya's boyfriend Andrei, who

was a friend of her son, know what had happened.
Then, early in March she received a tip-off from a
friend of a friend saying that her daughter had been
seen living in a town called Glubokoye, where she had
been squatting in a cellar. But again the police were
not interested. They told her to go and check for
herself. As was established later, Tanya had met a
couple of boys her age on a local train at the end of
January and had gone off with them. The boys were
heavy drinkers and petty criminals who were known
to the police. But she liked them and they were good
fun. They spent more than a week together, drinking
and having sex in a squalid ménage à trois in the
cellar under a house at number 8 Jubilee Street.

It didn't last, and by the beginning of March, Ryzhova had gravitated back to Shakhti and was literally walking the streets. A single girl, she was alone
and with no friends, but still too proud to go back to
her home to her school. The days spent sleeping out
were also taking their toll. There was little left now of
the pretty teenager she had used to be. Her drinking,
too, was getting worse. These days, even by lunchtime,
she had often drunk so much vodka or cheap port that
she could barely stand up straight.

More than anything else, it was this unsteadiness
on her feet which drew Chikatilo's attention to her
when he saw her outside the city's railroad station.
He took it all in with the quick expert eye of a professional: the dirty clothes, the unkempt hair tumbling
out of the winter hat and, above all, the smell of
alcohol on her breath. His approach was direct but
effective, his confidence enhanced by the knowledge
that his daughter's apartment in nearby Lenin Street
was empty and that he had the keys in his pocket. He
offered her food and drink, and like many before her,
she willingly went off with him. A few minutes later,
they had reached the typical crumbling tenement

block at number 206 and were inside the small ground-floor apartment with number 40 on the door.

Chikatilo's daughter, Lyudmila, had lived here before. But once she had gotten her divorce, Chikatilo was given the job of trying to swap the state-owned apartment for two smaller ones in which his daughter and her husband could both live separate lives. He was taking his time, though. He had given up the old broken-down house in Mezhevoi Pereulok some time before and the prospect of a new place all to himself for secret meetings was to good to pass up.

Tatyana got some food and some drink, although not as much as she would have liked. But she didn't put up much resistance when Chikatilo pushed her down on the floor in the corner of the living room and tried to have sex with her. As usual, though, the spirit was willing but the flesh was weak. Tatyana, too, was getting upset. Only now was she realizing what a mistake it had been going off with this elderly man, who tried so hard to get her into his apartment, and then couldn't do anything once he had gotten her there. Angry, she told him that she wanted 500 rubles or she was going to go home. She had good connections in the Rostov underworld, she said, and if he didn't pay, she would denounce him to them. Chikatilo tried in vain to calm her down. In the back of his mind, he was still hoping against hope that somehow, this time, he could actually make it. He couldn't. And the more he failed, the more the girl screamed.

He had already killed once before inside; his first victim, Lena Zakotnova, back in 1978, had died in the living room of the house on Mezhevoi Pereulok. That, though, had been a detached cottage situated a good few yards away from the nearest buildings. This was a small apartment with thin walls in the middle of a building. It was the kind of place where you could almost hear the neighbors breathing. There was also the risk that he had been seen coming in with her. In a throwback to village life, most Russian buildings have a bench outside on which the old women sit and gossip late into the night. The apartments had balconies too, which also looked over the courtyard. Nor would anyone have had trouble identifying him. In the time before Lyudmila's divorce, he had been a regular sight around the place, often coming to see his little grandson there. In another coincidence, who should live upstairs but Nina Dovgan, who had worked with him around the corner in Shakhti in the offices of Rostovnerud.

Dovgan, who lives at the top of the building, did not notice anything unusual that evening. Others that lived farther down did, though. Several recalled afterward having distinctly heard women's screams which apparently came from Lyudmila's apartment. But everything had quickly become quiet again and the neighbors did nothing. As they settled back in front of their television sets, they did not realize that the deadly drama down in number 40 was moving into its final act. And the ending was the usual bloody one.

Desperate about his inability to silence his victim, Chikatilo whipped a folding knife out of his pocket and stabbed her in the mouth. The action not only silenced her, it also bought him the pleasure that his halfhearted attempts at intercourse with her had failed to give him. After a few minutes the madness had taken him over completely, and she was dead.

Then he was faced with a problem. Usually he killed outside and left his victims where they were lying. This time was different. He had to get her out of there. But how? The main thing was to disguise the body. The method he chose was the most grisly one imaginable. Fetching a sturdy knife from the kitchen, he began hacking his way through her lifeless corpse, cutting off first the head and then both legs. He wrapped them in her clothes, put the horrific bundle in the cellar and cleaned up the blood all over the floor of the flat with a mop. Then he went outside to look for something in which to transport her away. There was snow on the ground and the best hope was a sled. After a long search around the neighborhood, he finally found one, lying against the wall in a nearby courtyard.

And so in the dark and in the snow, he set off toward the railroad, dragging behind him the sled with the remains of Ryzhova tied on it. No one seemed to notice him as he walked along, a solitary figure bundled up against the cold with what looked like his belongings slithering along behind him. That is, until he reached the railroad crossing. It was almost spring, the snow cover was only thin and parts of the rail protruded through it, jamming the sled. He began to panic as a passerby came toward him. He needn't have done so. Without saying a word, the other man bent down and helped him lift up the sled, pausing only momentarily with surprise when he felt how heavy it was. He soon disappeared away into the night. Chikatilo waited until he was completely out of sight and then began to stuff the contents of his bundle into a some large pipes which ran near the railroad track.

Ryzhova's remains were found nine days later. Like the rest of the killings, though, there were no more clues. The only thing it really told investigators for sure was that the murderer was back in their area. Yet for all the lack of evidence in the whole long and fruitless investigation, there was one common factor that kept coming up: the railroad. The initial theory that the murderer transported his victims by road had come to nothing. Despite all the police's efforts, none of the more than 150,000 motorists they had checked gave them grounds for suspicion. They were also convinced that if the killer had used a car, then someone would have seen it parked somewhere at the scene of the crime. There had been nothing, beyond a few vague and unconfirmed sightings. There were other reasons to favor the train theory. To start with, most of the bodies, Ryzhova's included, were found alongside the railroad line. Many of the victims had also last been seen alive at the railroad station.

So they began to pursue the new theory with the same determination with which they had followed the others before it. As the operation got underway, plainclothes police were positioned everywhere on the railroad. At any one time, there were as many as 500 or 600 of them. Some were at the stations themselves, disguised as passengers or in the woods nearby pretending to be picking mushrooms, a favorite Russian pastime. The more unfortunate ones had to lie in pits, especially dug along the side of the line, covered over with branches and leaves. Meanwhile, each train would have between four and six officers on board. Starting at opposite ends, they would gradually work their way through the carriages towards the middle.

Among them were policewomen, especially decked out in short skirts and heavy makeup. Some pretended to be drunk. If that was the kind of woman that turned the killer on, then they were ready. Although none of them were armed, each had several burly male plainclothes officers standing nearby with their service pistols in their pockets. The women, themselves, had also received special training in karate and other martial arts. However tasty the bait, though, Chikatilo never bit it.

Investigators could be forgiven a feeling of desperation. Although the killer had already single-handedly murdered forty people, they still did not even have a decent description of him. Not one victim had escaped from his clutches. Yet should it have been so difficult for police to notice him as he made his way back and forth on the train? The answer is no if one judges by the accounts given to police after Chikatilo's arrest by people who knew him. For while the police saw nothing, they seemed to be running into him the whole time.

The picture of Chikatilo's activity which emerges from their accounts is of a man hunting with the same enthusiasm and determination as he had done on the night in 1984 when he was followed across Rostov by inspector Zanasovski. An anonymous figure blending into the background of a carriage full of strangers, he could pick a victim at his leisure, lure them off the train, and take them away to their death. And he kept on doing so, in what he seemed to believe was the certain knowledge that no one was watching him. But sometimes even a big city can unexpectedly turn into a village. And Rostov, let alone Shakhti or Novocherkassk, was no Moscow.

Lyudmila Pilenko was one of those who kept running into him. A placid, middle-aged woman, she worked in the bookkeeping department of Chikatilo's factory in Novocherkassk. Like thousands of other city dwellers, she used to spend summer weekends working in the vegetable garden on her allotment of ground, leaving home maybe as early as six or seven A.M. She did not like Chikatilo any more than did most of her other colleagues. They used to meet each other often; every time he came back from one of his business trips, he had to give her his receipts. He used to come into her office, hand in the little scraps of paper and then go. He rarely said anything at all. Pilenko had never even seen him smile.

Imagine her surprise, therefore, one morning as she sat bleary eyed on the train to see her surly colleague from work. He was transformed. And he certainly wasn't behaving like someone off for a day of gardening. To start with, he wasn't dressed for it. Despite the early hour, he was already wearing a suit and tie. It looked as if he hadn't been to bed at all. His behavior was also strange, to say the least. He was like a man possessed, moving quickly from car to car. And all the time, his eyes were darting around him as if he were looking for someone. She saw him several times and it was always the same. He was also always carrying a large black nylon bag.

"Why is he always wandering around in the train with that bag?" she asked Gubernatorov, their mutual colleague, at work one day. "What is he doing? Collecting empty bottles or something?"

Gubernatorov said he didn't think so. He had seen him on the train a couple of times himself, and he couldn't work out why he was behaving so oddly either. So, one day, as he caught sight of Chikatilo walking past through the train car, he tapped him on the shoulder and asked him. Chikatilo looked shocked to have been recognized and paused for a few seconds before mumbling out an answer.

"I used to live in Shakhti, I've still got a little cottage there," he said. He didn't explain the bag.

They were not the only ones who noticed Chikatilo. Another woman, Yektarina Pustovoitova, who used to travel on the train, also kept noticing the strange behavior of a man she had known at work. Pilenko and Gubernatorov did not know her. Pustovoitova belonged to an earlier phase of Chikatilo's life; she had worked with him at his previous job in Shakhti. But she, too, disliked him, remembering him as a troublemaker who was always complaining about this or that. Pustovoitova's daughter was building a country cottage in the nearby town of Kamenolomni and she traveled early on summer Saturday mornings to visit her there. Always, she would sit in the second to last car to avoid having to walk too much at the other end. And always she would see him working his way through the car.

One particular occasion late that October particularly stuck in her mind. She was sitting in her usual place, when Chikatilo appeared. As usual, he was carrying his bag and had a faraway look in his eyes. He seemed to be searching, but it was not clear to her for what—or whom. She never saw him even talking to anyone. This time, though, she was determined to find out what he was up to and even stood up to confront him. He simply looked straight through her and went on. It was the last time that she saw him on the train.

Chikatilo killed four more times that summer. Three of the victims were little boys. It was not the first time that his victims were male. However, it was clear to those trying to track him down that the balance was shifting. Back in the early days of 1982 and 1983, most of the murders had been of females: from innocent little girls at one extreme to prostitutes at the other, with a few mixed-up teenagers in between. How to explain this apparent new preference? Was Chikatilo gradually turning from heterosexual to homosexual? Or indeed can one really describe him as ever having been either?

Many of the world's worst serial killers have been distinguished by the specific nature of their victims. Jeffrey Dahmer concentrated his attention largely on young black homosexual men. Others, from Jack the Ripper onwards, have murdered prostitutes. By contrast, Chikatilo had shown from the start an apparent ambivalence to the characteristics of those he killed. The differences between them were not only of sex, but also of age, background, and lifestyle. To take just two of his victims, it would be difficult to find any link between Marta Ryabyenko, the forty-four-year-old alcoholic and prostitute whom Chikatilo killed in Rostov in February 1984 and Dima Ptashinkov, the eleven-year-old boy who died a month later. The only similarity was their willingness to go with him to what was to be their place of execution, a willingness shared by almost all his victims.

There is an explanation for this apparent indifference. Chikatilo was not so much a rapist in the usual sense of the word as a sadist forever trying to take out his own feeling of inferiority and inadequacy on others. Misunderstood and looked down upon by society, he was convinced that he was different from other men, but at the same time would not accept it. He was desperate to prove to himself and to others that he was normal, yet ironically, he chose the most abnormal way in which to do it. For Chikatilo, there was no getting away from the fact that he obtained his sexual fulfillment from domination and from suffering, from seeing the agony of his victims. For this reason, the cries of pain of a little boy were just as stimulating as those of a woman.

In most cases, Chikatilo appears to have started out with the aim of rape—either heterosexual or homosexual—and almost all his attacks began with attempts at intercourse. But his claim later, in his own defense, that he had not initially intended to kill appears little more than an attempt to deceive not just investigators but also himself. He knew his own sexual tastes well enough to be aware in advance of which things would arouse him. And conventional intercourse was not one of them. He needed blood and he needed suffering and every attempt he made at sex in those years ended in it. Sometimes, as with the killing of Tatyana Ryzhova in his daughter's apartment, the first blow was struck to silence the screams of a victim. Other times, it was pure sadism. Underlying his actions was the certainty that every blow he struck with his knife or hammer or stone would bring him one step closer to orgasm.

When he was interviewed after his capture, Chikatilo made clear that he never set out in search either of a man or a woman. If the victim turned out to be an adult woman, all was well. But it was just as good if it was a prepubescent girl or a fourteen-year-old boy. He was the ultimate opportunist—the main thing for him was to kill.

The different sexes, though, were necessarily wooed in different ways. The most obvious difference between his male and female victims was over how and why they decided to follow him. A good number of the girls and women who went with Chikatilo were predominantly in their late teens or older; with the exception of a one or two, many accepted the invitation to go with him in the clear expectation that their encounter would end in sex.

The same was not true of the boys whom he killed. The American Dahmer, one of the few other murderers who came close to the horror of Chikatilo, only killed males and he lured them to their death by offering them money in order to pose for naked photographs. But Chikatilo was operating in a very different society. There was no evidence to suggest that any of the boys were homosexual, let alone a male prostitute. In fact, such prostitution appears to have been virtually nonexistent in Russia in those days, particularly in a provincial town such as Rostov.

The younger boys among Chikatilo's victims were instead tempted with promises of the chance to look at rare stamps or watch videos. The older ones were attracted by promises of food and drink. With a kind of naivety which was itself a product of Soviet society's prudish attitude towards sex, none of the boys seemed able to foresee the sexual designs which this apparently normal, elderly man could have upon them.

It is this which also explains the complete absence of adult males from Chikatilo's victims. To the extent that any homosexual community existed in the country, it was small and secretive. Indeed, Chikatilo did not consider himself homosexual and had no desire to associate with them; in fact, he even seemed repelled by them.

As for finding victims among heterosexual men, that was virtually impossible. A heterosexual man was unlikely to go off into the woods with another man, particularly one like Chikatilo, who as his work colleagues repeatedly complained had problems getting on with the same sex. Given Chikatilo's cowardice, it would also have been an illogical move. Although he was tall and strong enough to overcome most normally built men, it would have meant a fight. And he did not like fights—particularly if there was the danger that his intended victim might get away. He didn't need them. There were enough boys and women around for him to concentrate on. And that is precisely what he did.

So what changed? According to Andrei Tkachenko, a psychiatrist and sex therapist from Moscow's Serbsky institute who later spent two months examining Chikatilo, it is common among sadists to move in the course of their lives gradually from heterosexual to homosexual objects, often also involving pedophilia. Equally common is the almost paradoxical rejection at the same time of conventional homosexuality as falling short of the goals of normality which they set themselves. "It is not the consequence of homosexuality in the usual sense of the word," Tkachenko said. "Rather, such abnormal sexual behavior is due to the transformation of all structures, of distorted sex-role behavior and stereotypes. He is unable to perform his male role to the end, and his sexual self-awareness is distorted so much as to include a change, an inversion of the sex object."

Another explanation may also lie with the victims, themselves. After years of rumors and warnings about the killer, all but the most foolhardy of teenage girls and young women realized that going off with a strange man into the woods would be folly. Not only that. He knew that if he tried too hard to pick them up and they refused, then it was more likely that they would report him to the police. By this time, even professional prostitutes had become wary of going off with their clients, particularly if it were a matter of walking with them in deserted stretches of woods. Nineteen-year-old Yelena Varga, whom Chikatilo killed in August 1989, was an exception. Little boys, especially those from broken homes, were more vulnerable. The offers that Chikatilo dreamed up proved too strong to resist. And, after years of practice, he was a good enough psychologist to know precisely with what he could tempt them in order to drown out their parents' warnings not to go off with strange men.

Not that authorities did not make attempts to warn the children. In fact, during the late 1980s, police mounted a massive propaganda campaign throughout the region's schools. Investigators claimed afterward that not one school or college had fallen through the net. Part of the aim was to reinforce warnings to young people not to go off with any strange man who tried to pick them up. There was another aim, too. Police were also convinced there must be children out there whom Chikatilo had tried to catch and failed. If any child remembered a man making the slightest attempt to pick them up, however unimportant it seemed, then he was asked to come forward and tell his teachers or the police. Thousands of forms were handed out for them to write down even the most marginal sighting. By then, there was considerable publicity both on radio and television. Yet, like the patrols on the trains, the campaign drew a blank. Not a single pickup attempt was reported to authorities.

The police didn't confine themselves to schools. They also turned their attention to all the places where children would spend time outside school hours. A particular focus were the so-called "video-salons", which by the late 1980s were beginning to spring up across the country alongside other Western imports such as electronic game rooms. They were generally sleazy places, often situated at railroad stations, and the films they showed were a predictable diet of B-movie sex and horror, often dubbed into one language and with subtitles in another. They were everything that the old heavy, formal Soviet movies were not—and Russian teenagers loved them. Little did they know that the usual woman sitting taking the change as they went in had been replaced by a policewoman. The same was true of the people working at more traditional points such as ice-cream stands.

As the investigation was stepped up, police also began to challenge men out walking with children, especially if the age difference between them did not correspond to the usual one between father and son. After showing their warrant cards, the police officers would take the child a few steps away to ensure that the man was, in fact, his or her father rather than some kind "uncle" who had invited them to walk with him. Making full use of the country's experience of secret KGB surveillance, hidden cameras were also out up in many public places to check up on people's movements. Illegal? It was difficult to tell. After all the pain and suffering caused over the years by the killer, there was no doubt to the investigators that the end justified the means. Again, all their efforts drew a blank.

Part of the reason was the publicity itself. In any operation of the scale and length of Forest Path, the media can be a double-edged sword. But for those brought up under the secretive regime of Brezhnev or Andropov it was a difficult lesson to learn. The arrival of Gorbachev with his policy of *glasnost* transformed the way the local press, in particular, treated the affair. If at the beginning of the investigation police had deliberately kept the people of Rostov in the dark, towards the end of the investigation they swung the other way. There was no longer any political reason to keep silent. Kostoyev, in particular, realized the enormous use that could be made of the media both to encourage witnesses to come forward and warn others to take care. Together with colleagues from the police, he frequently appeared on Rostov's radio and television stations.

There was another side to it, too. Chikatilo's success in evading capture for so many years was partly a result of his awareness of how the police worked. As he traveled on the local train, he used to watch how police first concentrated their attention on one point and then shifted it to another, and he acted accordingly. The list of places where his victims' bodies were found shows clearly how he stayed one step ahead of those pursuing him by dodging from town to town and place to place and then back again. Every time police came on local television to announce they had found another body and to appeal for witnesses, Chikatilo knew that he had to keep away from the last place he had killed. He could also learn with satisfaction from the media of how little progress had been made in determining his identity.

The publicity also necessarily intensifies the caution which Chikatilo had always employed in approaching and then picking up his victims. If children did not come forward to denounce him, then it was not just because of a typical child's fear of authority. It was also because many of them probably did not realize how close they had come to becoming his victim. Chikatilo's age, apparent respectability, and gift of speaking worked clearly in his favor. But so too did his manner, which was dictated always by reason rather than impulse.

Vitaly Kalyukhin, who worked on the case from 1988 as deputy Public Prosecutor of the Rostov region, was struck more than anything by Chikatilo's extreme caution. "Even if he encountered only the smallest resistance from his planned victim, then he would immediately abandon the attempt," he said. "He never tried too hard to persuade anyone. He never used force. For his victims the attack that killed them was always a complete surprise."

Never was the element of surprise stronger than with Sasha Dyakonov, who was murdered on May 11, 1989, the day after his eighth birthday, in the center of Rostov. That day, Chikatilo had been to the shops on the edge of town looking for new wallpaper for his flat and was on his way home. The bus was full and he had little alternative but to walk. It was then that he first saw the little boy in school uniform walking beside the main road. As he caught sight of him, he could feel his pulse racing. Normally, he would have tried to lure him away to another point. But he didn't want to wait and the desire was so strong that he threw caution to the wind.

Waiting until the boy was shielded from the road by a row of bushes, Chikatilo jumped on him from behind and started to stab him. The sheer quantity of traffic on the road saved him from detection. The rumble of trucks, cars, and of the nearby railroad was so great that the little boy's cries were inaudible. And so he killed him, and left the body almost where it lay in the bushes—a mere 20 yards from the road. Despite the summer heat, it was some fifty-five days before anyone found it.

Alyosha Khobotov, by contrast, got only too good a look at his killer. A ten-year-old boy from a happy family, he was fascinated by the films that they used to show at a new videosalon which had just opened in the center of Shakhti. He liked the horror films best— or at least that was what he told the man who approached him as he was standing outside the building on the corner of Karl Marx Street and Soviet Street on August 28 of that year.

"I can show you some great horror films if you like," Chikatilo replied. "I've got a big collection in my cottage. Why don't you come with me and have a look?"

As they started to walk through the town, a plan began to form in Chikatilo's mind. A couple of years before, when he had been near the bottom of one of his frequent bouts of depression, he had come close to committing suicide. He had even gone to a graveyard and especially dug himself a grave. It seemed a nice, peaceful site for a final resting place, just beyond the cemetery itself amid some blackthorn bushes. Now, however, he had decided that the grave was to have a different occupant.

When the two of them reached the cemetery, Chikatilo led Khobotov first along the main path, and then off to the side. Confused, the boy asked him where they were going.

"It's just a shortcut," he replied.

When they arrived at what Chikatilo remembered as the point, he was pleased to see that the trench he had dug was still there. So too was the spade, propped up against the trunk of a nearby tree where he had left it. Trembling with pleasure, he flung himself on the boy and, after hitting him over the head, bit off his tongue and cut off his sexual organs. Then he threw his body into the pit and covered it with earth.

Chikatilo turned out to be a good gravedigger. Although Khobotov's parents promptly reported the disappearance of their son, all attempts by the police to find him either alive or dead ended in failure. It was not until after his arrest that Chikatilo confessed to the killing and led police exactly to the point where the boy's body lay. By then it was little more than a skeleton.

14

At the end of Rodnikovskaya Street, on the edge of Rostov's Botanic Gardens, lives a Georgian called Mikhail Dzhidzhelava. A former warehouse worker, he is now a pensioner. But despite decades of living in Russia, he has lost nothing of his love for women, good food, and good wine, nor the hospitality which is typical of his homeland beyond the Caucasus. Even a casual visitor to his home cannot leave without being plied with plates of *shashlik*, a Georgian kebab, washed down with glasses of strong red wine and vodka. Early in 1990, he saw Chikatilo.

Or rather Fog, his Caucasian shepherd dog, did. Dzhidzhelava was taking the ferocious animal out for its normal early morning walk, when it began barking and straining at the leash. The object at which he was trying to lunge did not seem worried. The middle-aged man in a brown jacket continued calmly walking past, his suitcase in his hand.

"Please take a step back," said Dzhidzhelava. "My dog is vicious. I don't think that I can hold him."

"He doesn't look so bad," Chikatilo replied. "I can take a chance."

Those few words marked the beginning of a strange friendship which was to develop over the next month or so. Dzhidzhelava was to keep seeing this man strolling past his house, either when he was out walking the dog or just working on the vegetables in his little front garden. Alone at home all day and with nothing else much to occupy him, his curiosity was aroused. His house was on the edge of town; there was no reason for a stranger to go there unless he was on his way to the Botanic Gardens. But this man did not look like the type to spend hours looking at the flowers. So what was he doing there? One day, maybe in April or May, he decided to try and find out a little more. So he asked the man where he worked.

"I'm a teacher," Chikatilo replied and went on farther toward the gardens.

A month or so later, they met again while Dzhidzhelava was out feeding his pet goats. He didn't like the way that the man was looking at them. Food was already getting scarce and expensive, and a goat was worth a lot in those days. And his were just wandering about freely in the garden.

"What are you staring at?" he asked him sharply. "Haven't you ever seen a goat before?"

While Chikatilo paused, Dzhidzhelava decided to try and engage him in conversation. So, again, he asked him where he worked.

"I'm a locksmith," Chikatilo replied.

"That's odd," the Georgian retorted. "Last time I asked, you said you were a teacher.

"Well, what's it to do with you anyway?" snapped back Chikatilo, angry about having been caught out.

"If your house was at the end of the row, then you'd be a bit particular about who was wandering around outside it," Dzhidzhelava replied. "Someone has already stolen my chickens. I'm not losing the goats as well."

But the harsh words were soon forgotten. As time went on, they would greet each other. Sometimes Chikatilo would even wash his hands in the man's pond. There was something odd about him, this teacher, or locksmith or whatever he was. Sometimes, he was well dressed in suit and tie; often he looked really rough, as if he had slept in his clothes. The only permanent feature was the little leather cap he used to wear. His mood, too, varied, from talkative to downright moody. If Dzhidzhelava asked him what was wrong, he said that he used to suffer badly with headaches. One morning, after he had seen the man lurking around outside at six A.M., Dzhidzhelava sent a couple of his neighbor's boys to follow him for a few hundred yards to see what he was up to. He was disappointed. When his spies came back all they had to report was that the man had gone off for breakfast in a nearby cafe.

If the boys had followed him a little longer, they would have found something more interesting. On March 7, about the time when Dzhidzhelava had first begun to see this strange passerby, Chikatilo had persuaded a ten-year-old boy called Yaroslav Makarov to walk with him along that same road. Makarov was an easy target, a sociable, talkative boy from what had been a happy home. Then, he started running away from home. The first time had been when he got bad marks at school, and then it kept on happening. He always turned up again, but his parents never quite knew what he had been up to in the meantime. That fateful afternoon, when the boy met Chikatilo in the square outside Rostov railroad station, he was just hanging around asking for money. Naturally, Chikatilo was happy to oblige with a few coins from his pocket.

Not that Chikatilo had set out that day with the intention to kill. He had come to Rostov for something else which gave him almost as much satisfaction: to complain. Some people were starting to build a garage outside his son's house in Shakhti, and he had gone to the post office to send a registered letter to the local Communist Party Committee protesting about it. Chikatilo had always been an enthusiastic writer of letters of complaint, whether about his bosses at work or about some supposed misdemeanor by the local council, but recently he had been surpassing himself. The whole thing had become an obsession for him. The garage was far too close and it was going to block out the light from the apartment. He also knew that normally, the council wouldn't have given permission, so the people building it, who were Assyrians by nationality, must have slipped someone a bribe.

It was not just the garage itself. It was also the principle of it. For all his horrific nocturnal activities, Chikatilo had a strong sense of what he felt was justice and didn't like people to get away with things. And, in his book, giving bribes was definitely wrong.

Now the whole thing had got rather out of hand. The others weren't giving up and the battle was beginning to have its toll on him. Like the other peoples of the Caucasus, the Assyrians have a strong sense of clan—and many also have links with organized crime. The longer the whole thing went on, the more Chikatilo became convinced that some Assyrian mafia band would get its revenge on him. Whenever he went out, he kept seeing what he thought were their cars parked in front of the house. He was afraid they were going to catch him and beat him up. As the whole saga continued, he ceased feeling safe even when he was at home. He used to lock the front door with all the bolts, and worry if his wife did not come home on time.

All his own fear was forgotten as he began to talk to this little boy with his jeans jacket worn awkwardly over his school uniform. Chikatilo did not waste any time. He told Makarov that he had some friends over at home and would be like to join them? The boy agreed, although even now it is difficult to understand why. What interest could an eleven-year-old have in going off with a man who was easily old enough to be his father, maybe even his grandfather.

In any case, the boy didn't get to spend much time with him nor did he ever meet the friends. Once Chikatilo had lost him in the depths of the Botanic Gardens, he jumped on him. The assault began with an attempt to have oral sex with the terrified boy; it ended in an orgy of hacking and stabbing during which Chikatilo sliced off the tip of the boy's tongue and genitals. Both were simply tossed away in the gardens after he covered the body with branches and leaves.

Then, after cleaning himself up, he made his way back past Dzhidzhelava's house to the station and toward the train which would take him home to his wife in Novocherkassk. He didn't normally go back home so quickly after a killing. He liked at least a day to pass. It was partly just a matter of cleaning himself up and making sure that there wasn't even the tiniest spot of blood on his clothes. Amazingly, Fayina had still guessed nothing about his secret life and he was determined it should stay that way. Psychologically, it was also part of his deliberate attempt to try and keep his two lives separate. This time it was different. The following day was a special one on the Soviet calendar: March 8, International Women's Day.

For 364 days a year, Russian men are among the most chauvinistic in the world. But for one day a year, all this changes. Sales of roses at the local peasant markets boom and, in a ritualistic display of hypocrisy, most men embark on an orgy of cleaning, doing dishes, and maybe even cooking as if their lives depended on it. Chikatilo was no exception. He knew he had to do everything to make the day a special occasion for his Fenya.

For Makarov's mother, it was the worst day of her life. On the morning of March 8, police found the body of her little son and promptly closed the Botanic Gardens. Officers were everywhere. Dzhidzhelava couldn't work out what all the commotion was about as they all went past his house. Not for the first time, though, the first trail that police followed turned out to have been a false one. Chikatilo was not the only "maniac" on the loose in the park; it seemed there was another too, too, and he quickly fell into the police net. However, this other man was not their killer; he wasn't a killer at all, he just got his kicks from touching children. Even so, police took him in and it took them two months to work out that they had made a mistake.

As time goes on, some serial killers shows signs of wanting to be caught, almost to be saved from themselves. Not Chikatilo. Maybe it would have been different if he had felt the police net was closing in around him. But it wasn't. The three months that he had spent in jail were a distant memory, more than five years behind him. To his relief, police had left him alone ever since.

At the same time, his murders were becoming more and more cruel. Ten years before, Chikatilo had found merely molesting children was not enough for him and, almost by accident, had killed for the first time. But now, simply killing did not do much for him. He had to intensify the suffering of his victims, by performing more and more unspeakable operations on them—many of which were carried out while they were still alive. Photographs in the files of the investigators show the state of the corpses after they were found. Even those that were "fresh" were virtually unrecognizable, as a result not just of stabbing and slashing but of deep wounds in the belly through which he extracted their internal organs. By now his knowledge of human anatomy was such that he knew exactly where to cut in order to get at them most easily. The agony for his victims must have been incredible. Many must have died literally of shock as the crazed surgeon made his incisions.

The cutting off and even chewing the genitals of those whom he killed had also became an established part of Chikatilo's ghastly ritual. Unlike a cannibal, he does not actually appear to have swallowed human flesh, let alone planned to do so in advance. It was more a spontaneous action at the height of his frenzy, a horrific variation of the innocent love bites of normal sex play. Subconsciously, he appeared to have been punishing his victims for being sexually adequate while he had always been weak and impotent. At the same time, he may also have believed the action would also help him acquire some of their sexual energy which he so badly craved.

If the victim were a boy, then Chikatilo would bite off the testicles and the scrotum and then throw them away almost immediately. His main obsession, though, was with the uterus and as time went on, he became more adept at cutting them out of the women he killed. "I did not want to bite them so much as chew them," he said later. "They were so beautiful and elastic."

Sometimes, after this orgy of stabbing and slicing and biting, Chikatilo appears to have felt some remorse for the victims, particularly for the children. But generally he closed the whole thing out of his mind, treating it as a minor incident which had no real importance for the future. Nor was there any sign that he returned afterward to the scene of the crime. For some sex killers, it is almost a part of their ritual.

As they stand again in the position where they killed, they are able to experience again the pleasure they felt the first time around. Not so with Chikatilo. And even though he did sometimes kill in the same place two, three, or even four times, his decision to do so was inspired not by nostalgia but by the realization that the place was one where he would be safe from detection.

Makarov was just one of eight victims whom Chikatilo killed in 1990, his deadliest year since 1984. It is difficult to say exactly why the tempo increased so dramatically, although, as had been the case six years before, it may have been triggered partly by problems at work. After five years of battles with his bosses in Novocherkassk, Chikatilo was finally persuaded to resign and early in the new year found work at another factory back in Rostov. It is also clear that his condition, even if it cannot be classified as mental illness, was a worsening one, which inevitably meant an acceleration in the rate of killing as time went on.

Andrei Kravchenko, a small eleven-year-boy with brown hair and an angelic expression, became the first victim of 1990 after meeting Chikatilo outside the Avrora Cinema in Shakhti on January 14. Like Alyosha Khobotov, the boy who had been killed and buried in the city graveyard, Kravchenko was a fan of horror films and even started to describe to Chikatilo the plot of one that he had just seen. He didn't realize that he was going to end up acting in a real life one.

By coincidence, the boy had lived upstairs in the same building as the offices of Rostovnerud, Chikatilo's former workplace. But it didn't help police to make the connection. After his body was found, they mounted a massive poster campaign in the town asking for anyone who had seen him on that day to come forward. The posters, showing a photograph of the boy in a white shirt and Young Pioneer scarf and describing his likely movements, were literally every-

where in Shakhti. But none of the information called
into the four specially set up police telephone numbers brought police any closer to Chikatilo.

The death toll continued to jump. Chikatilo again
took a stroll past Dzhidzhelava's house in July on the
way to Rostov's Botanic Gardens, taking with him
thirteen-year-old Vitya Petrov, and killing the boy
when he reached a suitably deserted spot. Another
young victim, Ivan Fomin, eleven, was slaughtered on
the river beach in Novocherkassk the following month
when the summer heat reached its peak. Chikatilo's
apparent new found predilection for boys continued;
of the fifteen murders he would commit from 1988
until his final capture, eleven of them were to be boys.

It is difficult to comprehend in full the anguish of
the parents. First, immediately after the child disappears, there are the attempts to convince themselves
that he will be back; maybe he was just gone to see
friends and lost track of the time, or perhaps gone off
to visit grandmother. Then, as the evening goes on,
the growing doubts and fears. Relatives and neighbors
are often there with reassuring words. "My son ran
away once, but he came back the next day," says one.
"Don't worry, all kids do it," says another. The police
don't seem very interested. But for those clinging to
every hope, their very indifference can seem a positive
thing, a sign that there is nothing to be concerned
about.

With the passing of the first sleepless night, everything begins to change. The words of reassurance
seem less and less convincing. The police begin to set
out with their dogs. The search begins. At first there
was hope, but now it is getting smaller and smaller,
until the fateful day when the body is finally found—
and then it is so horribly mutilated that police don't
want to let a mother see her own son.

Fomin's remains were found fairly quickly—within
three days. After his son disappeared on August 14,

his father Oleg, a captain in the prison service at Novocherkassk jail, organized a massive search. Dozens of colleagues joined him, not merely the other warders but even the typists and bookkeepers from the offices. During the first night of the search, they found some ten runaway children, a sign of the sheer extent of the problem. But Ivan was not among them. The parents had first assumed that the boy had gone off to his grandmothers to tinker with a moped which he was trying to put back together. Instead, he somehow ended up on the river beach where Chikatilo had murdered him.

The next day, around one hundred soldiers and officers from the camp resumed the search on land, while divers went off in a rowing boat to check the river. When the body was found, it had some forty-five different knife wounds. Fomin's father had witnessed some horrors during his time in the prison service. However, his son's body was so badly mutilated that he fainted when he saw it.

The anguish was even greater for the other parents; the thirty-five days that it took before Kravchenko's body emerged through the snow was not the longest. The remains of ten-year-old Lyosha Moiseyev, who was murdered by Chikatilo the previous year during a trip to the Vladimir region, near Moscow, lay undisturbed for sixty-six days. That of Petrov, just six days less.

Petrov's mother, though, had a further reason for anguish, which was linked with the manner in which her son disappeared. That evening in July, she had been traveling with Vitya and her other two children and arrived in Rostov late in the evening. They were only halfway home and the last bus had already gone. And since the bus station closed at night, they decided to go instead to the waiting room in the nearby railroad terminal.

Chikatilo, too, had decided to spend the night there.

He had been working late in his job in Rostov that day and had planned to go home to Novocherkassk. But he missed the seven-thirty P.M. train, and, not wanting to waste too much time, he went to the video salon to watch a film: a horror one, as usual. However, he found it so gripping that he lost track of the time and missed the next train as well. And that was the last one. He had little alternative but to stay there until the next morning. He was determined to make good use of his time and began to hang about near the mineral water machine.

When Vitya and his family came in, his smaller brother Sasha paused by the machine and Chikatilo edged towards him. When the boy's mother saw him, she shouted out.

"What are you doing with my son," she screamed. "Leave him alone."

Chikatilo shrank away and the woman dragged all three of them to the first floor where there were benches to sleep on. But tragically, that was not the end of it. At about one-thirty A.M. Vitya—or Viktor for full—was suddenly thirsty and asked his mother for some kopeck coins to go back to the same water machine. He never came back. Chikatilo's patience paid off. He persuaded the boy to go off with him and killed him.

The only exception to the pattern in those months was Lyubov Zuyeva, a mentally handicapped woman whom Chikatilo met on the train on April 4 on the way from Novocherkassk to Shakhti. After accepting an offer to have sex with him, they got off the train together and he murdered her in the woods in a particularly deserted stretch near the little station of Donleskhoz. No one sounded the alarm that she had disappeared and it took police some three months before they found the body, by which time it was virtually unrecognizable.

Only later, following Chikatilo's capture and several

appeals on regional television and in the local papers, did her former lover come forward. The man, who, like her, was mentally handicapped, told police she had left home in April 1990 and he had not seen her since.

By the autumn of 1990, Chikatilo was getting more and more tangled up in the affair of the garages which his son's Assyrian neighbors were still threatening to build. At the start, he had seized on the whole affair simply to have an excuse for spending yet more time traveling back and forth on the train in his search for victims. If his wife asked him why he had been away from home for so long, Chikatilo could always tell her that he had been in Shakhti, trying to straighten out the garage problem. However, what had begun as little more than a way of getting time away from his wife, quickly became a matter of principle, also, to him, especially because of the unyielding attitude of the Assyrians. He became more and more determined to torpedo the project.

Another such matter of principle followed swiftly, in the form of a toilet which a musical school was trying to build outside not far from the very same flat. Chikatilo wrote to them immediately, opposing the project on grounds of the likely smell, which he claimed would make it impossible to open the window of his son Yuri's apartment. More letters of complaint followed, most of them to the leadership of the local Communist Party, who were by now getting as fed up with Chikatilo as everyone else was.

This time, though, he went further. In a sign of his bizarre view of the world, Chikatilo decided to denounce the rogue builders to President Gorbachev and to parliamentary head, Anatoly Lukyanov and went to Moscow especially to try to see them. Not surprisingly, neither of them found time for him. But Chikatilo was not going to give up.

At that time, a spontaneous "tent city" was beginning to spring up near the Kremlin, inhabited by people with complaints about everything from persecution by the KGB to poverty and lack of decent housing. The community, literally on the doorstep of the giant Rossiya Hotel, formed an almost surreal contrast to the expanse of Red Square and the dome of St. Basil's Cathedral behind. It also provided a source of entertainment and sometimes puzzlement to the groups of Western tourists heading in and out of the hotel. While some of the inmates had set up home in proper tents, others made do with a collection of homemade structures. Many had their specific complaint written on a piece of cardboard hanging on the front of their home like a nameplate.

Chikatilo readily joined in, put up his tent and decorated it with the then still unofficial red white and blue Russian tricolor—an odd choice for a committed Communist. The atmosphere of the tent city should have suited him: It was full of people who were as convinced as he was that they were getting a rough deal from society and felt they had no other way of getting their message across. Unlike most of them, though, Chikatilo still had a job to go to, and so stayed only a few days camping out in the capital before going back home again.

15

Irina Belova was seventeen and out for a good time. Tall, with a shapely figure and glossy brown hair, she was a hit with the boys and she knew it. Some might have considered her a flirt. Her parents were always worried about what she was up to, but for her it was just a matter of having fun. She and her best friend had thought up a new pastime: meeting strange men on the street, talking with them, and then accepting their invitations to go to a restaurant. It was clear, of course, what the men wanted and the two of them were happy enough to string them along in return for a free evening out.

Soviet restaurants were not the kind of place where you went if you wanted merely to eat. You could do that just as well—and often much better—at home. With the price of a meal for two the equivalent of several weeks wages, a restaurant was for special occasions only, for some people just on their wedding day. The food paled in insignificance beside the

pounding music from the band and the bottles waiting on the table when you walked in.

The music and the alcohol would inevitably have
their effect. As the evenings wore on, Irina and her
friend would dance with their newly found partners:
first fast and furious to the Western-style music and
then slow to the smoochy ballads. Then, as closing
time neared and the men got more and more optimistic about the night ahead, they would both disappear
with the excuse of going to the ladies' room. Instead,
they would slip out of the side door and be at home
with their respective parents before their jilted partners realized what had hit them. Like many men
before him, Chikatilo could easily have joined the
girls' long list of "victims." This time, however, things
turned out differently.

He met her at the railway station, this time in
Novocherkassk. It was already October, but the southern climate meant the weather was still mild. Belova
was studying food science at one of the city's technical
schools but had been away for the day in Rostov doing
some practical work. The working day over, she
stopped off in Novocherkassk to see some friends and
was waiting for the local train to take her home to
Shakhti. Chikatilo, too, was free, but he had very
different intentions. He was looking for prey, and
there was something promising about her. She looked
like the kind of girl who would be easy to persuade to
take a walk in the woods.

As Belova stood on the platform, she suddenly became aware of him, too, with his suit and briefcase,
he looked little different from all the other office
workers. Already, though, she noticed the way that he
seemed to be moving around the women one by one
and trying to talk to them. Then, sure enough, he
came over to her, as well.

"Where are you off to, then?" he asked cheerily,
emerging from behind her.

"To Shakhti," Belova replied, without thinking.

"I'm going that way myself," he continued. "It's not far. Why don't we go together?"

It was typical of the kind of approach that Chikatilo had already used in various forms to lure more than forty women and children to their death over the previous decade. There was nothing clever or subtle about it. It did not seem to Belova that he was really trying to flirt with her, let alone pick her up. It seemed far more innocent than that. It had to be, at least by the late 1980s, when almost everyone in the Rostov region knew from the barrage of reports in the local newspapers and television that there was a dangerous killer on the loose. If someone arrived out of the blue and suggested a walk in the woods, then of course it would arouse suspicion. But what if he just started by talking about the weather or the price of vegetables?

When the train arrived, Belova climbed aboard and Chikatilo sat down opposite her. Although it was only afternoon, maybe three or four P.M., there were few other people on board. Soon the two of them were deep in conversation, with Chikatilo asking question after question and his young companion answering without paying him too much attention. After about half an hour, when the train had passed the little station of Persyanovka, he made his next move.

"Damn," he said. "That was my station. We were talking so much that I missed it. Never mind. I'll go on to Kamenolomni and get the train going the other way back from there. I won't take me much longer."

To Belova's surprise, he didn't get out at Kamenolomni either, although the train stood in the station for more than ten minutes. Things were going too well for him. Sometimes it was a real struggle to win the confidence of someone he met just like that on the street. But this girl was different. She was chatting away with him as if they had been friends for years. He moved closer to her on the pretext of being able to hear her better over the din of the train and put his hand on her knee. She flinched.

"What are you up to?" she said, putting his hand firmly back on his own knee. "You are an old man. You should be ashamed of yourself trying to touch a girl like me."

"Women always used to like that." he replied. "You mean you don't?"

"No, I don't," she replied.

Chikatilo didn't let his little miscalculation spoil things. Cursing himself for having almost blown things, he decided to keep his hands to himself for the time being, and steered the conversation back toward safer ground like college and her plans for the future. Having found out where she studying, he told her that he was a teacher. It was a calculated move. He still always told people that he was a teacher rather than a supply clerk because it sounded better. Somehow, people would respect a schoolmaster. Or if not respect him, they would at least not expect him to be a dangerous killer. Feeling that he had more or less repaired the damage, he then set off on a different tack.

By now, he had abandoned any idea of going home. All that was going through his mind was this girl sitting so close to him and how he could get her into the woods. As the train rattled along, he was even rehearsing in his mind the horrors that he was going to carry out on her. He could almost hear her screams. But how to get her alone? He suggested a movie. As a precaution, he made sure of always knowing the program of the various theaters and proposed to Belova that they should go to the Avrora in Shakhti. That evening a film was a particularly good one, he assured her.

She was not impressed. If he had invited her out for a meal, then it would have been different. A trip to the restaurant was not something any self-respecting girl out for a good time could turn down. But movie invitations were different. After all, it cost only a few kopecks to get in and she could do it at any time she liked. She wasn't much in the mood today, anyway, especially with this rather strange middle-aged teacher.

Nevertheless, she didn't think it strange when they reached Shakhti and Chikatilo followed her out of the train. She assumed he must have changed his plans and was going somewhere else instead. Nor did she object when he said he would walk with her a little before turning around and going back to the station. Although she didn't fancy him, she was flattered by all the attention. He wouldn't have been the first man who had fallen for her, but even so . . .

"What have I got to worry about," she thought to herself as they began to walk. She read the papers and she knew as much as anyone else about the killer. But it was only five o'clock and although the sun had already gone down, it was not yet dark. Home was just thirty minutes away through crowded streets. If the man so much as lay a finger on her, she could easily have cried out for help and dozens of people would have come running. All the same, she wondered why he was giving her all this attention.

"I think you've walked enough with me," she said after a while. "Why don't you just go home now?"

Chikatilo still hadn't given up the idea of the movie, and as they approached the block of apartment buildings, he made one final attempt.

"I've got an idea," he said. "Why don't you drop your bags off at home and tell your mother that you are going off to see a girl friend. Then we can both go to the movie. I'll be waiting for you out here."

Again she refused, and Chikatilo finally realized that there was little more that he could do—at least not for that day. The girl had been more strong-willed than he had expected, and trying to force her could lead to an embarrassing scene. In fact, with the police net closing around him, anything that smacked of coercion could end in disaster. But the time was not wasted. He now knew exactly where she lived and where she studied—both of which he recorded in a small notebook. And since he knew that she went back and forth on the train every day, arranging to bump into her supposedly by chance some time in the future would not be difficult. Much better to part on good terms now and greet her like an old friend several days or even weeks later, he thought as he walked away from the house. Luckily for Belova, that meeting never happened.

It was only months later, when investigators tracked her down at the college where she was studying in St. Petersburg, then still known as Leningrad, that Belova realized the risk that she had run. Police had found that little notebook—and in it her name and home address. When they began to question her about Chikatilo, she said there was very little that she could tell them about him. The only thing that had really struck her was how polite and gentlemanly he had been. Not at all how she would have imagined a sex killer. And, despite the more than thirty years age difference between them, she had to admit that she had found him rather attractive as well.

A few stops north from Shakhti is the village of Krasny Sulin. As you drive in along the main road, a plaque proudly announces that the place was founded in 1797. There is little to show for all those years, though. The village is little more than a collection of modest single-floor houses, with wooden walls and outside toilets. In a country where most housing was state owned, these were the exception: private houses, built mostly by their occupiers themselves at a time when it was still possible to buy planks and other basic building materials. It was at one of these little houses on a bumpy, unmade lane called Parkovaya Street that the doorbell rang later one morning in October 1990.

Lyudmila Sokolova tethered the family dog and opened the front door. She would normally have been away at her job as a hospital orderly at this time, but this week she was on vacation. She couldn't believe her eyes. There, in front of her on the porch, stood Andrei Chikatilo. She paused to take breath.

"How on earth did you find us here, Andrei?" she exclaimed.

"It wasn't that difficult," he replied with a smile. "I just went to the local passport office. Aren't you going to invite me in?"

"Of course, of course," she said. "Come in."

And so he slipped off his coat and heavy shoes and walked in to the living room. He had a leather hold-all with him, the sort a lot of Russian men carry with them. They went back a long way, Andrei and her, she thought, as they sat down and began to chat. They had first met in the late 1960s when they had been next door neighbors in the little town of Rodionovo-Nesvetayevski. They had gotten on well together, she and her husband and Chikatilo and his wife. In many ways, both couples were quite similar. Both women were fairly dominant, and both men tended to do what they were told. She and Fayina used to joke about it. "We are a real matriarchal society, here," she said to her one day.

To be honest, she always used to be a little jealous of Fayina. Chikatilo always seemed so ambitious, always trying to better himself. Of course, she didn't have any inkling of his sexual problems. It wasn't the kind of subject you discussed with friends. As Lyudmila saw it, the main thing was that he was good tempered, always smiling and, above all, never drank too much. He was good with the children, too. A real gentlemen, in fact, and you couldn't say there were many of those around. She had actually rather fancied him. Not that there had been anything between them, though.

The two couples' children were roughly the same age. When the time came to christen their son, Fayina had been the godmother. And she, in turn, had been the godmother of little Lyudmila Chikatilo. Neither of their husbands had gone to the ceremony. Both of them were members of the Communist Party and although her husband wasn't as serious about it as Chikatilo, it would have been very embarrassing for both if it had come out that they had baptized their children.

Those Communists could not stop her believing, though. It was a tradition in her own family, and Fayina thought much the same. So the two women went off on their own to the church with their children. Although her husband had not been there, she had enjoyed the ceremony. And all these years is still seemed to have created a kind of special bond between their two families.

But then in 1971, Chikatilo had gotten the job as a teacher in Novoshakhtinsk, so he had his family had moved away. Swapping apartments was always such a complicated business and it was a tribute to his ability to get things done that they managed to get one so quickly. She and her husband tried at the same time but did not succeed. It took them until 1973 before they were finally able to move out and come to Krasnosulin.

She had seen Chikatilo a few times since, just by chance, in Shakhti. If she wanted to buy fruit and vegetables, then she used to have to go to the market there because there was barely anything to buy in the local shops in Krasnosulin. They had been brief meetings and although she had told him roughly where she was living, they had never got around to exchanging addresses. But suddenly here he was in her house.

Out of the blue. She wondered why he had come and asked him.

"I'm on a business trip," he said. "I have to leave to go back to Rostov early tomorrow morning and I was wondering if I could stay the night here."

Of course he could, she said. She could easily make up a bed for him in the room where the children usually slept. They could sleep at their grandmother's a couple of roads away. And so he stayed, and while she got on with cooking lunch, they began to talk. The conversation was the usual one between people who had once been close friends. Chikatilo seemed calm and relaxed and happy. As she was to recall later, there did not seem anything odd about him at all, certainly nothing to give any indication of the tragic course that his life had taken since the days when they had been neighbors.

After all, they had a lot of catching up to do, particularly on the family. They joked about their children: her daughter was sixteen and Chikatilo's son, Yuri, was already twenty and doing his military service. What a great couple the two of them would make, they joked. But despite the happy reminiscences and the laughter, she couldn't help thinking as they sat there that there was something strange about this unexpected guest. If this was meant to be a working trip, what was the point of coming especially to spend the night in Krasnosulin? After all, his home in Novocherkassk was hardly a million miles away: It was only just over a couple of hours by train. He could easily have set out in the morning and been back by the same evening. It seemed rather mysterious. But she didn't press him.

The next day the mystery only deepened. She got up as usual at six to see off her husband to work and expected Chikatilo to be up and gone already. But he wasn't. In fact he slept for a couple of hours longer.

So much for his early start. She woke him and asked what had happened.

"Don't worry," he said, "I was just very tired. It doesn't matter."

And that was that. He dressed, packed his things and left.

"Thanks and see you soon. I hope." he said as he disappeared down the road in the direction of the railway station. They did see each other soon, but not quite under the circumstances that either of them had expected.

16

Vadim Gromov did not have much going for him. Sixteen years old and mentally handicapped from birth, he had been at a special school in Shakhti. But in April 1990 he dropped out. Unable to get a job in what was meant to be the land of full employment, he spent much of his time hanging about, either at home, on the streets, or simply riding up and down on the train. It was during one such trip on October 17 that he met Chikatilo.

The boy was doing what he always did. Walking through the cars and talking to passengers and smoking. With his experienced eye, Chikatilo quickly took in everything about him, this skinny kid who was barely five foot tall: his white sweater and trousers just that little bit too thick for the season and the manner which made clear that he had nothing to do and nowhere to go. So far so good.

"You shouldn't smoke," Chikatilo said, catching up with the boy as he stood in the passageway connecting two cars. It was a strange opening gambit, but by now he could consider himself an expert. And when they started talking, and Gromov revealed that he used to study at a school for the mentally handicapped, Chikatilo knew immediately that he had another potential victim on his hands. The follow-up was easy: He asked the boy his immediate plans and when he said he didn't have any, suggested he join him at his nearby cottage.

"Will there be girls there?" Gromov asked, his interest perking up.

"If you really want them, I suppose it can be arranged," Chikatilo replied.

The cottage, he said was a few stops farther at Donleskhoz, and the boy agreed to go there with him. It was one of Chikatilo's favorite spots, the perfect killing field. Quiet, surrounded by thick woods, and literally in the middle of nowhere. He had only come across the place a couple of years before, almost by accident when he had killed fifteen-year-old Zhenya Muratov there, and he knew it had taken the police months and months afterward to find the body. It was one of the rare occasions when he felt sorry about what he had done: Such a well-brought-up boy, he had only agreed to come with him at all because Chikatilo had pretended he needed his help.

The remorse hadn't stopped him going back again this spring, though, when he had killed Lyubov Zuyeva, a mentally handicapped woman, there. The beauty of the place was that you only needed to take a couple of steps away from the platform, and you were immediately on your own. Nor did the police seem to be keeping any more of an eye on it than before. Despite what was intended to be a huge increase in patrols all the way along the railroad, it still seemed miraculously free of them as he walked past with Gromov.

As Chikatilo described it later, this was to be one of his most fiendish of killings. After they had gone some three hundred yards together, he suddenly began to shake and to feel sexually aroused. Taking the boy completely by surprise, he jumped on him from behind and forced him to the ground, ripping off his trousers. As his victim lay pinned on his face, Chikatilo stripped off his own trousers and underpants, and rubbed his penis against Gromov's buttocks until he ejaculated. At that moment, with the last ounce of his energy, the boy tried to escape.

Chikatilo was too fast and too strong; taking a length of rope from his bag, he tied his hands and, turning him on his back, began to strip off the rest of his clothes. Then as the animal in him took over, he bit off the tip of the boy's tongue and began to strike at him wildly in the head and stomach with his knife. Gromov died within seconds, and in a gruesome finale, Chikatilo took the blade and cut off his genitals, tossing them away into the undergrowth.

As the euphoria faded, he untied the hands, removed the few scraps of clothing still left on him and dragged the naked body off to the bushes, where he covered it with leaves. He used the clothes to clean the blood off his hands. Then they, too, were tossed into the bushes. After straightening his own clothes, he left as calmly as he had arrived, going back to the station and taking the train home to Novocherkassk.

The pink-handled knife that Chikatilo used to kill that day was cleaned carefully and put back in the kitchen drawer of the family home at 36 Gvardeyskaya Street. His wife was not there at the time. She had gone off to see her daughter in Kharkov. Officially, he was supposed to have gone there himself on a business trip for his factory. However, Fayina hadn't seen her daughter much since she moved away and she offered to go instead. It was against the rules, of course, but no one needed to find out. There was only a simple job to do in Kharkov which even his wife, with no real knowledge of supply work, could do. In any case, if she had problems, Lyudmila could always help her out. She had learned the ropes from her father when she worked with him in Novocherkassk, and knew some of the people in the Kharkov factories that her mother would have to deal with.

It was an elegant solution which made everyone happy. Fayina and her daughter were happy because they had a chance to get together again. Since the job was done properly, the factory did not have to find out about it afterward. Happiest of all, though, was Chikatilo. Not only did he get the apartment to himself for a few days to wind down after the emotional trauma of the killing; he also had what he thought was a perfect alibi in the event anyone linked him with the killing. As far as the factory records were concerned, the evening that Gromov died he had been in Kharkov.

The discovery of Gromov's clothes two weeks later, and then his body the next day, galvanized police—but with anger as much as anything else. It was clear that the killer was playing games with them. "First he would kill in Rostov so we sealed off the city, and then he killed in Novocherkassk," said Kalyukhin, one of the Rostov prosecutors. "We threw all our forces into Novocherkassk and to some extent weakened our numbers in Rostov. He realized that we were looking for him in those two cities, so he killed in Shakhti. Then we put all our forces there and he went back to Rostov. And so it went on."

Vladimir Kolesnikov, head of the regional criminal police, went to the scene, so he could direct police work on the spot. So did Kostoyev, bringing with him the whole operational headquarters from Rostov. About sixty of them set up in Shakhti, the nearest major town to Donleskhoz, the specialists from the Public Prosecutor's Office and from the criminal police. They were joined by regular police, drafted from their normal work and assigned to the operation. Some were sent out on the beat, others took up positions on railroad lines along the ditches. A contingent of 100 of feared OMON riot troops were also sent in from their barracks in Rostov.

It turned out to be good timing. The very day that Kostoyev and his colleagues arrived in Shakhti, the local police told them that another boy the same age as Gromov named Vitya Tishchenko had just been reported missing. The distraught parents did not know what to do. Their son, a clean-cut sixteen-year-old, had gone to the railroad station in Shakhti to pick up some tickets the day before and had not been seen since. Three days later, on November 3, he, too, was found dead.

The last person who had seen him alive was the woman who worked at the ticket counter, so Kalyukhin's colleague, Yandiyev, from the prosecutor's office went to see her. As they sat in her little house near the railway station, the woman described how she had caught a glimpse of a middle-aged man lurking in the background behind Tishchenko while he was buying the tickets. All she could say about the man was that he was tall, wore glasses, and was probably in his fifties. At that moment, the woman's teenage daughter came in. When she saw the prosecutor and heard what they were talking about, she suddenly broke in.

"I was on the train a few days ago and I saw a man there trying to pick up a boy as well," she said.

According to her account, she had been on her way back from her institute in the town of Gornaya, just beyond Sovleskhoz, toward the end of October when she caught sight of a middle-aged man with glasses talking to a boy. Although she was too far away to hear what they were talking about, it was clear to her that they did not know each other, and that the man was trying to persuade the boy to get off the train with him. However, the man didn't succeed, and when

the train stopped at Shakhti station, the boy sprang
up and got off in a hurry. To her surprise, the man had
not tried to follow him. He stayed sitting where he
was on the train for a few more minutes and then, as
it started to move, he, too, had stood up and headed
off toward another compartment.

Yandiyev was convinced that the man they had both
seen must be the same one. Although the girl had not
heard her mother's account, their descriptions
matched. It could have been coincidence, of course.
Who was to say that the man standing next to this
latest victim, Tishchenko, had been responsible for
his disappearance? He could have been an innocent
passerby. Nor was there anything criminal in what
the ticket seller's daughter had seen him doing on the
train. Nevertheless, it was the first solid lead that they
had received in years, and they weren't going to waste
it just like that. Nor would it be difficult to follow up.
The girl said that it hadn't been the first time she had
seen the man; he was on the train quite often.

It was clear to investigators that the murderer was
beginning to step up the pace of his killings. Because
of what the girl had said, there was no longer any
doubt that the railroad was the key to everything.
After months of random checks at the stations and on
the trains themselves, it was decided to move to a
system of so-called total control. Around 600 police
were deployed at various points on the forest path
along the track as it ran through the Rostov region,
their orders being to check up on everyone who went
through. As many as three or four of them were
allocated to each of the country stations, many of
them simple stopping points serving a tiny community of a few houses. Given the killer's liking for
deserted countryside, police rightly believed that
those like Donleskhoz were the most important to
watch. It was now intended to be virtually impossible
for a passenger to get off the train without having

their documents checked by one of the plainclothes officers hanging about on the platform.

Yandiyev, meanwhile, began to work on the other lead. After some persuasion, the ticket seller's daughter agreed to take part in an experiment. With plainclothes police deployed around her at strategic points, she was going to repeat her journey from Gornaya to Shakhti at about the same time she had traveled before in the hope of seeing the man again. The ideal variant would have been for the man to try and pick her up. However, even if all that happened was that she saw him and identified him, then it would be a large step forward.

As they drew up plans for the journey, the investigators felt strangely optimistic. Of course the murderer could easily seek his next victim hundreds of miles away, as he had done before. They had no illusion about that. This time, though, it felt somehow different. They had a hunch that the man they had been seeking for so many years had already killed for the last time.

17

It was November 6, 1990, and the whole of Russia was winding down for the annual Revolution Day holiday, November 7. This was the high point of the Soviet calendar, a display of military might intended to frighten the country's enemies and show off the achievements of socialism to the people at home. In Moscow, the weeks of rehearsals were over, and everything was ready for the great day. The portraits of the holy Communist trinity of Marx, Engels, and Lenin had been put up in Red Square, and the reviewing stand atop the mausoleum on which Gorbachev was to lead out the Politburo had been dusted down. The prerecorded patriotic music was prepared, as usual with taped "hurrahs" to encourage the crowd standing below.

Admittedly, it was not as much of a show as it used to be. Gorbachev clearly thought it inappropriate to be seen flexing his muscles too much at a time when the Cold War was supposed to be almost over. So, although the missile and the tanks and the troops were all going to be there, there would be far fewer of them rumbling across the cobblestones. Western military attaches, for whom the parade used to the high point of the working year, were getting nostalgic for the old days.

For several years now the parade had been getting shorter and the emphasis changed. With his love of compromise, the Soviet leader was phasing out the whole thing gradually in a way he hoped would not antagonize the military. However, little did anyone know that this was to be the last such display of muscle on November 7. By the following year, the country was to have been transformed beyond recognition, and the 1917 revolution derided by many of the democrats then coming into positions of power as anything but glorious.

For millions of ordinary Russians, though, the whole thing was as much a bore as usual. It had never been a genuine popular holiday like New Year's, just a purely political one that had been forced down their throats. Any enthusiasm that once existed for the events of 1917 had long since been replaced by anger at rising prices and empty shop shelves. As for the tanks and missiles, they were increasingly a source not of pride but of resentment at how many of the country's precious resources were being devoured by the monstrous military sector. Now that they were no longer obliged by their employers to join the official parades staged across the country, people were doing what they always did: treating November 7 like any other public holiday and taking advantage of the time off to stay at home or visit friends.

Sergeant Igor Rybakov was no more enthusiastic about the whole thing than anyone else. In fact, this year it didn't look like it was going to be much of a holiday for him at all. In his early twenties and a newcomer to the force, he had been working until a few days before in his usual job handling drunks at

a district drying-out station in the little town of Do-
netsk, about 20 miles away. It was hardly very satisfying, but at least it meant a fairly quiet life. Then
suddenly they told him that he was being drafted into
Forest Path. Like hundreds of others of his colleagues,
he was first sent to the local headquarters and then
allocated a position. They had given him the railroad
station in Donleskhoz. So it was four P.M. and there
he was, standing in the cold November drizzle waiting
on the platform and keeping his eyes peeled for anything untoward.

At that moment, almost right on cue, Rybakov
caught sight of a man coming out of the woods. He
was walking towards him from the direction of Leso-
typ, the next little station along the line, a middle-
aged man, probably in his fifties: gray suit, tie,
glasses, and a bag with a shoulder strap. Rybakov had
plenty of time to watch him. There were never many
people around there at the best of time; now it was
deserted.

At the far end of the platform there was a small
water hydrant, and as the man approached, he
paused, bent down and started to wash his hands in
the trickle of water coming out of it. He was not the
first. Since coming on duty a few hours earlier, Rybakov had watched a virtual parade of mushroom pickers emerging from among the trees with bags slung
over their shoulder and stopping to clean up there. It
had been raining for several days now and it was
impossible to bend down in the thick undergrowth
without covering yourself in mud up to the elbows.

Then, as the man came closer, Rybakov noticed that
his finger was bandaged and that there was a red stain
on his cheek. The policeman couldn't really tell what
it was. It looked like it could have been blood, but
really it was difficult to tell at that distance. It might
equally well have been from the berries that also grew
in the forest. Or even paint. Besides the stain, the

man's clothes were covered with leaves, and his boots were muddy, as if he had been walking through a particularly dense stretch of forest. Rybakov waited for him to stop. Then he walked over to the man and asked for his documents.

The policeman was not worried. He had his gun in his pocket. "Chikatilo, Andrei Romanovich," he read off the man's passport. He was not the first policeman to see the name and think it odd. Nevertheless, it did not mean anything to him. How was he, a regular officer from a local anti-alcohol unit, meant to know that the very same man had been questioned during two separate murder inquiries over the previous years? Nor did the man's behavior give him any real cause for suspicion. Of course, the fact that any outsider was wandering around in this sleepy little settlement was strange, particularly as he was hardly dressed as a mushroom picker. But Chikatilo had an explanation for being there: When Rybakov asked him what he had been doing, he said he had been visiting a friend in the neighborhood.

There seemed little reason to check the story with the friend. If Chikatilo hadn't committed a crime, Rybakov certainly hadn't any right to detain him. So after writing down his name and passport number in his notebook, the policemen told Chikatilo he was free to go and watched him disappear into a group of other passengers boarding a train which had just pulled into the station.

Already as the train rolled out south towards Shakhti, Rybakov began to have his doubts. There was something about the man that hadn't been quite right, he thought as he stood there on the windswept platform. So, when he finished his duty for the day, he went back to the police station in the nearby town of Krasny Sulin to which he had been temporarily attached and wrote out a report for his boss which he then left on his desk. And that was where the report sat for the next few days, unread and forgotten, as the whole country closed down for a couple of days of relaxing, eating, and above all drinking.

What happened to that report in the few days that followed is still open to dispute. According to the police version, it got no farther than the local police chief. Another, more damning version backed by sources within the Prosecutor's Office is that the report was handed upward to senior police officers, only for the word to come back down that Chikatilo had been arrested, checked, and released in 1984 and was therefore now, in a sense, in the clear.

What is certain, though, is that once the holiday was over, the prosecutors in operational headquarters in Shakhti were beginning to wonder what was happening at Donleskhoz. It had been two weeks since the remains of Gromov had been found there, and there had been no reports of any fresh evidence. The lack of results seemed partly due to the fact that they did not have any of their own people there on the spot, so they drafted in a man called Manukyan, who had been previously working in the nearby town of Kamensk. By this stage, though, the prosecutors had still been told nothing by the police about Rybakov's sighting.

As soon as Manukyan arrived he asked one of the local district prosecutors, Pokhodayev, to show him the point where Gromov's body had been found. Pokhodayev was convinced that there was little point in going there yet again. After the body was found, they had been through the whole area with a fine-toothed comb. All the possible clues had already been found, he insisted. Even so, he understood his new colleague's wish to see the place with his own eyes and was happy to lead him there. And it was then that he realized that he had been mistaken.

After the two of them had been poking around for a few minutes in the undergrowth, Manukyan suddenly looked upwards and caught sight of a piece of blue nylon hanging on a tree. It looked like a pocket which had been ripped out of a coat, and Pokhodayev stared at it, stunned. He had been the last one to leave the scene of the crime, and he could swear the branches had been clear. There was no way that it had been missed. A team of police had gone through the whole area, too. There was only one explanation. The murderer had slipped back under their very noses and killed again.

The next morning, November 13, the two of them returned, but this time accompanied by forty police officers and twenty dogs. The orders they gave the men were simple: Keep working their way through the forest until they found a body. So, starting from the railroad track, they formed a line and began to push their way out into the woods. It was foggy and the temperature was dropping below freezing; the heavy rain of the last few days was turning to snow as they worked through the dense undergrowth, stumbling over roots and fallen branches as they went. It didn't take long. About fifty yards from the track, not far from the point where three bodies had already been found in the past, one of the officers came across the naked remains of a young blond woman half buried under a pile of leaves. She looked to have been in her early twenties and had been horribly mutilated. If the killing had happened a month later, she would have stayed undetected until the spring. But the snow had not yet settled.

   Checks run against the list of missing people identified her as Svetlana Korostik, age twenty-two. The autopsy suggested that she had been killed some six to seven days before. The official record put the cause of death as multiple knife wounds to the vital organs, including stabbing of the stomach and amputation of the genitals. The tip of her tongue had been cut off and was nowhere to be found; nor were the nipples. It was clear from the look of the wounds on her body that there had been a struggle and that the killer had eventually succeeded in overpowering her and tying up her hands.

The discovery of the body brought Kostoyev and the other leaders of the investigating group back to Donleskhoz. Two weeks earlier, they had all been standing in almost exactly the same place after the killing of Vadim Gromov, vowing that his killing was to be the last. Three days later, they had found Vitya Tishchenko, and now this. Kostoyev was understandably angry. What was the point of his investigators working themselves into the ground if there could be such gaping holes in the police presence? What about the regime of total control meant to have been provided by the hundreds of police all along the railroad?

If the latest murder had happened anywhere else, it might have been easier to understand. But here, by this little station, was precisely the point where three people had already died. Kostoyev wanted to know who had been on duty, and who had apparently let the killer slip through the net twice—first, going into the woods with his victim and then, after he had murdered her, coming out again.

Kostoyev wanted an explanation and summoned officers from the Krasny Sulin police station. The deputy head immediately began to tell him about Rybakov's report of the week before, describing how his officer had seen a man with what could have been a bloodstain on his face walking out of the woods on to the platform and had checked his documents. The man's name was Andrei Romanovich Chikatilo. He was married with two children and worked in the supply department of a Rostov factory.

Even though Kostoyev had been heading the entire investigation for the last five years, the name Chikatilo didn't mean any more to him that it had to

Rybakov. After all, there were more than 20,000 people in the card index by now and although Chikatilo's entry was one of the earliest, he had not been prominent among the suspects. Indeed, the very fact that he had the wrong blood type meant he had instead been virtually excluded from the investigation. The few months Chikatilo spent in detention in 1984 had also been well before Kostoyev had become involved in the case.

For once though, luck was on their side. At that moment, Fetisov, then head of the regional crime squad, was passing nearby. Oblivious of the discovery of the latest body, he was on his way to the funeral of one of his officers who had been killed on active duty earlier that week elsewhere in the region. He had the police radio on in his official car and when he heard the news, he changed his plans. Radioing back to Rostov to tell a deputy to take his place at the graveside, Fetisov went straight to the scene of the crime. Unlike the others, Fetisov had met Chikatilo when he was arrested six years before, and he still remembered the name.

"We had a man named Chikatilo here in 1984," he told Kostoyev.

By the time they got back to their temporary headquarters in Shakhti, the net had already begun to close around Chikatilo. As investigators began to go more carefully through the card index, they began to find out some interesting details about their suspect. It was not just the confirmation of his arrest in September 1984 and the fact that he had been questioned at the time about the murder of Dima Ptashnikov. There were other interesting little snippets from his earlier life, such as the way he had been forced out of his teaching jobs in the 1970s over his lecherous advances to children and the fact that he had been a suspect in the Zakotnova killing of 1978. There was also the list of items that had been found in Chikatilo's suitcase when Zanasovksi had detained him on September 13: the knife and the lengths of rope and the small jar with petroleum jelly—not to mention the child's toy gun that was found later in his locker in the offices of Sevkavenergoavtomatika.

But that was only the beginning. The operation moved forward on two fronts during the days that followed. While plainclothes police stationed around the clock outside Chikatilo's home began to watch his every move, the prosecutors began to probe his past. Yandiyev was given the job of finding out about him. It made fascinating reading; it was not just his succession of jobs in various supply departments in Rostov, Shakhti, and Novocherkassk, and the freedom that this gave him to travel around. There was also the proximity of his workplace at Sevkavenergoavtomatika in August and September 1984 to the point in Rostov where the bodies of four victims were found. His final job, from January 1990 at the city's Elektrovozoremontny factory, was also very close to the railroad station from which Makarov and Petrov had disappeared that year.

Alone, of course, this did not prove anything. Rostov was a big city. There were other coincidences, though, which would be much more difficult to explain away—like the revelation that, according to his work records from Novocherkassk, Chikatilo had been on a business trip in the Ukrainian town of Ilovaisk on May 14, 1988, the day when little Lyosha Voronko was killed.

Now, even the gap in the killers in 1985 and 1986 which had thrown the investigation began to fit the pattern, once Kostoyev slotted into the puzzle the three months that Chikatilo had spent in jail and the temporary deterrent effect that this appeared to have had on him. As far as their records showed, the problem of the blood type still remained. But then the test had been only a cursory one, and they could not completely exclude mistakes.

There was also the recent Japanese research pointing out the possibility, in a tiny minority of people, of a discrepancy between blood and sperm groups. Once they had pulled him in again, they could do the tests once more and eliminate any doubts. When Yandiyev reported all his findings back to headquarters, the questions the investigators had been asking suddenly changed: It was no longer, "Is this the right man?" The line now was: "How did we allow him to slip through our net for so long?" Yet this did not help them to decide how—and when—to pull him in.

With Chikatilo under permanent surveillance it would have been easy to arrest him there and then. But despite their belief in his guilt, the investigators wanted to wait and allow him to incriminate himself, if possible even detain him as he was about to commit his next murder. Of course, there were dangers, not least for the next potential victim, although they were confident that they could surround him or her with enough plainclothes men to stop Chikatilo at just at the right moment. Kostoyev and Yandiyev had other worries, too. Chikatilo was not a young man and anything could happen: Maybe he would have a heart attack or perhaps a road accident. The chances were small. Yet they were alarmed by even the faintest possibility that death would cheat them of the man whom they had been pursuing for so many years. Or what if he realized they were at last on his trail and committed suicide? With him would die the truth not only about the killings that they had already attributed to him but also about many others which were perhaps still unknown to them.

Despite the risk, they decided to wait, at least for a little. So, for the next few days, they watched Chikatilo's every movement as he traveled from his home in

Novocherkassk to work in Rostov. More revealingly, they also watched what were clearly his attempts to pick up victims. His behavior was every bit as suspicious as Zanasovski had described it when he pursued him in 1984. Whenever Chikatilo boarded the train either to or from work, he would systematically seek out a seat next to a single boy or girl, sit down next to them, and engage them in conversation. If they got up and left, he would sit for a few minutes, and then he, too, would stand up and look for another such conversation partner. It was not only on trains that Chikatilo was behaving like that. He did the same on the city buses and trams, too. Yet his apparent determination to find a victim was still tempered with caution. Whenever he met the slightest resistance, he would give up with good grace and try elsewhere.

Then on November 20, Chikatilo made what appeared his most serious attempt to pick up a victim since they had begun watching him. During a morning trip on the train, he sat down next to a boy and apparently tried to persuade him to go off with him. Just at that moment, though, a group of other people came into the carriage and Chikatilo slipped away quietly. A policeman immediately asked the boy what the man had said to him.

"He offered me some beer and suggested I go with him to his place to watch some videos," the boy replied.

When Kostoyev and the other bosses sat down later that morning in their headquarters, they decided enough was enough. Over the previous few days, they had noticed Chikatilo getting more and more agitated. Although he had gone home every night to his wife, they were convinced he was getting ready for a kill and they decided they didn't want to risk it anymore. And, in any case, they had seen enough over the previous few days to dispel any doubts which they might once have had.

"We decided not to tempt fate," said Kalyukhin. "Although he was covered by our men, we decided to take him." Police chief Kolesnikov travelled the 25 miles to Novocherkassk to personally supervise the operation.

At precisely three-forty P.M. three plainclothes police officers in leather jackets and jeans stepped out of an unmarked Lada car and approached Chikatilo as he was standing outside a cafe. The few seconds were captured by another officer with a hidden video camera.

"What is your name?" Kolesnikov asked as they strode over and stopped suddenly next to him.

"Chikatilo," he replied.

Without saying a word, Kolesnikov's men put Chikatilo's arms behind his back, snapped on the handcuffs, and pushed him gently into the car. He made no attempt to resist.

It was a low-key end to a hunt which had preoccupied thousands of people for more than a decade. Yet it was difficult to avoid the impression that it could have ended so differently. If Fetisov had not been coming past at that time, then it is quite possible that no one would have made the connection, and Chikatilo would have remained at large to kill again.

Criticism focused particularly on Rybakov. How could he have seen a man with blood on his face emerge from the woods and still let him go? The police hastened to defend his conduct. Under Soviet law, they argued, it would have been difficult for him to do anything else. Certainly, Chikatilo had a red stain on his face, but he could have just cut himself on the branches. Nor was it so unusual for someone to wash their hands when they came out of the forest. The mushroom pickers did it all the time. Under the rules then in force, they had the right to pull someone in for three hours on suspicion only if it is a matter of establishing their identity. On this occasion there was no such doubt about identity. Chikatilo had his passport and work papers with him, and presented then when asked to do so. In fact, he always made sure his documents were in order, apparently so as not to give police any pretext on which to pick him up. As if to defend their own, police later rewarded Rybakov with a prize and promotion.

There were also technical factors working against him. The first thing any Western officer would have done in such a situation would have been to radio headquarters while he still had Chikatilo. By running his name and address through the computer, they would have quickly pulled out his previous conviction and found the criminal record of the man that they had on their hands. But Rybakov had no radio. The only way he had of communicating with headquarters was through a courier who traveled all day back and forth between the various police posts. And even if he had a radio, he would not have found a helpful computer operator at the other end when he got through. After years of working with little more than pen and paper, the police had finally got some computers at the beginning of 1990 and had begun punching the data from the card index into them. It was a long job. By November, they had barely managed 20,000 names, and that was out of a total of more than 250,000. And, anyway, who could he have got to search through all those cards on the afternoon when the whole country was winding down for November 7?

All in all, the Revolution Day holiday had a lot to answer for. Had it been a normal day, then the report would have been studied by Rybakov's superior immediately, or at least by the next morning. But while the country relaxed, the report lay untouched in the empty office in the police station.

Even that was far from being the most damning point. The question should perhaps be not so much how Chikatilo was allowed to walk free as how he had been able to walk past the same point, together with his last victim Korostik, a few hours before. And again the finger points at the police. Despite the supposed round-the-clock surveillance, the first shift at Svies-khoz station did not start until nine A.M., and that day Rybakov's colleague was late. He did not turn up until eleven A.M. By that time Chikatilo was already past the post and in the forest.

It was not the first time that it happened either. Chikatilo had slipped through the very same loophole to bring Vadim Gromov to his death just over three weeks before. The fact that he literally led the boy to his death past them three weeks before and then came back alone was clear evidence that they had not been doing their job properly. In the case of Vitya Tish-chenko, killed on October 30 in nearby Shakhti, Chi-katilo had been fortunate enough to turn up with his victim at a time when there were no patrols either. The reason? Staff shortages and an apparent police decision to divert their men to other work.

Why stop there? What of all the other mistakes and miscalculations which had occurred during the course of the entire investigation. The release of Chi-katilo from jail in 1984 was the most glaring one. But even that was not the beginning. Move farther back and you come to the fiasco of the false suspects and then, inexorably, to 1978 and the killing of Zakotnova. If Chikatilo had been convicted at the time, then it would have meant more than saving the life of an-other, apparently innocent man, who was shot in his place. It would have saved more than fifty other people from the most grisly deaths imaginable.

In terms of police blunders, the whole operation must count as one of the largest in crime history. The investigation currently underway may bring some answers. Some of those responsible for the most glaring errors may eventually be punished. But there is nothing they can do to bring back those fifty-three innocent people.

18

He came quietly. Too quietly. When the policemen made Chikatilo climb into the car, he did not even demand to see their warrant cards, let alone ask why he was being pulled in. Strange for an innocent man. And as they drove the 25 miles back to Rostov with Chikatilo pressed between two burly officers in the back, no one said a thing. It was Kolesnikov's idea. If there was complete silence in the car, then he expected Chikatilo to break down and say something. Surely he would start to complain or demand his rights. But he didn't. He said nothing for the entire forty minutes, not even as they crossed over the bridge into Rostov and drove down Bolshaya Sadovaya Street, past Gorky Park where he had once hunted victims, and up to the gray building housing police headquarters.

His hands handcuffed behind his back, Chikatilo was led on to the first floor and in to Fetisov's spacious office. Despite its size, the room was full, and there was a feeling of anticipation in the air. Not counting the guards, there were ten of them, all straining to get a glimpse of the man they had been hunting for so long. Fetisov, himself, of course, as well as Kostoyev, Kalyukhin, and Valentin Panichev, Public Prosecutor of the Rostov Region. Kolesnikov came into the room with Chikatilo. Medical experts were also on hand.

The only person missing was a lawyer. At that time, under Soviet law, the defendant had the right to an attorney only from the moment when charges were pressed, not from the moment of arrest. (The right was finally extended the following year, in 1991, by Mikhail Gorbachev, himself a lawyer by training, as part of his doomed attempt to turn the Soviet Union into what he called a "law-based state.")

After Kolesnikov had given a brief description of how they had arrested Chikatilo, they got down to business. Kalyukhin acted as master of ceremonies. He introduced all the people present to Chikatilo by name and by position and began the first, routine round of questioning.

"Are you Chikatilo?" he asked.

"Yes," came the reply.

"Your first name and patronymic, please."

"Andrei Romanovich."

Kalyukhin continued: "Do you have any questions?"

Chikatilo's response staggered them. Again, he made no protest and asked no questions. He simply shook his head.

While a stenographer sat taking notes, Kalyukhin tried again, if only for the record.

"Maybe you would like to make a complaint or a statement or an appeal," he asked.

Again, the same reply.

"No, nothing."

With the first formalities behind them, a police photographer took mugshots of Chikatilo against Fetisov's plain wall. The pictures show him just as he was when he walked in off the street: an elderly man with a black mock-leather cap and coat and a large black briefcase in his hand. Samples of his blood were taken.

Any lingering doubts that they had got the right man disappeared when they searched his bag: There were no papers inside; instead, two lengths of rope, a pocket mirror, and a kitchen knife with a nine-inch blade.

One by one, they began to ask Chikatilo questions, focusing in particular on his movements over the previous few weeks. Gradually working their way backward, so as not to arouse his suspicions, they finally asked him about the evening of November 6.

"I don't remember," he replied.

"What do you mean? It was the day before the holiday. You must remember what you were doing the day before the holiday."

Chikatilo paused. "Oh, yes," he said. "I was at work all day and then I went home and stayed there all evening."

"You didn't go anywhere?"

"No, nowhere."

"Not even on the train?"

"Only from Rostov home to Novocherkassk and that was it."

"And you didn't go farther . . . to Shakhti perhaps?"

"No, I never went beyond Novocherkassk. Not on the sixth, or on the fifth, or any time."

From the way Chikatilo was lying, it was clear to Kostoyev and the others assembled there, that the whole thing could take some time. They broke up shortly afterward to decide how best to proceed with him. As for their suspect, he was taken downstairs in the building, which they shared with the KGB, and put in a cell.

The next day, the experts brought in the results of the blood test. Fetisov's heart sank. Again, the same result: type A. When Chikatilo was tested after his arrest in 1984, a regular doctor had taken a couple of pin pricks of blood from his finger and sent the result off to the laboratory with several other samples. They were hoping that a mistake had been made. This time, though, the whole operation had been handled by specialists, and, to be absolutely certain, they had drawn the blood straight from the vein. Now, though, there was no doubt. Chikatilo had type A, and they were looking for AB.

It was the same dilemma again. Although they had been able to build a convincing picture of Chikatilo's killings, they still did not have any firm evidence, anymore than they had had it in 1984. And again the same problem with the blood test. They had to be careful with him. He was not a simple worker with whom they could take liberties. He was well-educated and knew his rights, and although he had taken it all calmly until now, things could easily change. It could become extremely embarrassing for all involved if they turned out to be mistaken.

Under Soviet law, they could hold him for up to three days before deciding whether or not to press charges. But then came the crunch. They would have to charge him with a specific crime, and to do that they would need some real evidence.

This time, though, they didn't leave it at the blood. They told experts to do other tests, including one of his sperm and one of his hair. Sperm was the key one, because it had actually been sperm rather than blood that had been found on the corpses. They could barely believe their ears when one of the doctors came in to tell them the result: Chikatilo's sperm was of a different group from his blood. And the sperm *was* AB.

Ever since they received the circular from Moscow back in 1988, they had known it was theoretically possible for a man's sperm and blood to be of different groups. But it was believed to be just one in a million and they hadn't given it much attention. It seemed unbelievable that this one-in-a-million man could also be the murderer they had been pursuing all these years.

Now, though, it all became clear how Chikatilo had passed the blood test when he was detained in 1984 and how he had never turned up in any of their subsequent probes. All those groups they had analyzed, from prisoners and policemen to car owners and sex offenders. Each time, in order to narrow down the field, they had confined themselves to those people with AB blood. And, in so doing, each time they had excluded Chikatilo from the probe even before they had started. At the time, they had seemed to have good reason: Without exception, all the sperm traces had been of the same group. Looking back, all they could think of was the waste—not just of time but also of the lives of those who had died unnecessarily in the six long years since Chikatilo had been released.

All the information they had collected over the last few days pointed to Chikatilo. Now, with the sperm-blood hurdle overcome, all they needed was a confession. But that did not mean it was going to be easy to get one.

For more than week, Kostoyev sat face to face with Chikatilo in a little room in the building the local KGB shared with the police. And, for a week, Chikatilo said nothing. Kostoyev had never seen anything like it. Despite years of handling some of Russia's toughest criminals, he had never come across such a hard nut to crack. It wasn't that he was lying or denying things. He just sat there and kept quiet, so quiet that by the end of it, Kostoyev was almost sick with exhaustion.

And even when Chikatilo did begin to speak, it did

not help. According to the official record of proceedings, he told Kostoyev that he had already been picked up in 1984 and checked for involvement in the killings, and had then been cleared. He wanted to know why he was being arrested for the same crime again and tried to make out that the whole thing was linked with the long saga about the garages. The Assyrian mafia clearly had friends in high places who were trying to frighten him into dropping the whole thing, Chikatilo said. Substantiating his claim, he made the following statement: "I think that I am being persecuted by the investigative bodies because I wrote complaints to the different official bodies about the illegal activities of individual officials from the city of Shakhti, who decided to build garages on the courtyard of the house in which my son lives."

Gradually, Kostoyev began to grind him down, forcing Chikatilo to talk about himself and about the inner conflicts which made his life a misery. In a statement made on November 22, Chikatilo spoke of his weakness for "perverted sexual displays" in films. He said he was sometimes unable to control his actions, adding: "From my childhood I was unable to realize myself as a man and a complete human being."

The next day Chikatilo opened up a little more, in the process revealing more about his attitude to the tramps and prostitutes who, by most reckoning, formed some 70 percent of his victims. It went some way to describing the mixture of attraction and repulsion that he felt as he dipped into the lowlife of Rostov:

"I often used to spend time at railroad stations, in trains, on suburban trains, and in buses," he said. "There are a lot of different tramps there, both young and old. They ask, demand, and take. They are drunk from the morning onwards . . . These tramps are dragging minors into their activities. From the railroad stations, they are crawling out in various directions aboard the trains. I used to see scenes from the sex lives of these tramps at the railroad stations and on the trains. And I used to recall my humiliation that I had never been able to realize myself as a complete male.

"The question arose of whether these degenerate elements had the right to exist . . . it is not difficult to become acquainted with these people. They don't try to hold themselves back. They crawl into your very soul, demanding money, food, vodka, and offering themselves for sex. I used to watch them as they walked away to secluded places."

Then, in a statement made on November 27, Chikatilo admitted in detail his lecherous activities towards his students while he was teaching in Novoshakhtinsk during the early 1970s. The next day, he gave the following insight into what was going on inside his mind.

"My inconsistent behavior should not be regarded as an attempt to evade responsibility for what I did. One could even argue that after my arrest I did not even realize its dangerous and serious nature. By its character, my case is an exceptional one . . . I am ready to give evidence of the crimes that I committed, but please do not torment me with the details, because my psyshe could not cope with this . . . It did not even occur to me to hide anything from the investigation . . . Everything which I have done makes me tremble . . . I feel only gratitude to the investigating bodies that they captured me."

By now, Chikatilo was behaving very differently from the way he had when he was held in 1984. Then, he had denied everything. It seemed this time that they would be able to get him to confess. Nervous, perched on the edge of his wooden seat and talking in short, breathless phrases, he seemed even to welcome the chance to talk about himself. Still, though, there was something holding him back.

It was not that he was protesting his innocence anymore. The detailed nature of the questions put by Kostoyev over the previous few days had convinced him that the police knew almost as much about his life as he did. He was still refusing to be more specific, though. The feeling of shame which had grown in him over the years was coming to the fore. He could not bring himself to confront his killing, let alone to describe it to another man. He was ready to talk only vaguely about "crimes" and about the "dangerous and serious nature" of what he had done.

Kostoyev needed more. He needed hard facts: the how, the when, and the why of the killings they had attributed to Chikatilo. And he needed them quickly. Nothing that Chikatilo had told him to date constituted a confession. Under Soviet law, the police could hold Chikatilo for only ten days without pressing charges. They had only one more day to make him talk.

Kostoyev decided to change tack. During the investigation, Aleksandr Bukhanovsky, the local psychiatrist, had worked with Burakov and other members of the local police on drawing up a couple of "psychological portraits" of the killer which, in retrospect, had proved a good likeness. Although they had not played any direct role in Chikatilo's ultimate capture, Bukhanovsky certainly knew the details of the case well. As Kostoyev saw it, a change of face across the table might well persuade him to talk. All the more so if the new conversation partner were a psychiatrist able to present himself not so much as an interrogator but as someone who wanted to help Chikatilo come to terms with his problems. Bukhanovsky was the obvious choice. So Kostoyev summoned him.

When the Volga police car arrived in the early morning of November 29 outside Bukhanovsky's book-filled apartment just off Bolshaya Sadovaya, the driver said little more than that he was to take him to local KGB headquarters. Once he arrived, he was told the news: The investigators were convinced they had at last got their man. At first, Bukhanovsky was skeptical. It was not the first time he had heard that line. He had been working on the case on and off for more than five years and they had already asked him in the past to interview suspects.

Once they began to describe Chikatilo, though, Bukhanovsky realized that this time was different. He felt he already knew the killer a little through the portraits he had drawn of him. Now, he was at last to meet him face to face—and do so alone.

What actually happened on that day has since been a subject of dispute. Like so much else in the case, it became a victim of the struggle between the main actors in the drama to claim credit and to apportion blame. Bukhanovsky's version, as described later in court, was simple: His task was to determine whether Chikatilo was the right man. If he found he was, then he had to help Chikatilo draw up a detailed list of his murders and describe the precise way in which he caught his victims and how and where he killed them.

However, the psychiatrist also set three conditions in return: First, he was going in to see Chikatilo as a doctor and not as a member of the investigating team, and as such was not obliged to try for a confession; second, he was to work with Chikatilo alone and be allowed to make his own notes rather than file an official statement; and third, if Chikatilo turned out to be the criminal, any confession he made during their conversation would not count as evidence against him. Kostoyev accepted the conditions and just before ten A.M. Bukhanovsky went into the little interview room. He introduced himself, handed Chikatilo his business card, and the two of them began to talk.

In a strange kind of way, the two of them soon started to hit it off. It may have been Bukhanovsky's skill as a psychiatrist, it may have been merely the change of face. By lunchtime Chikatilo had begun to pour out his heart. Starting with his childhood persecution by the other children, he went on to tell the story of his life. Running through it all was the feeling of inadequacy and of bitterness: Other people had never accepted him for what he was, he said; they had always done him down, always taken advantage of him and persecuted him. After twenty years in which he had hidden his innermost thoughts from the rest of the world, Chikatilo seemed almost relieved to be able to share them with someone. Bukhanovsky, slipping into the role of therapist, began in return giving him advice. Then, toward evening, again according to Bukhanovsky's account, Chikatilo admitted for the first time that he had killed.

Was this the crucial stage in breaking Chikatilo? Judging by his evidence in court, Bukhanovsky is convinced that it was. Kostoyev and other investigators have expressed skepticism. One even said: "You could have sent anyone in there with him in a white coat and Chikatilo would have started to talk." In a sense that is not the point. The main thing is that from then on Chikatilo began to confess and to do so in the terms that the prosecutors needed.

The following day, Kostoyev formally charged Chikatilo with thirty-six premeditated killings of women and of children of both sexes in the period from 1982 to 1990. He was also accused of carrying out rape and homosexual acts. Over the following week, he admitted thirty-four of them, although denied two dating from 1986. Speaking often in little more than a hoarse whisper, Chikatilo said the killings had been sexually motivated, but denied that he had raped or sodomized his victims. He insisted his impotence would have made it physically impossible.

That was only the beginning. To the surprise of Kostoyev, as the interrogation continued, Chikatilo admitted that his first killing had been in 1978, four years earlier than they had originally thought. They already knew that he had been questioned at the time in connection with the killing in Shakhti of nine-year-old Lena Zakotnova. However, until then they had not had any reason to challenge the accepted version that Kravchenko had been the killer.

Chikatilo's account was vague at first, and Kostoyev was dubious. However, it was understandable if he had forgotten a few points. After all, the murder had been almost twelve years before, and since then he had claimed more than fifty more victims. Gradually, though, he began to modify his story, adding more description and details until the doubts began to fade. It was then, and only then, that Chikatilo learned that another man had been shot in his place.

There was more to come. Over the next few weeks, Chikatilo admitted to a staggering eighteen more killings. Many of them were outside the Rostov region and, as a result, no one had linked them with him. They included Lyuba Volobuyeva, one of his first victims, who was killed in the southern region of Krasnodar in July 1982; the two murders in Tashkent during his business trip there in August 1984; Oleg Makarenkov, killed near the Urals town of Ekaterinburg in May 1987 and Ivan Bilovetski, killed in the Ukrainian city of Zaporozhye almost two weeks later; Yura Tereshonok, killed that September in St. Petersburg and Lyosha Moiseyev, killed in the Vladimir region, east of Moscow, in June 1989.

There were also others in their own area in Rostov, which they had missed. In some cases, such as the killing of Larisa Tkachenko, in September 1981, police had found a body but had not realized that it had been part of the series. In the case of Oleg Pozhidayev, killed in August 1982, and Laura Sarkisyan, who died in June 1983, they had not even found a body.

The same was true of ten-year-old Alyosha Khobotov, whom Chikatilo had buried in August 1989 in the grave in Shakhti that he had originally dug for himself. Police had searched for months for the boy after he disappeared, but had eventually given up. Just over a year later, on December 5, Chikatilo admitted after being shown a photograph of the dead boy by police that he had killed him, and, what is more, said that he remembered vividly the point where he had buried him. When he first took police to show them the point, they came across a cap and a pair of tennis shoes which Khobotov's mother was later to identify as her son's. On the next visit they found the body.

There were two more murders, too, which Chikatilo admitted, both of them dating back to the early years. Despite his description of both of the victims and of the places where he had killed them, the investigators were unable either to identify the victims or to find the bodies. They had little alternative but to give up the two as lost.

This was the exception, though. In the weeks that followed, as Chikatilo took the prosecutors to the scenes of his crimes across the Rostov region, they were struck by the accuracy with which he could pinpoint the place where he had killed. Most times, he would draw a rough sketch for them in advance while he was sitting in the interview room. Sometimes there were errors: a road pointing in the wrong direction or a junction inaccurately drawn; but it was the exception and easily remedied on the spot. Almost without exception, they found what they were looking for—and once, more. When Chikatilo took them to Aviators' Park in Rostov in search of the point where he had killed forty-four-year-old Marta Ryabyenko, his oldest victim, in February 1984, he almost stumbled over the point where he is believed to have murdered Sveta Tsana, a young prostitute, several months later. Although Chikatilo confessed to killing the prostitute, he later denied it in court.

Most days, they were ten or more, as they retraced his path: Chikatilo, of course, as well as Kazakov, sometimes Kostoyev as well as other prosecutors, police, and the bodyguards, their tour recorded on a police video which was to form part of the evidence for the court. They made a bizarre group, in their jackets and ties, as they picked their way through the muddy forest paths where Chikatilo had murdered his victims. On the film, they sometimes looked more like a group of Communist Party functionaries embarking on a tour of a collective farm rather than a serial killer and his captors.

Since so much of their case rested on Chikatilo's confession, they relied heavily on his ability to reconstruct the murders, and on being able to show the court that he had done so without any promting from them. In order to dispel any suspicion that they had led him, he did not wear conventional handcuffs during the tour. Instead, they attached him to the guard with a long piece of thick wire allowing freedom of movement. They also carried with them a tailor's dummy. Whenever they reached a point where Chikatilo said that he had killed, they told him to take the dummy and run through again the last seconds of that victim's life. Initially, he would often hesitate as if it were painful for him to remember. But then, he would agree and stab the dummy with the piece of wood that they gave him in precisely the same way that he had stabbed the victim.

Particular care was needed with the case of Zakotnova. Given that the unfortunate Kravchenko had already been executed for the murder, it was vital to show beyond all doubt that his confession was genuine. Accompanied that time by Kazakov, the group squeezed into the little cottage on Mezhevoi Pereulok to watch Chikatilo demonstrate with the dummy precisely how he had throttled the little girl with his right elbow on the floor next to the dining-room table. Then, the dummy tucked under his arm, he led them outside and across the fields to the point where he had thrown her body into the river.

Despite Chikatilo's apparent newfound candor, he was still finding it difficult to come to terms with what he had done. His shyness with the dummies was part of it. At first, he would not even use words like "murder" or "killing." He talked instead only about having done "this" or "that." The successful breaking down of this barrier was due, in part, to the skill and determination of Kostoyev and Kazakov. In moments of desperation, other less experienced investigators would have broken down and asked him outright: "How could you commit such terrible crimes?" If they had, though, he would probably have clammed up completely. Kostoyev was more careful and with a combination of strength of will and gentleness managed to get him to talk.

Bukhanovsky, too, played a role, meeting Chikatilo again some two weeks after they had first come face to face. Other sessions followed. "I had to help Chikatilo overcome the automatic psychological defense," he said. The defense became more of a problem as the investigation moved from the sterile dates, names, and places to the gory details of his killings. One such block concerned the fate of the sexual organs and other body parts which Chikatilo cut and removed from his victims. Thanks, in part to Bukhanovsky's prompting, Chikatilo revealed for the first time on December 13 how he had chewed them and then spat them out. Just over a month later, on January 18, he described to Bukhanovsky the various methods he had used to pick up his victims. To help Chikatilo open up,

Bukhanovsky told him to write compositions on given subjects.

Yet Kostoyev suspected Chikatilo was still not telling them the full truth, particularly about the planning which he had put into the killings. For the first few months that Chikatilo spent with the investigators, he continued to insist that he had not set out with the intention of murder: When he took his victims to secluded places, it was merely with the aim of having sex with them. He claimed it was only then, when they mocked his inability to perform sexually, that he had been overcome by a kind of madness which turned him into a killer. As for the knives and ropes which he used to kill, these were everyday household objects which he carried with him for innocent purposes.

This may have been the result, again, of the internal barriers which Bukhanovsky was trying to help him break down. Confronted with the full horror of what he had done, Chikatilo may subconsciously have been trying to convince himself that it was not his fault but rather that of the victims: He would not have killed them if only they had behaved differently. Even though it was far from a defense in law, it may have made the memories easier to bear.

There were also, undoubtedly, more conscious motives. Even after his arrest, the full horror of what now lay in store had not really sunk in to Chikatilo. Of course, he knew the crimes he had committed carried the death penalty. At times, when talking almost nostalgically about his past thoughts of suicide, he even said that as far as he was concerned, his life was now effectively over. Live or die, it did not really make any difference. Yet the investigators who worked with him said he did not appear to grasp the fact that he would eventually face the firing squad. At one stage, he even argued that the very number of killings that he had carried out turned him into a kind of unique specimen who could be of use to science.

Gradually, though, the hopelessness of his situation dawned on Chikatilo. And he was sane enough to realize that insanity was the only thing that could save him from the firing squad. Not complete insanity. It was too late to start imitating that. Instead, he appeared to think he could claim a temporary madness, under the influence of which he had lost control and had killed.

If it had been a matter of one murder, it might have been convincing. But it could hardly explain the sheer carnage made by Chikatilo. After all, if he had been so horrified by what he had done, how could he explain why he killed again and again? There was other evidence of the premeditated nature of the murders: the long pause after his release from jail at the end of 1984, for example, and the decision to kill far from home in the years that immediately followed. There was also the apparent energy he devoted to finding places to kill and his successful efforts to keep one step ahead of the police. Kostoyev was convinced: These were no mere crimes of passion carried out in the heat of the moment. These were premeditated killings by a cold, calculating professional.

The care with which Chikatilo had planned the whole thing became even more apparent when investigators sought out those who had known him, going all the way back to people who had sat in the same classroom with him in primary school almost fifty years earlier. Their stories to a great extent coincided with Chikatilo's own account of his life: the same sense of his isolation and inability to fit in with any group. Yet as they reached the period from the 1970s onwards, the investigators were most staggered by the success with which Chikatilo hid his double life from all of them. Not one of those whose path he had crossed claimed to have had the smallest suspicion that he could have been a killer. And that went even for those who had taught with him in Novoshakhtinsk and Shakhti and had seen him in action, molesting little boys and girls from school. Most amazing was the reaction of his wife.

Immediately after Chikatilo was arrested, Yandiyev from the prosecutor's office went to the family flat in Novocherkassk to search for murder weapons. When Fayina opened the door and led him into the dirty and untidy living room, he informed her that her husband had been arrested, but did not yet tell her why. She was angry and convinced that it must have been linked with the protests that he had been making about the garages.

"I kept telling him not to make such a fuss about the whole thing," she said.

When Yandiyev gave her the real reason the next day, she was stunned and refused to believe it. True, she had been only too aware of his sexual problems and had known the reason why he was drummed out of teaching—although she had apparently laughed it off as nothing. Yet, she still refused to believe that she had lived under the same roof for more than twenty-five years with a man who carried out such horrendous deeds. For her, the most difficult to understand was the fact that he had killed children, since she remembered how fond he had been of his own.

A particular incident also stuck in her mind. One day, a couple of months before his arrest, Chikatilo had gone on a business trip to their daughter Lyudmila's new home in Kharkov. By that time, she already had a second child by her new husband and was finding it difficult to cope. As a favor, Chikatilo offered to take his older grandson back with him to Novocherkassk for a while. Fayina told Yandiyev that she had been furious.

"How do you expect me to look after him?" she

recalled having told her husband. "I'm tired and busy with my job, too. It's Lyudmila's baby. She had him, she should bring him up herself."

The irony of Chikatilo's reply was chilling. "You are heartless," he had said. "It's our own grandchild. You don't care about children at all. If I wasn't working, I would bring him up myself." The child stayed with them for a short time.

The prosecutors believed her story. Having seen the way that Chikatilo had fooled everyone else, it was not going much further to accept that he had fooled her, too. The nature of his work and the frequency of the business trips, coupled with the access to several other flats to clean up in had also apparently helped him to keep the truth from her. After all, it was not as if he had come home with bloodstained clothes. In his account, he had made clear how he deliberately waited days or sometimes even more than a week before going home to her. In any case, if she had known, it was difficult to see what kind of motive she would have had to cover up for him. As for the murder weapons, a gory collection of sharp-bladed knives, Yandiyev found them mixed in with the normal cutlery as he searched their flat.

And, just as the prosecutors believed her innocence, so Fayina gradually came to believe them. According to Yandiyev, the decisive moment came after the discovery of the body of Khobotov buried in the cemetery in Shakhti. After hearing how her husband had led them to the exact place where the remains lay, Fayina was forced finally to accept the truth.

She only met Chikatilo again once and even then, she did not really want to. She needed access to the family savings and for that she had to have Chikatilo's signature on the bank book. The prosecutors could probably have arranged it for her, but Yandiyev thought the two should see each other. And so, after some persuasion, she agreed.

The meeting was short but painful. When Fayina asked Chikatilo outright why he had done so many terrible things, he did not answer her. Just like their first meeting all those years before, he was so embarrassed that he could not even bring himself to look her in the eye. At last, he mumbled a few words, addressing her by the diminutive that they had used in their few tender moments in the past.

"If only I had listened to you, Fenyuchka," he said. "If only I had followed your advice and got treatment."

The final months of the investigation took Chikatilo and his captors out of the Rostov region and across the Soviet Union to the other cities in which he had killed. Most of the time, he had not known the places in advance and not been back to them afterwards. Even so, it often went smoothly, as when they went to Leningrad, where he had murdered Yura Tereshonok in 1987. Although Chikatilo could not remember at which of the city's stations he had made the initial contact with his victim, he was able to identify it after they drove around them all. Once they had the right starting point, the rest proved fairly easy.

Other murders proved more of a challenge. The killing of Lyuba Volobuyeva, for example, somewhere in the countryside in the region of Krasnodar, south of Rostov, was especially hard to reconstruct. The whole area was a mass of woods and paths, and it was not easy to pinpoint the exact one where he had picked her up and killed her. To make it more difficult, it had also been more than eight years before. In the end, they found the point, but only after they had taken a helicopter and cruised low for hours over the countryside until Chikatilo spotted a piece of scenery which looked familiar.

Also problematic was the murder of Oleg Makarenkov, in a tiny village called Revda on the border of

Siberia near the city of Ekaterinburg. The boy had been reported missing, but no body had been found and no one knew exactly where it lay. If, as Chikatilo claimed, he had killed the boy in the middle of the *taiga,* a vast featureless expanse of open ground, then there seemed little chance of finding him. But again, he demonstrated his incredible memory.

"It's somewhere here," Chikatilo told Kazakov as their party arrived literally in the middle of nowhere.

"How far out were you?" Kazakov asked.

"Maybe one hundred yards or so," he replied.

Sure enough, when they consulted local police they found that some unidentified fragments of bone had been found there a year before.

By the summer of 1991, investigators had virtually completed their case against Chikatilo. The months since his capture had been traumatic ones for the country as a whole, amid signs that Gorbachev's *perestroika* was going sour. Ever since Foreign Minister Eduard Shevardnadze's resignation in December 1990 with an ominous warning of "looming dictatorship," the country appeared to have been sliding to the right. Inexplicably, Gorbachev filled leading posts in his government with reactionary old Communists, while hardliners in the Russian parliament stepped up their challenge to Gorbachev's old radical rival, Boris Yeltsin. Meanwhile, several of the old Union republics were refusing to join the new looser Soviet Union which Gorbachev and Yeltsin had finally appeared to have cobbled together. By summer, when the Soviet leader headed south for his fateful holiday in the Crimea, things were looking grim.

The investigation continued regardless. Besides the weeks and weeks spent with Chikatilo, himself, the investigators from the Public Prosecutor's department had interviewed hundreds of people who had known him and visited hundreds of places which had played a role in the fifty-five years of his life. The enormity of the task was shown by the sheer amount of evidence which they collected: More than 200 fat volumes of it were eventually to be presented to the court.

It was not just the quantity of this evidence which convinced them but also the quality of it, the way in which Chikatilo's own account meshed with that of the other witnesses. They believed that had a clear and conclusive case for fifty-three killings—and that included the most controversial one of them all: the murder of Lena Zakotnova in 1978, for which Kravchenko had already been shot. Their only failure had been to find any evidence to back the fifty-fourth and fifty-fifth killings, to which Chikatilo had confessed. And since they had still neither established the victims identities nor found their bodies, it was concluded that Chikatilo had simply been mistaken.

There was only one real question left: Was Chikatilo sane or was he insane? Despite the terrible nature of the crimes, the prosecutors were convinced of the former. Their impression had also been confirmed by a brief examination which had been carried out by a local psychiatrist in Rostov.

However, given the seriousness of the charges, they needed a more detailed analysis. And so before Chikatilo could be sent for trial, he was taken to experts at Moscow's Serbsky psychiatric institute. The choice was an ironic one. During the worst days of the Brezhnev era, the place had become infamous for the part it played in branding dissidents as mentally ill and confining them to hospitals.

But times had changed. The dissidents had all been freed, at least so the authorities claimed, and some of them had even gone on to become opposition members of the Soviet parliament. And although many of the old doctors were still in place, they had been joined by a new generation determined to change psychiatry from a tool in the hands of Communist politicians into what it should be—a pure branch of medicine. And it was into those hands that Chikatilo was passed.

There was still one piece of unfinished business, prompted by Chikatilo's confession to the killing of Zakotnova. The prosecutors realized that they had to admit to Kravchenko's family that he had been executed for a crime which it now seemed he had not committed.

After much searching, they tracked down his mother in the north of Russia and told her the news. When she heard it, she broke down and cried; she had not even known that her son had been shot in the first place.

19

In a little side street just inside Moscow's ring road, a few doors away from Kropotkinskaya 36, one of the capital's first and still best private restaurants, lies a formidable-looking building, surrounded by a high wall. Inside the door there is a Spartan waiting room, with a small window set in one of its walls. It is positioned low, so that visitors have to bend their heads to speak to the woman sitting in the little cubicle on the other side. Entry into the heart of the building is only with her consent: The only other door out is operated by a switch in her office. Security is tight.

It was even tighter the day they brought in Chikatilo. Just over twenty-four hours earlier, on Monday, August 19, 1991, a group of Kremlin hardliners led by KGB chief Vladimir Kryuchkov had announced that Gorbachev was sick and said they were taking over from him. Despite the drama outside on the streets, work was going as normal at the institute, which was formally a part of the Interior Ministry.

It is not clear what thoughts went through Chikatilo's head as the car taking him to the institute weaved its way around streets blocked with tanks and lines of soldiers. As a committed Communist, did he welcome the conservatives' attempt to put an end to what they saw as Gorbachev's dangerous flirtation with liberalism?

In any case, the coup was all over by the next day, Chikatilo, however, was to stay in the institute for almost two months, during which he underwent a detailed medical examination and a series of psychiatric tests. Most important, he was to talk about everything from his childhood to his inner feelings as he sat in jail awaiting his trial.

The doctors' final conclusion was clear and unequivocal. If sanity is the ability to be in control of one's own actions, then Chikatilo was undoubtedly sane. He was ready to face trial.

Leading their work was Andrei Tkachenko, one of the institute's senior psychiatrists. Despite his youth—he was then only twenty-nine—he was already a major name in his field.

A year later, as Russia prepared to celebrate the first anniversary of the coup, Tkachenko sat in his little office in the institute and was asked about Chikatilo. He was still as convinced as ever of their findings. He was first questioned about the likely role of Chikatilo's childhood and of his relationship with his parents:

ANSWER: It is a difficult question. It would be going too far to say categorically that one or another event in his earlier life played a decisive role in the development of his pathological condition. The fact is that it developed due to a whole tangle of factors, most of which lie within the sphere of the patient's biological functions.

To a great extent, abnormal functioning of his brain played the most important role: structural lesion of brain, disturbance of biological balance, of the body homeostasis, and so on. It's quite another thing that in the course of life every human being distributes and molds those resources under the influence of circumstances, including the relationship with his mother, father, and so on. But it is hard to tell which of these factors plays the decisive role.

QUESTION: What about his childhood? What role was played by the various problems at home and at school with his eyesight, with relating to other children, and so on?

ANSWER: Certainly, the situation was real and dramatic enough. There were many things which happened which were traumatic particularly for a boy who already had these organic problems. Another child as shortsighted as Chikatilo might have coped with the defect and it would not have prevented him from mixing with his peers. But with Chikatilo everything was drawn to the extreme. He feared wearing glasses, he was afraid of being mocked, he thought everybody was looking at him. And you should add to that a certain mental ridigity which was evident in his exaggerated enthusiasms for certain things. Such a combination is extremely inauspicious, because it makes one's surroundings seem hostile. Accordingly, the surroundings could not treat him naturally. He was practically rejected by the collective. His father's late arrival on the family scene was also significant. Indeed, his father fought in the war, was then imprisoned in a camp.

QUESTION: To what extent were his sexual problems a physiological thing and to what extent were they psychological?

ANSWER: At the beginning it might have been the effect of his peculiar psyche, of his hypochondria, and of his inability to find adequate forms for heterosexual relations. He had difficulty establishing contact with girls or women. Of course, many boys have such problems, which are more or less pronounced. But in his case, it was acute. Each case is unique because apparently banal things combine in highly varying proportions. Taken by itself, none of the factors is unique. But in combination they produce a unique picture. He had certain physiological peculiarities which our Russian sexopathologists explain by lesion of certain brain structures. Children like him usually suffer from incontinence. In principle, incontinence is physiological until a certain age, but later it may be pathological. Premature ejaculation, often unrelated to sex, is also typical. For example, ejaculating out of fright, or because of physical tension, not during intercourse but before.

QUESTION: Why do you think that politics obsessed him so much, even starting from early in life? How did he become such a staunch believer in Communism?

ANSWER: It was all very peculiar. His obsession with politics was more than just normal conviction, it came close even to mental disorder. Such disorders are due to arrest of development. He was retarded both mentally and physically, that is sexually. Such phenomena are generally accompanied by heightened suggestibility, that is the tendency to accept other people's opinions. These people can fall easy prey to any idea that is suggested to them. Before a doctor begins hypnotic suggestion, he must test his patient's suggestibility, because it varies from one person to another. Chikatilo was highly suggestible, especially in his teens. Generally speaking, suggestibility is an adolescent quality and a suggestible teenager might easily embrace certain antisocial ideas. He might be easily led on. Anywhere.

QUESTION: How can you explain the leap from a boy with such problems to the pervert and the criminal that he was to become as an adult?

ANSWER: Certain predispositions for such behavior evolve before actual behavioral patterns become evident. In fact all peculiarities of his heterosexual life give evidence of such predispositions. Incidentally, in adolescence they often manifest themselves quite conspicuously. For instance, in sadistic fantasies. He began to have them as a child. It was not that he actually imagined what he was going to do later. It never happens like this, it is a very gradual process. Fantasies may supersede one another, but never—and certainly not in childhood, do they take the form of what eventually is performed. I mean, these fantasies may be more or less socially acceptable. For instance, one might imagine oneself as being a strong man dealing with evil forces, and acting quite violently. Such fantasies bear witness to sadistic tendencies in one's character.

One's subsequent behavior only *appears* to be unexpected. It seems so because it begins with the forms usually far removed from what one is already prepared for, and one gradually approaches what one is prepared for. It means those fantasies begin slowly but increasingly to be translated into actions. You will note that most of those processes are unconscious. That is to say, one seldom realizes beforehand that one wants to commit a murder, and more specifically, commit it the way Chikatilo did.

With Chikatilo everything developed little by little, gradually. First he began deviating from what is considered usual, normal sexual life: from a heterosexual partner and the usual method. First, while he was working at school, he suddenly realized that he was attracted to girls below twelve. And then, his actions became increasingly aggressive. And eventually, when the situation allowed, his gradually revealed impulses took the form of murder.

After the first murder there was a long pause. In principle, some of the restraining mechanisms were still working. You see, the general dynamic, the general regularities or pathological attraction and its evolution consist in gradual escalation of behavioral manifestations. Actions become more violent, more frequent. Quite often the person accepts these actions and recognizes the attractions, but the process is gradual, and at earlier stages self-control and restraint are still possible. His second victim appears not to have been a child, but a grown woman. In fact it is rather difficult to trace the exact dynamic. But on the whole the process is clear enough. By and by, gradually, he fully realized what form of sexual behavior fully met his true motives.

QUESTION: The pause between 1978 and 1981 was not the only pause. There were other ones. In 1986, for example, and smaller ones often in the winter. Other times saw dramatic increases in the frequency of the killings. How can you explain all that?

ANSWER: Despite lengthy investigation one cannot be sure everything has been clarified down to the last detail. Nobody knows everything except Chikatilo, himself. Yet these winter periods are evidence of his still being perfectly in control of the situation. He was still able to restrain his impulses.

As for the rise in his activity, there is no unambiguous scientific explanation for that, either. But one can in principle assume that such a deviational pattern of activity may not only serve to satisfy pathological yearnings as such but also to discharge psychic tension. If we again draw an analogy with normal sexual intercourse, it is also followed by a psychic discharge. In a person like Chikatilo with all his brain anomalies, it might have been a more acute condition which resulted in greater relaxation. In other words, whenever he felt tension due to certain anxiety or depression, he had a ready method to achieve relaxation and escape tension.

QUESTION: Does that mean that killing for Chikatilo came to play the same role as sexual intercourse?

ANSWER: Of course the motivation was distorted, but many usual motivational elements were still there, some of the motives predetermining normal behavior likewise predetermines an abnormal one. For instance, to achieve sexual satisfaction, to relax. But a normal person has a different method, and a different object. Chikatilo had his own. However, the stages were the same: establishing contact, excitement, intercourse proper, and relaxation. All those stages were present, although each of them was modified, of course. And the objective was the same.

QUESTION: What about Chikatilo's relationship with his wife? They had a normal sex life to start with, didn't they?

ANSWER: Of course, they had sex and gave birth to two children. But as with other people with retarded sexual development, there was also a reduction of the sexual function. The arrest of development led to comparatively faster aging. At the time of examination we also found signs of beginning cerebral atherosclerosis, which could also play its part. But the primary factor was the general deformation of his whole sex life. He had found a different object, and a different method of realization which satisfied him better. Therefore, a heterosexual relationship could no longer satisfy him. He wanted something quite different.

QUESTION: Yet for some time in the 1970s, the two seemed to coincide—sex with his wife and his molesting of children?

ANSWER: These are two different processes. One appears and the other gradually disappears. It does not happen overnight. It is not as if he sees a child is satisfied and cuts off all other possibilities. He had sex with his wife less and less often. In the later stages she began asking him why he did not sleep with her, and he responded by causing an argument. Since he did not want to have sex with her, and anyway no longer could, he tried to keep the spheres strictly apart.

The family and the man-woman relations in general were a taboo for him. Constrained by his own inadequacy and social rules, he was hardly likely to mix the two spheres. Other people, even those with sadistic tendencies, often do. They can have sadistic fantasies during sexual intercourse, or resort to certain actions, but for him those were two different spheres.

He might have such fantasies when he masturbated, deliberately fantasized or dreamed. In fact he has the same sadistic fantasies to this day. At any rate that was what he told me during the latest examination.

QUESTION: How would you characterize Chikatilo? Was he bisexual?

ANSWER: In essence, Chikatilo, like so many other sadists, was deviating from a heterosexual object in his activity. The normal object is heterosexual and mature. Every deviation, every sexual abnormality, is specifically characterized by a deviation from the normal object. More often than not sadists gradually switch over to homosexual objects, to homosexual pedophilic objects. And so, as with other serial killers, boys began predominating at later stages. It wasn't because women were beginning to turn him down, it was the consequence of certain biological irregularities underlying the process. Such abnormal sexual behavior is due to transformation of all structures, of distorted sex-role behavior and stereotypes. He is unable to perform his male role to the end, and his sexual self-awareness is distorted so much as to include a change, an inversion of the sex object.

Even by the end, you could not call him a regular homosexual. Moreover, sadists like him deny homosexuality and homosexuals as having anything to do with them. They detest homosexuals because they fall short of the acceptability standards I have mentioned earlier. Inwardly they begin gradually approaching the homosexual object, but their mode of realization is different. It is violence. It is sometimes said that the actual sex of their object is insignificant to them. In fact, it is insignificant on the conscious level, and yet the tendency is there, most definitely. As the result, if the process is well-advanced, as in Chikatilo's case, homosexual and pedophilic objects are invariably found at the latter stages.

In a way, it is difficult to reveal the exact personal significance of each element of his behavior. Because more often than not he behaved automatically, although there was a certain consistency and repetitiveness about his actions. According to him, he derived pleasure from performing this or that act. Another sadist might derive pleasure from different actions. It is extremely individual.

Slivkov (and another Russian killer Tkachenko worked with) used to hang Young Pioneers. That is, they all had to have red ties around their necks, and wear well-polished shoes. Kujik (another one) used to thrust something—a stick, or a broken bottle—into his victims' genitalia. And Chikatilo enjoyed cutting. He said he liked the uterus, it was so elastic he felt like chewing it. Thus, his behavioral patterns became fixed once he found them satisfying. Once he derived pleasure from this or that action he tried to repeat it again so that he could get satisfaction. The range may gradually expand, as he tries other actions and finds them satisfying. Each sadist has his own individual range. Every person's sexual life is individual. Some people have normal sex, others have abnormal.

QUESTION: You have said that Chikatilo derived the greatest pleasure from cutting out and chewing the uterus of his victim. How important was the cannibalistic aspect of his killing?

ANSWER: Cannibalism and vampirism are modifications of sadism. Also, they could be accidental, because bites and bloodletting are common in normal sexual intercourse, too. Therefore I don't think he actually chewed or swallowed.

You must imagine him in this highly agitated condition, manipulating the dead body, often chaotically, with his hands and his teeth. Suppose, when he bites, he bites the dead woman's nipple off. He said he might have bit and swallowed. This happens at the height of sexual excitement, when all sorts of actions are possible as long as they lead to sexual satisfaction. After normal intercourse, too, a woman might complain to her partner, "You hurt me." And he would say, "Sorry. I did not mean to. I was carried away by passion." Something similar, though more complicated, happened in Chikatilo's case. He was carried away by his perverse passion.

QUESTION: After all that you have said, how could you still declare Chikatilo to be sane and responsible for his actions?

ANSWER: What is responsibility is a concept determining a person's ability to be aware of his behavior and control it while performing a crime or a criminal act. The concept of responsibility comprises two criteria. The legal and the medical one. The legal criterion was to go with the awareness of one's actions, and ability to control them. And there are four medical criteria covering practically the entire field of psychic pathology: chronic psychic diseases, feeble-mindedness, a temporarily diseased state, and other diseased states.

Thus, the acknowledgment of a certain psychic disorder does not automatically lead to irresponsibility. To pronounce a person irresponsible, it must be proved that his psychic disorder has prevented him from being aware of his actions and being able to control them. Therefore, a forensic psychiatrist's examination always consists of two stages: first, doctors diagnose psychic disorders as such, and then they try to determine how bad they are, now pronounced, and whether or not they can prevent the person under examination from being aware of his actions and controlling them, in particular in relation to the criminal act in question.

A certain person might suffer from a psychic disorder and yet commit a robbery, a burglary, or multiple murders, like Chikatilo. Even if the disorder is identical, the medical verdict for each of these criminal offenses will be different, absolutely different. Because each of them puts different demands on the person's resources, and involves a different degree of awareness of misdoing and possibility of restraint.

Now, let us look at the combination of Chikatilo's psychic disorders. His diagnosis reads as follows: organic lesion of brain with certain psychopathic peculiars and a sadistic tendency. After ascertaining these peculiarities, we must try and understand if they deprived him, in his concrete behavior, of the ability to be aware of his actions and control them. What does this mean? It means we must understand how adequately he could assess the situation. How purposeful his behavior was. Whether or not there were certain disorders at the moment of crime which deprived him of all controls by robbing him of all willpower and making him unable to resist his passion.

And when we analyzed in detail each of Chikatilo's killings, a very definite picture emerged. Most of his crimes were carefully thought out, his actions preprogrammed. In fact he told us he had learnt to dodge out of the way to avoid spurts of blood from his victim's bodies which would stain his clothing. Or, look at the way he captured his victims. These were carefully thought out and differentiated actions, depending on his object. There were also no lapses of memory which could indicate mental disorder. There was nothing of the sort. He recollected the sequence of his actions down to the smallest detail. There are known cases when epileptic patients suddenly performed normal sexual actions at the moment of the blackout and psychic discharge. Such things happen. But it was not Chikatilo's case. There was no situation in which his mind suddenly misconnected itself. Also after performing his actions he methodically set out to cover his tracks. He buried the victim's clothes and destroyed all evidence of his being there to prevent identification. After analyzing every episode we came to the conclusion that there was no question of irresponsibility in the given case. He is a responsible individual.

Maybe we should have found differently, if Russian law had the category of limited responsibility, as is the case in several other countries. As we stated in our report, his diagnosed disorders were certainly connected with his needs and predetermined his motivation. We have written about that. But as long as there is no category of limited responsibility in Russia, it is not worth speculating about it. In any case, the category is normally used for people committing less grave offenses. As I said, it is easier to commit robbery than a murder. Homicide is a very grave offense, socially. And it takes very serious disorders of psychic activity for you to fully forget what you are doing. One must be very deeply deranged to commit murder unconsciously, totally without control—and Chikatilo was not.

20

It was a typical Russian crowd, aggressive and ill-tempered. There were more than 150 of them, both men and women, standing outside courtroom number one in the Rostov Regional Court, and the young policeman at the door was not letting anyone in. In the middle, making the most noise of all, was a little man, probably about sixty years old, in a flat cap and creased working overalls.

"Make an exception for me, son," the man pleaded. "I'm a hero of socialist labor. Look, I've got the card to prove it. My wife told me not to come. She said it would be bad for my heart. But I want to see this bastard. I want to look him in the face."

For the people pushing and shoving in the entrance hall, Chikatilo's trial was nothing less than a sensation. For years they had lived with the idea of the "maniac," first as rumor, then later, through appeals in the newspapers and on local television. It had been worst for those with children. All those warnings not to talk to strangers, all that worry every time they were a few minutes late coming home. Then it had ended. Soon after police caught Chikatilo in November 1990, they called a press conference to announce the news.

Wallowing in the gory details, the Russian press had provided colorful accounts of the way in which the killer had terrorized the country and gruesome descriptions of his murders. Yet people still knew so little about him. Who was this monster who had been living all this time in their midst. What was his name? What did he look like? Was he married? Did he have children? Until then no one had given an answer to any of these questions. According to Russian practice, the newspapers did not even name the accused, referring to him only as "Citizen Ch." The nearest the public came to seeing his picture was the inaccurate composite sketch, which had been drawn up after the March 1984 murder of Dima Ptashnikov. However, at ten A.M. sharp on April 14, 1992, all that had changed.

The atmosphere inside the wood-paneled courtroom was tense. Admission was restricted to relatives of the victims, experts, and the media, but space was nevertheless tight. The first journalists began arriving half an hour before the trial opened, the television crews and photographers fighting their usual battle for the best position. The relatives, many of them in black, came in more slowly. Some of the women among them were already in tears. As they squeezed onto the wooden benches, the only thing uniting them was their grief. Otherwise they were as different from one another as Chikatilo's victims: simple peasants from the countryside who looked as if they had come in straight from the farm, more sophisticated city dwellers in suits and ties and, most noticeable, the *babushki* (grandmothers) in their head scarves. All were on the edge of their seats, their eyes fixed on an empty metal cage prepared for Chikatilo on the right side of the courtroom. They were all straining to catch a first glimpse of the man who had murdered their son or daughter, brother or sister, grandson or grand-daughter.

As the minutes ticked by, the room began to fill to bursting point. Some of the relatives had now joined the reporters around the empty cage, trying to get close. Barring their way were four burly young soldiers, whose job was less to prevent Chikatilo from escaping than to stop the crowd from getting their hands on him and ripping him apart. Already, the tension was getting too much to bear for some of them: a couple of white-coated doctors who had taken seats in the front row had started administering to those who were feeling faint.

Then, just before ten, came the sound from below of a heavy door opening and of army boots walking up the steps which lead from the basement to the door of the cage: First to appear was a soldier, then two more behind him walking side by side. Finally, came the man they had all been waiting for. The crowd surged forward, almost pinning the soldiers against the bars.

Tall, even gangly, looking older than his fifty-six years, he was dressed in a faded shirt decorated with the rings of the 1980 Moscow Olympics and a pair of plain gray trousers. His head was completely shaved, apparently at his own request. There was little left about him to suggest the kindly uncle or grandfather figure who had lured children to their death. To the crowd in the courtroom he looked strange and evil, almost like a monster from another planet. He was led into the cage with his hands tied behind his back, and the door was slammed shut behind him.

The whole courtroom was in pandemonium; men were shouting, women were crying and screaming, a group of them trying to push their way through the guard to the cage. From his podium at the front of the courtroom, Judge Leonid Akubzhanov, a quiet school-masterly type, was trying in vain to bring order. The press and spectators were refusing to sit down, the doctors darting around to comfort the spectators. But then finally, after about ten minutes, the judge succeeded in calming the crowd. Peering down through his glasses at the courtroom, the judge began to speak.

It was clear from the start that the trial was going to be both long and emotional. The sheer quantity of the murders and their gruesome nature ensured that. With the court sitting every day for some three hours, it took Judge Akubzhanov three days to read the charges, starting from the various child molesting incidents of the 1970s through to the killing of Sveta Korostik on November 6, 1990, two weeks before Chikatilo's arrest. While Akubzhanov ran through the unbearable details of the killings in a flat voice, gasps went up from the crowd. The relatives of the victims were not the only ones to need the help of the doctors: even a couple of the young soldiers keeled over as the judge reached a particularly gruesome passage.

Questioned about the killings one by one, Chikatilo gave a chilling insight into his own indifference to the suffering of his victims and the ease with which he had picked them up over the years and killed them. "I did not need to look for them," he said from his cage. "Every step I took they were there."

The evidence largely confirmed what Chikatilo had already told prosecutors, proof of the incredible memory for detail that his captors had already remarked upon. But even he was sometimes at a loss: "I don't remember, there were so many of them," he said in exasperation when pressed for details about one of the killings.

Despite the horrors, many of the witnesses gave their evidence calmly, among them some of the parents of the victims. The passage of time, in some cases as long as seven or eight years, had helped ease some of their pain. But those who had lost their children more recently found the ordeal too much to bear: The father of Vanya Fomin, the eleven-year-old boy killed in August 1990, was among those who broke down and were unable to give testimony at all.

Other witnesses were petrified by the whole process. When the court began to discuss the 1989 murder of Tatyana Ryzhova, witness Anastasaya Kalshnikova was asked to testify how Chikatilo had allegedly stolen a sled from outside her apartment on which to transport away the dead girl's body. The woman, a plump, badly dressed worker broke down and begged the judge not to lock her up. "I don't know anything. Let me go," she blurted out and started crying.

Echoing the sentiment of many in the room, other witnesses openly questioned the point of having a trial at all. Chikatilo had already confessed, they said, so why run through all the horrors again? When the court began to investigate the case of Zhenya Muratov, the fifteen-year-old boy murdered in July 1988 near Donleskhoz, his aunt suddenly broke in: "This trial is just rubbing salt into the wounds of the relatives of the victims," she screamed. "We should stop all this and just liquidate the criminal. Too much money is being spent on supporting his life."

One of the most conspicious absences from the trial was that of Chikatilo's wife, Fayina. Although she had cooperated fully with the investigation, the prosecutors realized it could be dangerous for her to appear in court. The desire for revenge among relatives of the victims was so great that it could easily have been directed against her. So, before the trial started, she had changed her name and gone away to start a new life, presumably with her daughter Lyudmila in Kharkov. Yandiyev, the man from the Public Prosecutor's Office who first told her the truth about her husband, helped arrange her relocation. Fayina had met with her husband only once since his arrest and did not have any desire to see him again. She wanted only to forget him and all the years that they had spent together.

Despite Chikatilo's earlier confessions, the prosecution quickly faced complications. During questioning the defendant unexpectedly withdrew his admission of killing Lena Zakotnova, the little girl who had died in Shakhti in December 1978 and for whose murder Aleksandr Kravchenko had already been executed in 1984.

"You can decide what you like," Chikatilo told the court. "But I didn't kill her." The reason for his sudden change of mind was unclear, least of all to the prosecutors who were convinced that his confession had been spontaneous and truthful. As they put it, Zakotnova's killing had already been closed at the time Chikatilo confessed; had he not brought up the murder himself, they never would have linked him with it. Furthermore, his final description of how he had killed the girl and disposed of the body fitted the evidence. Some even suspected that pressure may have been put on him by police to retract his confession to save the embarrassment of those involved in the earlier investigation of Kravchenko.

That was not all, though: Chikatilo also denied five more killings: that of Larisa Tkachenko, dating from 1981, Vatalya Stalmachenok from 1982, Nataty Shalapinina and Sveta Tsana from 1984, and Ivan Bilovetski from 1987. As far as the prosecution was concerned, the case for these five—and indeed for Zakotnova—was just as good as for the remaining forty-seven killings. Prosecutors maintained that Chikatilo's strategy was simply to waste time and sow confusion. Yet it nonetheless made them uncomfortable.

In a sense, it would have been easier for them if Chikatilo had suddenly pleaded not guilty and denied all 53 murders of which he was accused. Then his denial could be dismissed simply as a normal desire to save himself from execution. However, six murders more or six murders less were not going to make any difference to his fate. And it was this which appeared to lend some credence to his claims and made the whole thing so disconcerting. Had the prosecutors made a mistake? Or had they simply taken advantage of Chikatilo's readiness to confess in order to clear a few unsolved murders from their books?

As the weeks and months passed, the courtoom atmosphere changed; the number of relatives in the audience dwindled to a hard core; the mother of Tatyana Ryzhova was invariably there, so too was the brother of Lyuba Alekseyeva, the woman killed in August 1984 in Rostov. After the initial burst of enthusiasm, the Western and even Russian press also quickly lost interest, leaving the press bench to a handful of the more determined locals. With most of the key witnesses already heard from, those who were left to testify had little of interest or relevance to say. The emotion and high drama of the first few days degraded into little more than a farce.

Much of this was due to behavior of Chikatilo himself. On the first day of the trial, he had delighted photographers and television crews by producing a pornographic magazine from his pocket and waving it briefly in the air, before it was confiscated by his wardens. Later, he became even more obstreperous, refusing to answer the questions put to him by the judge and interrupting proceedings with shouts. The motive was clear: Whether consciously or subconsciously he was trying to prolong proceedings and with them, his own life. He did not succeed.

"Chikatilo, I command you to keep quiet," the judge kept repeating as the interruptions became longer and louder. But Chikatilo ignored him and continued talking and shouting until the guards would come over, sometimes dragging him out of the cage on the way back down to the cell.

Drawing on his Ukrainian orgins, Chikatilo began to demand he be provided with an interpreter to translate the proceedings from Russian into Ukrainian—an act of nonsense, since he had spoken Russian all his life. He also called for the dismissal of his defense lawyer and his replacement with one from the Ukrainian independence movement Rukh, whom he named only as Shevchenko. It was not clear whether such a man actually existed, let along whether he was prepared to defend Chikatilo. Despite repeated questioning from the judge, Chikatilo was unable to give any more details about the lawyer, and his request was eventually overruled. In one of his greater flights of fantasy, he also began claiming that the trial was political and likening his fate to that of the former top Communists still in jail awaiting trial for the 1991 coup.

In July, the farce reached a high point. After a particularly noisy standoff with the bench, Chikatilo stripped off all his clothes and began waving his penis at the court. "Look at this useless thing," he declared. "What do you think I could do with that?" He was taken away and, as a punishment, barred from the courtroom for several days. When he was finally allowed back into the court, he was more subdued. His hands, which had been untied for the previous weeks, were clamped back firmly again by handcuffs. It didn't stop him from one last disruption, though. On the final day of the trial he was again to succeed in removing his trousers, revealing the naked flesh below.

Chikatilo was not the only source of farce. In another strange incident during the summer, the courtroom had to be evacuated and the proceedings abandoned for several days after it was reported that more than two pounds of highly poisonous mercury had been released in the court building. Officials spent hours frantically scrubbing, and eventually it was claimed that the danger had passed. However, there was never any adequate explanation for what happened.

That the trial was being held in Rostov, at all, had proved controversial from the start. Some people involved with the case argued that the charges were of such gravity that the proceeding should have been staged on a Moscow court rather than in a small, provincial one. After all, although most of the murders had been carried out in and around Rostov, a number of them had been committed outside the region; the case was therefore more than a local one. Not without good reason, it was suggested that the quality not just of the judge but also of the prosecution and defense would have been far greater in the capital. There was also a certain irony in the fact that a court which all those years earlier had convicted Aleksandr Kravchenko for the killing of Lena Zakotnova should be handling the same murder again. This time as one of Chikatilo's fifty-three.

Nor did the behavior of Judge Akubzhanov inspire much admiration. His style was often more of a schoolteacher than a judge, hectoring nervous witnesses and interrupting proceedings to scold a journalist for chewing gum. At times, he seemed to be completely out of his depth. Of particular concern to the defense, however, was the way he handled Chikatilo.

Under the legal system which independent Russia inherited from the Soviet Union, the judge necessarily plays a dominant role in any trial. Flanked by two lay assessors, whose function sometimes appears little more than decorative, he leads the questioning both of witnesses and of the accused. It is only after he has finished that the defense and prosecution have their say. With no jury, it is also in the end his job to give both the verdict and the sentence. All in all, it is virtually a one-man show.

Even by Russian standards, though, Akubzhanov was trying to dominate things. And in May, defense council Marat Khabibulin struck back. A state-paid lawyer who had been allocated the case, he was in the unenviable position of organizing the defense of a man almost everyone in the courtroom already considered guilty. Until then, the harmony had been relatively passive, making little use of his right to cross-examine witnesses. But as the trial began to head into its second month, he had clearly had enough of Akubzhanov's way of running things, and made a formal complaint. In front of the court, he accused the judge of violating his client's rights and demanded he be replaced by someone more impartial.

Akubzhanov was stunned by the criticism and turned on prosecutor Nikolai Gerasimyenko for support. But in a rare sign of cooperation between the defense and the prosectuion, Gerasimyenko actually backed his opponent. He, too, agreed that the judge was behaving improperly. Put in the strange position of deciding his own fate, Akubzhanov adjourned proceedings and withdrew for a few minutes with his two deputies to decide further action. However, the judge was obviously not in a mood for self-criticism. When he returned a few minutes later, he formally rejected Khabibulin's appeal and continued with the trial.

Gerasimyenko soon paid the price for his defiance. A few days later, Akubzhanov got his revenge. Unexpectedly, the father of one of the victims stood up and declared that the prosecution was not pursuing the case forcefully enough. Again, Akubzhanov withdrew for a few minutes. When he returned, he upheld the man's complaint and ordered Gerasimyenko out of the courtroom.

The unhappy prosecutor was eventually replaced a

week later by two men. Anatoly Zadorozhni, a department head in the regional Public Prosecutor's Office, and Aleksandr Kuyumdzhi, one of his deputies. In a clear breach of usual practice, however, the proceedings had continued in the meantime without the prosecution at all. Cynics said that the judge, himself, was already behaving so much like a prosecutor that there was no need for one anyway.

Sentiments were running high outside the courtroom, too, as the latest tensions which had built up during the years of the investigation exploded to the surface. Much of the controversy appeared to settle around the Rostov psychiatrist, Aleksandr Bukhanovsky and the degree to which his "psychological portraits" had played a role in catching Chikatilo. It was a big enough blow to his pride that the court decided to hear him as a normal witness rather than as an expert, which effectively barred him from most of the early part of the proceedings. But even worse, he faced the added indignity of being attacked in the press by the prosecutors with whom he had worked on the case.

In an interview published in May 1992 in the newspaper *Moskovskaya Pravda*, investigating group head Kostoyev poured scorn on Bukhanovsky's alleged contribution to the investigation, claiming that his portrait had been full of errors, and implied that he was using publicity around the case to boost his career. Bukhanovsky wasted no time in hitting back. Visiting journalists were read extracts from his psychological portrait intended to discredit Kostoyev's criticism and to show, in retrospect, how accurate he had been. He claimed that he eventually intended to publish the complete portrait, himself. Other prosecutors, meanwhile, joined in on Kostoyev's side.

There were also signs of rivalry between prosecutors and police, as the brief burst of self-congratula-

tion that followed Chikatilo's arrest gave way to re-
criminations over why it had taken so long to catch
him. Kostoyev's men were often openly critical of the
way in which the police had handled their part of the
operation. They complained that leading police officers had spent too much time on paperwork in their
offices, and not enough time out on the streets. One of
the prosecutors even described many of the ordinary
police drafted into the operation as being incompe-
tents who deserted their posts at key moments and
even turned up drunk for work. There were also mut-
terings about the medal given to Rybakov, the policeman who had challenged Chikatilo on November 6,
1990, when he emerged from the woods around Sovleskhoz after killing his last victim. Shouldn't he instead have been reprimanded for letting the killer go
on his way? they asked.

Fetisov and Burakov, the two top policemen who
played a leading role in the investigation, were bitter
about the criticism. "For the week after each murder
was committed and the body was found, it was work
around the clock for us," said Fetisov. "No Saturdays,
no Sundays. It was hard. But it is even harder when
they start to blame us unfairly." For his part, Burakov
said he was considering writing his own book about
the case as the only way of insuring the objectivity
that he claimed was missing in press accounts.

In fact, the role played by the press in the entire
affair was controversial. Decades of censorship and
self-censorship under the Communists have proved a
heavy burden for the Russian media. Journalists are
poorly paid and often alarmingly unconcerned about
sources or facts, while many articles are an infuriat-
ing mixture of comment and fact. *Glasnost* had not
only shaken up the existing press but also spawned a
number of new publications every bit as irresponsible
and sensationalist as the Western tabloids.

In the weeks before the trial started, it was tradition

rather than law which drove the newspapers to describe the defendant in their articles as "Citizen Ch," rather than Chikatilo. And that was about the only example of self-restraint which they exercised. Once proceedings got underway, the gloves came off. Many journalists reported the case in a starkly sensational manner. This, in turn, confirmed the belief of many involved in the investigation that it had been a mistake to allow proceedings to be open in the first place.

A blatant example of sensationalism was a full-page article published in the weekly *Moscow News*, under the title of "Vampire for Sale." The bizarre title came from a rumor, reported in the text, that the Japanese wanted to buy the killer's brain once he had been executed. And this was one of the country's most respected newspapers; other, lesser publications were even more sensationalist in their handling of the case.

By summer 1992, the case was drawing to an end and Chikatilo's behavior was becoming ever more bizarre. Sometimes, he was almost boisterous; at other times, he barely seemed to be following proceedings at all, sitting motionless with his mouth open in the cage or making grimaces. Asked a question by the judge, he would often give an answer to a completely different one. For those observing Chikatilo, it was unclear whether he was really losing touch or else merely feigning insanity to save himself from likely execution. Judge Akubzhanov therefore called back the psychiatrists who had earlier certified him as sane and responsible for his actions to see if there had been any change for the worse in his condition.

The examination was carried out by three of them; Andrei Tkachenko and Inna Ushakova from the Serbsky Institute, who had both worked with Chikatilo in Moscow, and Ivan Bakumyenko, top psychiatrist of the Rostov region and head of the local commission which had examined him briefly that May. After reading reports of Chikatilo's behavior in his cell and during the trial, the doctors went into the courtroom on July 7 after proceedings had broken for the day and questioned and examined the defendant for a few hours. Having already spent so much time with Chikatilo, Tkachenko maintained, there was no need for a long examination to establish any change in his condition.

The verdict they gave to the court the following day was unequivocal: Chikatilo was as sane as he had been when they examined him before. Although convinced that his behavior in the courtroom was more than just playacting, they maintained that it did not prevent him in any way from understanding and taking part in court proceedings. With the witnesses now heard, the trial could move on August 10 into its final and decisive phase: the summing up of the case by both sides.

The prosecution case, as put by Zadorozhni, was straightforward. After running through the charges, he made the expected appeal for the death sentence. The defense case, however, was more complex: In his speech, Khabibulin chose a two-pronged attack, both challenging the quality of the evidence, particularly relating to the crimes that Chikatilo had denied during the course of the proceedings and questioning his client's responsibility for his actions.

He appeared to have a good argument for both points: Certainly, despite all the 222 volumes of evidence, the prosecution did not have a single witness who had actually *seen* Chikatilo kill. Much of the evidence was purely circumstantial. Some experts, Bukhanovsky in particular, were also skeptical about claims that Chikatilo was sane. But with the judge apparently bent from the start on conviction, Khabilulin looked as if he faced an impossible task.

Nor did the attorney receive much help from his client. When Zadorozhni began his summing up, Chikatilo started singing the socialist anthem, "The Internationale" in a loud tuneless voice and continued shouting and singing until he was again thrown out of the courtroom by the judge. He did not even hear the speech made by his own defense council. When he was allowed back in afterward in order to make any last statement in his own defense, he refused to say anything, instead remaining seated in the cage with his head slumped.

"The accused said nothing," Akubzhanov told the court stenographer. "Fix it in the court record." And with that, the judge ordered the case adjourned and withdrew with his two assessors to another room to consider and then write the verdict.

They almost didn't have a defendant; as the courtroom began to empty, Volodya Alekseyev, whose seventeen-year-old sister was killed by Chikatilo in 1984, stood up from the public benches. Slipping his hand into his pocket, he produced a small, heavy metal ball and sent it flying through the air toward the cage. His aim was good, but not quite good enough—the ball came within an inch or so of grazing Chikatilo's ear before crashing against the wall behind. Chikatilo's guards rushed toward Alekseyev. But several members of the audience who had gotten to know the sad, quiet man during the trial, formed a ring around him and prevented the guards from getting anywhere near.

The guards' commander paused for a moment. Alekseyev's face was white and his hands were shaking. After looking around to check that the judge had not seen the incident, the commander waved him away. Chikatilo, clearly shaken by the event, was taken back down to the cells.

The verdict was set for September 15 and then postponed until October 14. It was not so much that the judge appeared to need time to decide Chikatilo's guilt; he had seemed convinced of it from the start. Rather, Russian court practice required that the final verdict contain as long and as detailed an account of all the crimes as had the initial charges. And, in a sign of the country's technological backwardness, it all had to be written by hand.

For Chikatilo, there was little cause for hope. With the psychiatrists having declared him sane, there was little doubt that he would be condemned as guilty and face the firing squad. One of many features that independent Russia has inherited from the Soviet Union is its extensive use of capital punishment— more than that of any other country except, perhaps, China. One murder is enough to ensure almost certain execution. It was difficult to see how a man who had killed fifty-three people, and done so in the most gruesome way imaginable, could escape such a fate.

In a sense, it was also the most humane solution. If Chikatilo had received the next punishment down, a jail term of fifteen years, then he would certainly have had to be kept in solitary confinement for his own protection. In the tough world of Russian prison camps, the inmates would show little mercy toward a man convicted of molesting children, let alone one who had killed and mutilated dozens of them.

It was a tragic end to a tragic life. The story of Chikatilo is not just one of police errors and incompetence. It is also the history of the unchecked descent of one man into depravity. The psychiatrists from the Serbsky Institute who examined Chikatilo insisted that he was not mad, and had been perfectly aware of what he was doing at the moment when he killed his victims.

When Chikatilo met his wife, Fayina, after his arrest, he told her he regretted never having accepted her advice to seek proper treatment for his sexual problems. Would it have helped? Perhaps not. By the time Chikatilo made his sole and abortive visit to a psychiatrist in 1984, he had already developed the thirst for blood and suffering which probably nothing, save imprisonment, could have stopped.

There is no doubt that Russia in recent years has produced a surprisingly large number of serial killers. After decades in which the problem was ignored, police and psychiatrists now talk of it openly—and admit that it is getting worse, in part because of the breakdown of society which accompanied the final collapse of Communism.

Many of those involved in the Chikatilo affair have since gone on to apply their expertise to other serial killer cases both in Rostov and elsewhere in the country. Andrei Tkachenko of the Serbsky Institute has already examined dozens of murderers in his little central Moscow office who, he says, differed from Chikatilo only in the number of their victims; and recently, Tkachenko interviewed another alleged killer who police feared may have killed even more people than Chikatilo.

Yet the questions remain. What if Chikatilo had been treated earlier, in the 1970s or even in the 1960s? Could the feelings of inadequacy and inferiority which were with him almost all his life have been treated effectively enough to stop them exploding into deadly violence? Would he still have turned into the monster he became if he had lived in a more liberal Western society, where it was possible to speak openly of such sexual problems and obtain treatment for them?

But there can only be so many "what ifs," and none of them will bring back the young lives of those he had murdered so brutally, nor will they ease the suffering of the victims' loved ones. As for Chikatilo himself, he had committed crimes of such depravity against society that he was doomed to pay the ultimate penalty.